Police Custody

This article reviews certain flow of control formations to show why the GO TO is hard to get rid of. A discussion of the control structures in BLISS follows with a defense that doing without the GO TO is a good thing.

[49] Wulf, W. A., "Report of workshop #3 'methodology'," Symposium on the High Cost of Software, Carnegie-Mellon University, September 17, 1973, pp. 1-12.

This paper discusses the qualitative differences among programs and explores means for consistently producing better programs. Also noted are the absolute cost of software, its cost relative to hardware and its cost escalation as time goes by. A number of software attributes are defined: maintainability, modifiability, robustness, clarity, performance, cost and portability.

[50] Zurcher, F. W. and B. Randell, "Iterative multi-level modeling — a methodology for computer system design," IFIP Congress, Edinburgh, 1968, pp. 867-871.

The paper presents a method of modeling a computer system design as it evolves so that evaluation can be made an integral part of the design process. The paper introduces the concept of concurrent existence, within a single model, of several representations of the system being modeled, at differing levels of abstraction.

[51] Datamation, December 1973, Issue on Structured Programming.

Five articles giving an overview of structured programming from the manager's point of view. Entertaining, but light on the technical side.

[52] Proceedings 1973 IEEE Symposium on Computer Software Reliability, April 1973.

A collection of papers covering subjects such as software testing, modeling and analysis of software, management techniques, programming methodology. Though spotty coverage, there are nice papers by people such as H. Mills, Ramamoorthy, B. Kernighan and P. Plauger.

[53] Structured Walk-Throughs: A Project Management Tool, IBM Corp. Data Processing Division, August 1973.

This short document defined the basic idea of the structured walk-through. This is a management technique designed to yield greater visibility of the software during development.

Police Custody

Governance, legitimacy and reform in the criminal justice process

Layla Skinns

Routledge
Taylor & Francis Group
LONDON AND NEW YORK

First published by Willan Publishing 2011
This edition published by Routledge 2011
2 Park Square, Milton Park, Abingdon, Oxon OX14 4RN
711 Third Avenue, New York, NY 10017 (8th Floor)

Routledge is an imprint of the Taylor & Francis Group

First issued in paperback 2012

ISBN 978-0-415-62775-7 paperback

ISBN 978-1-84392-813-3 hardback

British Library Cataloguing-in-Publication Data

A catalogue record for this book is available from the British Library

Project managed by Deer Park Productions, Tavistock, Devon
Typeset by TW Typesetting, Plymouth, Devon

For Kay and Len

Contents

List of figures and tables

Figures

Tables

List of abbreviations

AA	Appropriate adult
ACPO	Association of Chief Police Officers
APAC	Assessment of Policing and Community Safety
AR	Arrest referral
CCTV	Close-circuit television
CDRP	Crime and Disorder Reduction Partnership
CDS Direct	Criminal Defence Service Direct
CEG	Community engagement group
CID	Criminal Investigation Department (for the police)
CJIT	Criminal Justice Integrated Team
CPS	Crown Prosecution Service
DDO	Designated detention officer
DFs	Dihydrochloride
DIP	Drug Intervention Programme
DP	Detained person
DS	Detention supervisor
DSCC	Defence Solicitor Call Centre
ECHR	European Convention on Human Rights
ECtHR	European Court of Human Rights
FME	Forensic medical examiner
GBH	Grievous Bodily Harm
HMIC	Her Majesty's Inspectorate of Constabularies
HMIP	Her Majesty's Inspectorate of Prisons
HRA	Human Rights Act 1998
IPCC	Independent Police Complaints Commission
MAPPA	Multi-Agency Public Protection Arrangements
MPS	Metropolitan Police Service
MQPL	Measuring the Quality of Prison Life
NPIA	National Policing Improvements Agency
NSPCC	National Society for the Protection and Care of Children
NSPIS	National Strategy for Police Information Systems

OHCHR	Office of the UN High Commissioner of Human Rights
OIC	Officer in the Case
OPCAT	Optional Protocol for the UN Convention Against Torture
PACE	Police and Criminal Evidence Act 1984
PCCG	Police–community consultation group
PCSO	Police Community Support Officer
PFI	Public Finance Initiatives
PRA	Police Reform Act 2002
RCCJ	Royal Commission on Criminal Justice 1993
RCCP	Royal Commission on Criminal Procedure 1981
RSPCA	Royal Society for the Protection and Care of Animals
SPT	UN Subcommittee on Prevention of Torture and other Cruel, Inhuman or Degrading Treatment or Punishment

Acknowledgements

With thanks to all the fascinating people that I have encountered throughout the course of conducting the research. I am also enormously grateful for the research monies I received from the Economic and Social Research Council (RES-000-22-1719). Thanks must also go to Melony Sanders, Martin Duffy and Amber Marks for their shrewd observational skills, as well as to Zelia Gallo for her help with the data entry and, more recently, Scott Spencer, for creating a fitting book cover. The support and kindness of colleagues spanning four institutions has been exemplary. At King's College London much thanks in the early days of the research go to Mike Hough, Paul Turnbull and Tiggey May. At the Institute of Criminology and Darwin College, University of Cambridge, my thanks go to Hilary Powell, Alpa Parmar, Nicky Padfield, Loraine Gelsthorpe and Mary Gower. From my new institution, the University of Sheffield, thanks go to Joanna Shapland, Simon Holdaway, Stephen Farrall, Gwen Robinson and Gilly Sharpe. More recently still, Andrew Sanders has provided sound words of advice and a wonderful foreword to the book. My heartfelt thanks also go to all those involved in the production of the book from start to finish, especially Brian and Julia Willan and Bill Antrobus. Last, but not least, my special thanks go to my family, particularly Jess, whose legal 'rows' with custody officers provided a seed of an idea, and David, who read countless drafts, but particularly to my partner Matthew for his calmness, kindness and gentle encouragement throughout.

Foreword

Policing is a crucial part of modern society. The police are allowed to do things that would be civil or criminal actions if ordinary people did them: bugging, forcible entry to our homes, intimate body searches, aggressive questioning and involuntary detention in usually unpleasant conditions are just some examples. At their best, these powers enable policing to protect the vulnerable from the unscrupulous. At their worst they put the vulnerable under such pressure that some people say and do things that work to their disadvantage – sometimes with fatal results. Clearly we need policing, but we need to control it. This book is about one of the most important aspects of policing – custody – and how effectively it is controlled. It therefore goes to the heart of policing, but also raises questions about the values embedded in 21st century Britain.

Policing is rarely out of the news. It is literally a life and death matter, from the death of Ian Tomlinson after being struck by a police officer in a demonstration in 2009 to the dozens of deaths in police custody that happen every year. Yet, as Layla Skinns notes in this book, there has been little research on policing in the last 10 years or so in the UK.

This book is therefore very welcome. Based on extensive observation and data collection in two police stations, it provides a unique insight into the problems police officers and suspects face after arrest and before charge. It also highlights neglected issues such as the use of 'civilians' in police custody areas, and the problems that arise from this.

Data does, of course, have to be interpreted. It is clear from Layla Skinns' data that controls on the police are fairly 'light touch'. It would be hard to envisage anything different. But whether these controls are effective or not, and whether making them more effective would create more problems than they would solve, depends on one's perspective. I do not share Layla Skinns' perspective in every respect. But the important point is that she raises vital issues and presents logical and powerful arguments that cannot be dismissed. The Home Office and research councils should take careful note of her proposed agenda for research at the end of the book. Policy makers, practitioners and newspaper editors should read the whole book.

I look forward to this book inaugurating a new phase of research on policing.

Andrew Sanders
University of Birmingham

Chapter 1

Introduction

To put it simply, this book is about police custody in England and Wales, focusing on processes and practices that occur once a suspect arrives at the police station until when they leave. Drawing on existing and current research, the aim of the book is to describe and critically assess the custody process from the perspectives of suspects and police, but also from the perspectives of the other practitioners who work there, in particular non-warranted civilians known as police staff,[1] legal advisors, doctors, appropriate adults and drug workers. A further aim of the book is to begin to theorize the custody process. To do this, I have situated the book within theories about procedural justice and police legitimacy, and governance. These theories are mainly explored in Chapter 2. The purpose of the present chapter, however, is to outline current policy and practice in police custody areas in England and Wales.

Police custody is an important but neglected area of scholarly research. With the exceptions of Newburn and Hayman (2002), Phillips and Brown (1998) and Choongh (1997), there have been few studies of the police custody process over the last decade, which contrasts with the flurry of research that emerged in the period immediately after the introduction of the Police and Criminal Evidence Act 1984 (PACE), an important piece of legislation which aimed to regulate police custody more closely as well as other police practices. And yet, police custody is also an important topic because there is a great deal at stake for staff and suspects in this gateway to the criminal justice process. Police custody can deeply affect suspects, particularly the vulnerable, whether that is to have the effect of frightening or angering them or worse still contributing to them admitting to something that they did not do or pushing them into self-harming behaviour. The police can also behave in ways that can fundamentally shape these experiences of police custody, as can aspects of the wider custody environment, such as the cleanliness and warmth of the cells or the availability of a shower before court. Changes to the ways that the police custody process works mean that it is no longer just the police who influence the experiences of suspects; now, so too can non-warranted police staff, along with legal advisors, medical staff, drug workers, appropriate adults and others.

In this chapter, I clarify the parameters of the police custody process. First, I critically assess the purposes of the police custody process. Second, I describe suspects' rights and entitlements under PACE and the key practitioners in police custody areas, while situating this description within a discussion of the history of PACE. Third, I provide a brief history of research on police custody, exploring how the present book diverges from it. Fourth, I examine some of the key features of the wider socio-political context and how they have impacted on police custody. Finally, I provide a brief outline of my analytical framework and the content of the book.

Police custody and its purposes

Police custody functions as a gateway to the criminal justice process. It is the place where suspects are taken on arrest and while the police or those working for the Crown Prosecution Service (CPS), based in the police station, reach a decision about whether to:

- charge the suspect with an offence;
- caution the suspect, which requires that he/she admits to the offence and, among other things, that the offence be minor and that the suspect has a short, if not non-existent, criminal record (Sanders and Young, 2006: 351);[2]
- give the suspect police bail either after they are charged or while a decision is reached about whether to charge them.[3] The latter is known as 'bail to return' and if the suspect fails to arrive for an agreed appointment, then a warrant can be issued for their arrest;
- take no further action, which may be necessary because there is insufficient evidence to charge the suspect;
- release the suspect without charge, which is different to no further action in that the suspect is wholly exonerated as it is decided that they are no longer even suspected of committing an offence.

Police custody is the first stop after arrest and the last stop before court. For this reason, it is a central part of the criminal justice process, particularly, as decisions made at this early stage can be reinforced by decisions later in the process; for example, those who do not receive police bail are unlikely to receive bail at court (Sanders and Young, 2006: 176), and so the momentum of the criminal justice process begins in police custody areas. However, as Choongh (1997: 40–1) notes, for a minority of suspects police custody is an undesirable end-point rather than the entrance to the criminal justice process; in these cases, police custody alone is used to pursue police objectives to maintain authority, deference and subordination, as well as exercise summary punishment and social control over those who come into regular contact with the police.

In theory, police custody contributes mainly to the role of the police in investigating and reducing crime. The investigatory function is of particular importance to the police custody process; after all, most suspected offences can lead to arrest and detention to 'allow for the prompt and effective investigation of the (suspected offence)' (Serious Organised Crime and Police Act 2005, s. 110). To this end, suspects in police custody can be interviewed and biometric data, such as fingerprints, photographs, results from drug tests and DNA, can also be collected from them. This also means that arrest (and detention) are the start not the end-point of the police investigation (Gearty, 2007: 102).

The collection of DNA has been a particularly controversial part of police investigations. Section 82 of the Criminal Justice and Police Act 2001 allows DNA and fingerprints to be taken from those arrested for, charged with, or informed that they are to be reported for a recordable offence and detained in a police station,[4] regardless of whether they are later released without charge or whether they are acquitted. Since the implementation of the Act, these data have been retained on the National DNA database and can be kept there for 100 years. The National database is used to cross-match suspects to verify their identity or to see if they are wanted for any outstanding matters. On 4 December 2008, the European Court of Human Rights (ECtHR) ruled that keeping the DNA of the innocent constitutes an infringement of their right to respect for private and family life, under the Human Rights Convention (*Guardian*, 2008).[5] In spite of this ruling, the Home Office has remained reluctant to remove the DNA of the innocent from the database, reasoning that it was too much of an administrative burden and that removal would undermine the possibilities of identifying future offenders through the database. More recently still, on 11 November 2009, the government announced plans to remove the DNA only of those arrested but not charged or convicted after six years and this was legislated for in the Crime and Security Act 2010, which received Royal Assent in April 2010.

The evidence collected and collated by officers while a suspect is in police custody is central to decisions about any charge and ultimately whether the suspect is convicted and punished. As the public debate about the retention of DNA demonstrates, there are concerns that police custody is largely used to build a case for the prosecution, albeit within the confines of due process controls such as PACE. As such, the police custody process can be seen as a prosecutorial 'sausage factory' churning out suspects once a case has been built against them by the police and charges have been laid by the CPS. The prosecutorial and routinized nature of the custody process and those working within it is also apparent in other ways, such as in relation to the authorization of detention. In theory, the sergeant booking in a suspect must decide, based on the information presented to them by the arresting officer, whether detention at the police station is necessary. In practice, the custody officers rarely reverse the decision of the arresting officer. For example, Phillips and Brown (1998: 49) found that there was only one case (out of 4,246) where a custody officer did not authorize a suspect's detention. Similarly, McConville *et al.* (1991: 45) found that for the majority of suspects, their detention was authorized without scrutiny. Therefore the purpose of the police custody process for the police, at least, is not just to investigate an offence, but to build as a strong a case as possible against the suspect.

In practice, police custody has other purposes too. Police custody areas are places where coercive policing is employed from time to time; when a suspect does not agree or consent to being policed, they may be coerced either through the threat of or use of force. Famously, Bittner (1970) argued that, within the context of the quest for peace in modern nation-states, the police alone have the monopoly over the use of unrestricted coercive force, if it is justified by the circumstances. He says '[a] society committed to the achievement of peace by pacific means has created an institution [the police] with the monopoly to employ non-negotiably coercive force in situations where its use is unavoidably necessary' (1970: 122).

In fact, it is the unrestricted nature of the legitimate use of force by the police which makes this competence unique and separates them from other kinds of organizations designated with the use of force in specified circumstances, such as prison officers or the military. Consequently, the forms of coercion employed by the police in police custody areas are varied; they range from physical forms of restraint such as the use of handcuffs, pepper spray or physically carrying suspects to their cells if they refuse to go of their own accord, to restraining them while they are strip-searched if they refuse to consent to a search. However, coercion is no longer the preserve of the police alone, at least within the police custody process in England and Wales. Workforce modernization, which I describe in more detail later in this chapter, has meant that civilians employed either by the police or by private security companies (known as police staff) are involved in the use of coercion along with fulfilling other roles in the police custody process.

However, coercion may not have to involve force. The 'Tough Choices' initiative introduced in 2006 under the umbrella of the Drug Intervention Programme (DIP) and as a result of the Drugs Act 2005 is used to encourage those suspected of 'trigger' offences to receive help with their drug problem, but under conditions which are arguably coercive. Trigger offences are mainly acquisitive crimes, such as shoplifting and burglary, which are believed to be drug-related.[6] If someone is arrested for such an offence within an intensive DIP area – that is, an area with large numbers of problematic drug users – they have to take a drug test on arrest, which looks for evidence of cocaine and opiates in the saliva. If a suspect declines to take the drug test, they have committed an offence, which carries a maximum tariff of up to three months in custody and a fine of £2,500. The police are responsible for administering this test and it is one of the few parts of the police custody process for which there is a performance target, which is known as Cozart.[7] Drug-testing on arrest suggests that the police have developed new coercive roles which may not have been fully anticipated by Bittner (1970).

A combination of factors including the discretionary and invisible nature of police power in police custody areas, a rank-and-file occupational culture (which expresses suspiciousness towards and solidarity against, for example, 'police property' (Reiner, 2010: 123–4)) and the possibility of coercion suggest that police custody may also be used to punish or retaliate against recalcitrant or uncooperative suspects or to teach them about the parameters of their relationship with the police. For example, Choongh (1997: 100) argues that police custody has been used as a form of social discipline. This meant that suspects who were locked into a regular relationship with the police and/or were non-compliant found that their length of detention was affected by whether or not the police wished to condition them into accepting their authority or to put pressure on them to confess, albeit in accordance with the rules.

These 'other' purposes of police custody can have lethal consequences as illustrated by the case of Christopher Alder. He died face-down on the floor of a Hull Police station in the early hours of 1 April 1998 after his uncharacteristically aggressive behaviour was blamed on his 'bad attitude' rather than the head injury incurred during an incident which had racist overtones (IPCC, 2006). Mr Alder had been involved in a fight outside a nightclub, which resulted in him being knocked unconscious for 11 minutes. He was taken to hospital, and was eventually arrested there after he became seen as being too aggressive to have been treated by staff. He was arrested for a breach of the peace at the hospital and taken to the police custody area, being dragged out of the back of a police van with his trousers around his ankles and doubly incontinent. In the custody area, the officers focused on 'processing' him. They claimed they believed him to be faking illness, even though there was no evidence of this. His last minutes of life were captured on CCTV. The most likely cause of death is believed by medical experts to have been asphyxiation due to the position he was left in.[8]

Thus far, I have pointed to the purposes of the police custody process for the police in terms of investigation and crime reduction, as well in terms of coercion, social discipline and the building of a case for the prosecution. However, it is important to acknowledge that police custody also has a purpose for suspects (e.g. to establish their innocence or enable a swift release), as well as for the other practitioners that work in police custody areas who are likely to have a variety of sometimes overlapping organizational objectives. These are discussed in Chapters 3 and 7. Moreover, police custody is underpinned by legislation used to regulate the police practices therein, which is largely through PACE.

Suspects' PACE rights and entitlements

Broadly speaking, suspects have ongoing rights and entitlements, which they can use at any time. These include:

- access to free and independent legal advice, as soon as is practicable;
- the right to notify someone of their arrest, such as a friend or family member, as soon as is practicable;
- the right to consult the PACE Codes of Practice, which is a lengthy, legalistic and somewhat difficult to read book detailing rights and entitlements available to suspects. Code C is of greatest relevance to non-terrorist suspects;
- a qualified right to silence, meaning that negative inferences can be drawn from their silence, that is, if they fail to mention something in an interview that they later rely on at court;
- access to a doctor, if a suspect is feeling unwell;
- access to an appropriate adult, if a suspect is a juvenile or mentally ill or intellectually impaired.[9]

Since the introduction of PACE, these rights and entitlements in police custody areas are predominantly provided by a combination of:

- police, including police constables, sergeants and inspectors;
- non-warranted civilians who are known as police staff and are employed directly by the police (and henceforth referred to as public police staff) or by private security companies (henceforth referred to as private police staff);
- legal advisors who are solicitors, accredited trainee solicitors or accredited legal representatives. Of the solicitors, aside from working for a law firm, some also register to be duty solicitors, who are on-call around the clock to respond to requests for publicly funded legal advice;

- appropriate adults who support vulnerable suspects, that is juveniles and adults who are mentally ill or intellectually impaired. Appropriate adults include parents, legal guardians, volunteers and social workers;
- doctors, who are known as forensic medical examiners, and also sometimes nurses;
- drug workers whose role grew out of the arrest referral initiatives of the 1980s in which drugs workers identified problematic drug users in police custody and referred them to local drug services. This role, however, was formalized by the Drug Intervention Programme in 2002 which introduced drug workers into all police custody areas;
- interpreters;
- independent custody visitors – formerly known as lay visitors – who were put on a statutory footing by the Police Reform Act 2002. They have to be allowed access to monitor police custody facilities, suspects and their records, even if their visit is unannounced.

To a lesser extent, the Crown Prosecution Service (CPS), particularly those workers based in the police station, also have a role in implementing PACE rights and entitlements, since they are responsible for making decisions about charging. The roles and responsibilities of these staff members, with the exception of the CPS, are described in more detail in Chapter 3.

For non-terrorist suspects, who are the focus of this book, under PACE and following amendments implemented as a result of the Criminal Justice Act 2003, suspects arrested for summary and indictable offences can be detained without charge for a maximum of 24 or 36 hours,[10] respectively, although for both the period of detention can be extended from 24 to 36 hours by a superintendent or person of a higher rank (Home Office, 2009: 18). In exceptional circumstances, those suspected of either summary or indictable offences can have their detention extended to 96 hours if the police successfully apply to a magistrate. In theory, the 'PACE clock', as it is known, puts pressure on officers to expedite cases so that suspects do not spend unnecessary time in police custody.

PACE emerged in the wake of public disturbances, such as the miners' strikes and the Brixton riots, with the Act demonstrating the strength of the state in the face of opposition to Margaret Thatcher and the then Conservative government.[11] Dixon argues that PACE was 'the distinctive product of a governing strategy – "authorize and regulate" – which fitted a particular juncture in twentieth-century liberal democratic societies. That juncture has now passed, and new ideologies, priorities and rhetoric have come to dominate our world' (2008: 43–4). Indeed, since its inception, PACE and the Codes of Practice have been regularly revised, although never substantially overhauled. For this reason, questions have been raised by some, including the Home Office, about whether PACE is fit for its purpose. The Home Office began a significant review of PACE in March 2007 which is ongoing;[12] so far, it has consisted of two rounds of public consultation, one of which has been responded to by the Home Office, and one meeting of the PACE Review Board (Home Office, 2008b). After a short delay,[13] in March 2010, information from the second round of consultation was published. At the time of writing, there was no governmental response to this round of consultation and the change of government after the general election on 6 May 2010 is likely to delay matters further.

Prior to PACE, the police custody process was regulated by the Judges' Rules. These rules arose in 1906 in response to uncertainties about police practices such as length of detention, access to legal advice and cautioning and were formalized and extended in 1912 and 1918. Even so, they remained 'unclear, self-contradictory and incomplete' (Dixon, 1997: 131). Later, the Judges' Rules were heavily criticized by the Royal Commission on Criminal Procedure for contributing to miscarriages of justice (RCCP, 1981). The RCCP was announced by the Labour government on 23 June 1977. Its main aim was to conduct a holistic review of the criminal process as for much of the previous century reforms had been piecemeal (Dixon, 1997: 142). In addition, there was mounting criticism about the use of police powers, particularly in the wake of the Maxwell Confait murder case. In the Confait case, the Court of Appeal quashed the convictions of three juveniles (who were also intellectually impaired): police malpractice in the handling of the investigation and mistreatment of suspects were believed to contribute to false confessions. In addition to this focus on malpractice, the terms of reference were also to take account of 'the need for the efficient and economical use of resources' (para 1.10, p. 4). Many of the principles and recommendations from the RCCP, for example about the length of detention, the right to legal advice, the recording of police interviews and the treatment of juveniles and the intellectually impaired, subsequently became embodied in PACE, albeit with some variations.[14]

Research on police custody in England and Wales: a short history

Much of the early research on police custody and, indeed, on other aspects of the criminal justice process was driven by concerns about police malpractice. This tendency was apparent from the RCCP and onwards.[15] Twelve research studies into police practices on topics such as arrest, police interviews (or interrogations as they were referred to then), charge, prosecution, the use of confessions in court and contested cases in magistrates' courts were considered by the Commission. These studies were undertaken by academics that subsequently went on to research and publish widely in the area of police custody and criminal justice, including Barrie Irving, David Brown, John Baldwin and Michael McConville. There was also other research at this time which critiqued police malpractice and the factors that enabled it to flourish. For example, Holdaway (1980) – using Goffman's notion of 'frontstage' and 'backstage', where the former is used to present an idealized image of order – argued that, in police custody, the police largely engaged in backstage behaviour, unless supervisors or doctors were present, in which case frontstage behaviour would be used, such as the shielding of supervisors from the 'questioning' of suspects where force had been used.

The flurry of research immediately after the implementation of PACE from the mid-1980s to the early 1990s was used to examine the impact of the Act on police (mal)practice (e.g. Maguire, 1988; Brown, 1989; Irving and MacKenzie, 1989; Sanders *et al.*, 1989; Dixon *et al.*, 1990; Bottomley *et al.*, 1991; Dixon, 1991; McConville *et al.*, 1991). PACE was found to have been variously received by the police. In one study, Maguire (1988: 32) showed that junior officers disliked what they saw as additional paperwork, as well as the threat of disciplinary action. Outside of London, these officers regarded PACE as punishment for the 'sins of the Met' (that is the Metropolitan Police Service, who police London). Sergeants, however, were more ambivalent; they also disliked the additional paperwork and rules created by PACE, as well as disliking the monotonous but independent job of being a custody officer (in charge of the treatment of suspects in police custody), but recognized the value of PACE in protecting them against allegations made by suspects about mistreatment. Maguire (1988) found that the greatest hostility to PACE arose from the Criminal Investigation Department (CID detectives), who disliked having to take notes in interviews, newly required in all cases by PACE, which they felt interrupted the flow.

PACE was also variously regarded in terms of its impact on suspects' access to their rights and entitlements. Some, such as Irving and McKenzie (1989), regarded it as a progressive change to police detention and interrogation practices. By contrast, others, such as academics from the 'Warwick School', regarded PACE as having been absorbed by the police but without making any changes to their priorities, culture and crime control commitments (McConville *et al.*, 1991: 189). That is, the police had made PACE 'work' for them. This was apparent, for example, in relation to access to legal advice, where the police were found to use ploys to dissuade suspects from requesting and consulting with a legal advisor, such as reading them their rights quickly, incomprehensibly or incompletely or telling suspects that they would have to wait or that they were only going to be in the station for a short time (e.g. Sanders *et al.*, 1989: 59). Consequently, it was argued that rather than regulating the police, PACE had facilitated and legitimated existing powers and practices.

This latter understanding of the impact of PACE was both influential and controversial.[16] Like Dixon (1997: 166–7), however, I am a sceptical optimist about the impact of PACE and, moreover, about the possibility of legal reform for changing police practices. PACE may be imperfect as a mechanism for regulating police practices, as this book shows. PACE may also have extended police powers, such as the storing of DNA and fingerprints on a national DNA database and, in the review of PACE in 2007, there are discussions about allowing the police to question suspects after charge. Nevertheless, it remains an important piece of legislation and it is better than having no legal framework at all.

In its defence, the murky nature of custody suites prior to 1984 meant that the value of PACE was in providing a framework of clearly specified and comprehensive rules, outlining police powers and suspects' rights (Maguire, 1988). While it may have formalized existing police practices in the police station and added to bureaucracy, it also clarified ambiguities, such as those regarding cautioning or a suspect's right to legal advice or the length of detention without charge, and meant that a record had to be kept of every suspect who came into custody. The value of having such a clear framework is all too apparent when one compares England and Wales to other jurisdictions, such as in the United States, where there is no equivalent legislation, or to other countries which were slower to develop such a framework, such as parts of Australia. In these jurisdictions, police officers working in custody areas are dependent on senior officers to translate case law into practice, for example through directives, and if this is not done effectively uncertainties about the treatment of suspects in police custody contribute to inconsistencies and unfairness. For example, Dixon (1997: 205–14) notes the uncertainties in New South Wales about the purpose of arrest, whether it was for questioning or for bringing someone before a court for charging, which arose because of ongoing discussion of this issue in the courts. In the absence of a clear framework, it is also possible for police officers to exploit uncertainties in the custody process to suit their own ends. For example, uncertainties about the maximum length of detention without charge might mean that suspects are held indefinitely (Skinns, 2010).

There was another flurry of research around the time of the next major review of the safeguarding of suspects in the police station. The Royal Commission on Criminal Justice (RCCJ) was announced in 1991, eventually reporting on its deliberations in 1993. Like the RCCP, it took place in the wake of miscarriages of justice which came to light between 1989 and 1991, even though they had occurred before the introduction of PACE (Reiner, 1992). These miscarriages of justice included the 'Guildford Four' and the 'Maguire Seven' and they shared in common the police suppressing evidence for the defence and obtaining incriminating evidence through oppressive means (Sanders and Young, 2006: 16). The RCCJ was chaired by Viscount Runciman and its terms of reference were to explore the effectiveness of the criminal justice process for securing convictions of the guilty and the acquittal of the innocent (Hirst, 1993: 27). As for the RCCP, 23 research studies were hurriedly prepared for consideration by the RCCJ on topics such as the tape-recording of interviews and the role of legal representatives (Baldwin, 1992); the role of police surgeons (Robertson, 1992); suspects' understanding of their rights (Clare and Gudjonsson, 1992); interviews with juveniles (Evans, 1993); the right to silence (Leng, 1993); the identification of vulnerable adult suspects (Gudjonsson *et al.*, 1993); custodial legal advice and its relationship with the right to silence (McConville *et al.*, 1993); and the questioning and interviewing of suspects outside the police station (Moston and Stephenson, 1993). In spite of the recommendations of the RCCJ in favour of keeping an unqualified right to silence, the government enacted the Criminal Justice and Public Order Act 1994 which allowed adverse inferences to be drawn (Sanders and Young, 2006: 235). Other recommendations, however, were heeded such as the creation of a Criminal Cases Review Commission to review alleged miscarriages of justice (Sanders and Young, 2006: 580).

In the early 1990s there were also other empirical studies of relevance to police custody, including McConville *et al.*'s (1994) study of the practices of defence solicitors. However, the empirical interest in police custody began to dwindle in the mid- to late-1990s. There were a few notable exceptions to this. In his qualitative study – in which a period of observing in two police custody areas was followed by interviews with 80 suspects – Choongh (1997) retained a focus on police malpractice. His main argument was that police custody has extra-legal functions, namely to discipline suspects, particularly the 'regulars', into accepting the boundaries of their relationship with the police. His study contrasted with the only other empirical research on police custody in this period, namely the policy-orientated research of Bucke and Brown (1997) and Phillips and Brown (1998) published by the Home Office. These two studies provided a wealth of useful information, not least because of the size of the studies,[17] but also because they were a review of key issues, such as the role of appropriate adults, access to legal advice, interviewing, bail decisions and entrance into the criminal justice process. At the same time, they did not fully explore how and why difficulties arose, and whether police malpractice was partially to blame. More recently, Newburn and Hayman (2002) have translated an evaluation study of the use of closed-circuit television (CCTV) in police stations, which was invited by the police, into an academic book which reflects on the advantages and disadvantages of surveillance, in that the cameras were used to watch the police, not just suspects.

Since then, there have been only two pieces of empirical research on police custody. The first was the mixed-method study on which this book is based for which the data were collected in 2007. Further details of the research base are in the appendix. Aspects of the research have already been written about in other publications, including the factors affecting access to legal advice (Skinns, 2009a, 2009b, 2011), length of detention (Skinns, 2010) and the lawfulness of legal advice at the police station (Pattenden and Skinns, 2010). Subsequent to this, researchers from the predominantly independent research arm of the Legal Services Commission conducted a survey of defendants and prisoners about their experiences of legal advice at court and in the police station (Kemp and Balmer, 2008) which was, later still, accompanied by an observational study of eight police stations (Kemp, 2010). More recently still, data from 30,921 police custody records have been used to explore access to custodial legal advice (Pleasence *et al.*, 2011).

The policy focus of much of the most recent research means that the present study, given its orientation towards theoretical matters such as governance and procedural justice and police legitimacy, which are discussed in Chapter 2, bears the most resemblance to Newburn and Hayman (2002) and particularly to Choongh (1997). Like me, Newburn and Hayman (2002) describe the nature of the suspect population, those working in the police custody area, as well as touching on inter-agency dynamics. However, this is only fleeting, given their focus on CCTV in police custody areas, which also means that they situate the book within theories about surveillance. Choongh (1997), as is the case in the present book, critically examines suspect experiences of police custody and access to their rights and entitlements. He also positions the book, to a degree, within ideas about due process and procedural justice. However, his work differs from the present study in two important ways. First, he focuses on suspect perspectives, not those of the police or other criminal justice practitioners, which means that he ends up with a 'lop-sided' view of police custody and an almost obsessive focus on its extra-legal purposes. Second, his legal background means that he examines the implications of the book for socio-legal matters such as the reliability of evidence in confessions, rather than the implications for theories about procedural justice.

Consequently, what is new in the book is the explicit focus on most of the important players in the police custody process, including suspects, police and civilian police staff, legal advisors, doctors, drug workers and appropriate adults. The starting point for the book is that all these actors have a role to play in enabling suspects' access to their rights and entitlements, rather than it being only down to the police. What is also new is the knitting together of the empirical findings with what have been hitherto separate theories about governance and police and prison legitimacy. Finally, since the studies in the late-1990s, there has been little empirical research on police custody. Yet the organizational context for the police and other key players has changed dramatically, prompted by changes in the wider socio-political environment, which I examine next. Therefore this book builds on, updates but also challenges some of the existing research on police custody.

Police custody and the wider context

Undeniably the socio-political context of the police custody process has altered over time. Neo-liberalism – referring to the 'the re-assertion of market disciplines' (Garland, 2001: 98) and resulting in greater economic freedom and greater individual choice for most but not all – has contributed to a new variant of managerialism. These terms refer to the application of private sector management techniques to the public sector – and have altered the role that the state plays in crime control.[18] Liberalism is no longer used in a way that expresses sympathy for the offender rather than the victim, treating them as a kind of victim lacking personal agency due to personal and social pathologies, deprivation and inequality.[19] Nor is liberalism used to convey the valorization of human rights expressed by the founders of the Enlightenment. The New Right has transformed the meaning of liberalism to express the need for personal and social responsibility moderated by top-down control by the state (Garland, 2001: 98). Hence, under this influence, we have seen the redistribution of responsibility for tasks of government to statutory, voluntary and commercial institutions, and citizens (e.g. to multi-agency partnerships such as the Crime and Disorder Reduction Partnerships), which are simultaneously micro-managed by central government. That is, government has become simultaneously centralized and decentralized in its use of power, leaving localized actors and organizations to 'row' while they 'steer' (Osborne and Gaebler, 1992: 146).

Governance, in relation to policing and security, has two different meanings. First, it refers to the 'constitutional and institutional arrangements for framing and directing the policies of the police' (Jones, 2003: 605). This understanding accords with older accounts of police governance, such as that by Lustgarten (1986: 178), which emphasized a prominent role for the state within policing arrangements. Within this perspective, the law is a fundamental part of the constitutional and institutional arrangements of the police (and other social actors involved in governing security). It provides a framework within which social actors should operate, although adherence with the law can be impeded by cultural and structural factors, a matter to be discussed later. Accountability mechanisms, such as the tripartite system (of chief constables, police authorities and the Home Secretary) or the police complaints system, are a part of the institutional arrangements of the police, contributing to the governance of security because they are used to check whether the police are fulfilling their role.

Second, it is concerned with the regulation and ordering of contemporary societies. It refers to 'any process that deliberately attempts to shape events. To govern, in this sense, is to intentionally seek to influence the flow of events . . . that are intended to promote security' (Shearing, 2007:

249). This second and perhaps more recent understanding of police governance recognizes the varied role that the police play within policing arrangements, as well as the involvement of others. For the purposes of this book, the concept of governance will be used to reflect both of these meanings. The first of these meanings is particularly important when examining how suspects' rights and entitlements, as set out in PACE, are put into practice in police custody, which is the subject of Chapter 5. The second meaning is particularly important in Chapters 6 and 7 which look at the roles of a range of criminal justice practitioners in custody areas; I argue that, alongside the police, these practitioners also play a (limited) role in regulating and ordering police custody.

Within this recent climate of neo-liberalism, with its preference for private sector management techniques and responsibilization, one of the ways that government has retained centralized control over localized social actors and organizations is through performance-monitoring regimes. This has been manifest in relation to the police with a more vigorous form of managerialism, which goes beyond a mere concern with expenditure and effectiveness, as was the case immediately after the First World War (Jones and Newburn, 2002). Similarly, Hough (2007) argues that, managerialism may have emerged with calls for 'value for money' in the public sector when the Conservative government came to power in 1979, but it has continued and been extended under New Labour who, for example, rebranded privatization and 'market-testing' as competition and contestability. This intensification of managerialism falls under the umbrella concept of 'new public management' (NPM), a term coined by Hood (1990b, cited in Hood, 1991); it might even be referred to as 'hyper-managerialism', in the light of movements towards simultaneously centralized and decentralized control.[20] On a practical level, this means that the police and other criminal justice agencies are subject to management practices derived from the private sector, including targets and key performance indicators, on which their funding partially depends, as well as the deliberate introduction of purchaser–provider splits, involving providers from the private sector and decentralized decision-making in the public sector.

These socio-political developments have left an indelible mark on the police custody process in three key ways. First, what is important in this climate of NPM is not just that criminal justice agencies pursue the goal of crime control, but that the manner in which they do this is as efficient and effective as possible. Efficient crime control, as well as, increasingly, public reassurance, are agendas that have been pushed by central government. This has been enabled by their role in 'steering' local policing matters (while also allowing responsibilized agents of the state and citizens to 'row' in partnership with the police). For example, the Police Act 1996 allowed the Home Secretary to set national policing objectives, and since then other key changes have included giving the Home

Secretary the power to dismiss underperforming chief constables and the establishment of the Police Standards Unit (now called the Police Community Standards Unit) and the National Policing Improvements Agency to monitor the performance of the police. More recently still, the resignation of Sir Ian Blair as the Commissioner of the Metropolitan Police, which was pre-empted, encouraged and possibly even coerced by the Mayor of London, Boris Johnson, goes to show the continuing power of those in government over chief constable posts.

Second, civilianization of key police roles has given way to privatization which is commonly referred to as 'workforce modernization' (Flanagan, 2008).[21] Since the 1980s, the police have employed civilians as detention officers who perform cell checks and look after the welfare of suspects in the cells. HMIC (2004) found that 32 of the 43 police services in England and Wales employed police staff as detention officers. Drawing on provisions in the Police Reform Act 2002 and funding by the Home Office, 16 of these 32 forces had designated these public police staff with powers to fingerprint, photograph, search and take non-intimate samples from suspects.[22] By employing civilian staff, HMIC (2004) argue that police custody areas become more cost-effective; civilians reduce bureaucratic burdens and free-up the time of experienced custody officers, who can then be re-deployed to supervise front-line duties such as arrest and detection (p. 168). Money is also saved, in theory, because civilian officers in police custody areas cost less than their police counterparts. For example, Greasley and Barlow simulated the reallocation of the tasks of custody officers (e.g. booking in suspects) to jailors and found that it would result in 'significant savings in staffing costs provided the staff time saved can be utilized effectively' (1998: 986). However, it remains to be seen whether custody officers have been effectively redeployed or whether costs are reduced by employing civilian staff in police custody areas, particularly as research on the privatization of prisons has shown that reforms do not always result in the anticipated savings.[23]

Without much public debate, privatization has also begun to take root in police custody areas with private companies becoming involved in building or refurbishing and managing custody areas through public finance initiatives (PFI), as well as supplying police staff. This lack of public debate is unsurprising, however, given that the extent of privatization of police custody areas remains unclear and, revealingly, the only information available is on the websites of security companies. The lack of public debate about the privatization of police custody areas may also be because of a lack of research or public knowledge of workforce modernization in police custody areas, although it may also suggest that the use of public–private criminal justice partnerships have become accepted as the status quo in the wake of the privatization of prisons. Either way, it is worrying given that the research on private prisons has failed to reach satisfactory conclusions about the relative advantages and disadvantages of privatization; in particular, questions about improved cost-effectiveness remain largely unanswered, the consequences for inmates' sense of justice unknown and the impact on prison accountability relatively unexplored.[24]

(Defence) legal advisors have also been subject to a form of 'workforce modernization'. Concerns about the cost of legal aid have meant that their role has been affected by the Carter Review in 2003. These reforms have resulted in changes to the way that legal advisors are paid; since October 2007 they are paid a fixed fee per police station visit, which is supposed to include any travel costs or time spent waiting at the police station, rather than each of these being paid for separately as they used to be. This is likely to add to legal advisors' reluctance to attend police stations in person until their client is ready to be interviewed and to increase their reliance on telephone legal advice in the first instance. Since April 2008, the Criminal Defence Service Direct, known as CDS Direct, was rolled out nationally, meaning that for specified and less serious offences, including drink-driving, publicly funded legal advice is only provided over the telephone.

Another important change is that since January 2008 all publicly funded requests for legal advice are routed through the Defence Solicitor Call Centre.[25] This service is provided by First Assist Ltd, who notify the appropriate legal advisor of the request. Since January 2008, if a suspect nominates a legal advisor the advisor will only be contacted three times for up to two hours and after that they are allocated the duty solicitor. If suspects are forced to opt for the duty solicitor (because their nominated solicitor cannot be contacted) they may, in fact, opt for no solicitor rather than a solicitor that they have never met, especially if the role of the duty solicitor is misunderstood by some suspects, who believe that they work for the police or are too busy to give them a personalized service (Choongh, 1997: 149, 152; Sanders *et al.*, 1989: 76).

Third, police custody areas are also an increasingly multi-professional context. Since the 1980s the police custody area has become host to a range of practitioners described in the section above. Police custody areas can be viewed, therefore, as a multi-professional context the development of which has been partly driven by the diverse nature of suspects' legal, mental, physical and drug-related needs. Failing to meet these needs can have serious, if not, lethal consequences. For example, in a recent report by the Independent Police Complaints Commission it was found that over a 12-month period when there were 28 deaths in custody, it was estimated that there were 1,000 'near misses' which were primarily related to attempted suicide/self-harm and drug consumption or possession (IPCC, 2008). The multi-professional context means that while the custody officer may have overall responsibility for the care and fair treatment of suspects, other actors also make a contribution and the stakes are high for *all* involved in the police custody process.

The analytical framework

Before setting out what the rest of the book is about, first I want to set out my analytical framework. The book is socio-legal – probably more 'socio-' than legal – in its orientation. Rather than focusing on the minutiae of the police custody environment or on individual decision-making within it, as (social) psychologists might, my aim is to situate suspects and staff within their broader socio-political-historical context, as well as trying to think about how the law is put into practice in the 'real world'. This has meant developing connections between the micro- and macro-levels of society, so between the micro-social world of the two custody areas in the research and the macro-social world of power, legitimacy and governance that are used to structure society. The socio-legal focus of the book means that another important strand to the book is an attempt to identify, throughout, the gulf between the 'is' and the 'ought', between practice and rhetoric, and between the empirical and the normative. For example, PACE may provide a framework for how police custody should function, but the reality, as the book shows, can be quite different. In so doing, I also step beyond merely exposing the moral choices of criminal justice practitioners and tentatively towards providing a view on what those moral choices should be.

Furthermore, there are three main themes to the book. First, in the light of previous research, it was difficult to avoid the idea that police custody could be a site for police malpractice. However, the intention was to provide as balanced a view as possible of police custody. Hence, I sought the views of suspects and a range of criminal justice practitioners. This also enabled an examination of the relationships between them and how this impacted on suspects' access to their rights and entitlements. At the same time, it sometimes also led to ambivalence about how the police exercised their authority, simply because I was able to see it from a range of perspectives. The second key theme that is developed in the book is the idea that different kinds of staff in different contexts, within the custody area, employ different philosophies and strategies for maintaining social order. These strategies can be, on the one hand, emblematic of aspects of procedural justice, thereby having the potential to enhance the legitimacy of those that use them and contribute to cooperation and compliance. On the other hand, they can be authoritarian, punitive and connected with a more utilitarian way of exercising power. The third, is the idea that police custody is like a bridge in the sense that it acts as a bridge between the police and, ultimately, prison (if the offence and the offender are serious enough to warrant it). Consequently, one of the conclusions of the book is that, even though it can be a fairly short-lived experience, police custody is more like prison than anticipated at the outset of the research. Police custody also acts as a bridge, for example, for civilian non-sworn staff who want to become police officers or for police officers who want some time in a more controlled environment than out on the streets before they retire.

In sum, the book examines what the custody environment is like, as well as exploring the experiences of those working within it and those who are on the receiving end of it. The account offered is both empirical and theoretical in its focus. The research is situated within two main theoretical debates about procedural justice and police legitimacy, and governance, and the intersections between them. These are explored in Chapter 2. The aim of the research was not to explicitly test these theories. However, it became apparent that these theories were a fundamental backdrop to the research. The empirical findings from the research are discussed and integrated with the existing research in Chapters 3 to 7. Chapter 3 examines the roles and responsibilities of those working in police custody areas and describes the features of the suspect population. Chapter 4 critically examines aspects of the custody environment, such as the cells, the showers and the buzzer systems. Chapter 5 examines suspects' access to their rights and entitlements such as phone calls and legal advice as well as their experiences of legal requirements such as detention reviews, and explores some of the circumstances in which police practices diverge from the law. Chapter 6 explores relationships between the police and police staff and suspects' differential experiences of the two. Chapter 7 broadens the discussion in Chapter 6 from plural policing to an exploration of relationships between the police/police staff and other criminal justice practitioners, including legal advisors, doctors, drug workers and appropriate adults.

Chapter 8 examines the implications of the research for the theoretical issues outlined in Chapter 2. The growing recognition of parallels between police custody and prison means that the implications of the findings from the research for theories about governance, procedural justice and legitimacy are discussed in terms of the police and prisons. Based on these theories and the empirical evidence, one of the aims of the book is to develop the key components of a model of how social order is created and maintained in police custody areas, which might be tested in future research, both in England and Wales and in other jurisdictions. This is the subject of Chapter 9, as are the implications of the research for improving the police custody process in the future.

Notes

1 Non-warranted means that they do not have warrant cards, which are carried by police officers to certify their identity and to indicate their authority.
2 Details of the caution may be added to the Police National Computer and retained for five to ten years, depending on the seriousness of the offence and whether the suspect is reconvicted in this period (ACPO, 2006).

3 The police make decisions about a suspect's suitability for bail as well as setting bail conditions for them, which takes place, in principle, in the presence of a legal advisor. These decisions take into account matters such as the seriousness of the offence, prior convictions, a suspect's record of failing to appear at court, the likelihood that the suspect might interfere with witnesses or with evidence and so on. Bail bonds are not used to ensure the suspect's appearance at court.
4 A recordable offence is one which is punishable by imprisonment or one of a list of 52 others. See the National Police Records (Recordable Offences) Regulations 2000 and the amendment regulations in 2007. A recordable offence means that details of cautions, convictions and the offender are kept on the Police National Computer.
5 Two separate cases were brought against South Yorkshire Police; in one case, the harassment charges against Michael Marper were dropped by the police and in the second 'S' was acquitted of a robbery charge against him. Both requested that South Yorkshire Police remove their DNA from the database, but the police refused, resulting in an initial ruling by the House of Lords and subsequently their cases being taken to the ECtHR.
6 The full list of trigger offences is: theft, attempted theft, robbery, attempted robbery, burglary, attempted burglary, aggravated burglary, aggravated vehicle taking, Fraud Act 2006, ss. 1, 6 or 7, handling stolen goods, attempted handling of stolen goods, taking without the owner's consent, going equipped, begging, persistent begging, production of a specified class A drug (crack, cocaine, heroin), supply of a specified class A drug, possession with intent to supply a specified class A drug.
7 The police are measured on the proportion of suspects arrested for a trigger offence who are successfully drug-tested.
8 An inquest into Christopher Alder's death found him to have been unlawfully killed. However, the officers involved were acquitted of manslaughter due to insufficient evidence and, for bureaucratic reasons, the Police Complaints Authority, who directed Humberside Police to conduct disciplinary hearings, concluded that there was no case to answer. More recently, in their review of the circumstances leading to his death, the IPCC described it as 'unnecessary, undignified and unnoticed' (2006: 9).
9 These rights can be delayed or denied under certain circumstances. For example, the right to legal advice can be delayed or denied for indictable or either-way offences if authorized by an inspector or above (PACE Code C: 5.6) and if using these rights interferes with evidence, causes harm to others, alerts other suspects or hinders the recovery of property (PACE Code C: Annexe B).
10 Indictable offences encompass, first, offences that have to be tried in front of a jury in a crown court or, second, 'either-way' offences which, depending on the defendant's wishes, can be tried, without a jury in a magistrates' court or, with a jury in a crown court. Indictable offences tend to be more serious than summary offences, which are only tried in a magistrates' court.
11 In fact, the delay with implementing the PACE – it was implemented in 1986 rather than in 1984 when it received Royal Assent – was because the police were too busy dealing with the miners' strikes (Zander, 2010).
12 A significant review of PACE was also conducted in May 2002, lasting six months. However, it was relatively superficial: it involved only four officials

from the Home Office and three officials from the Cabinet Office, as well as eight interviews with PACE experts and limited consideration of academic evidence (Zander, 2010). The review led to the Serious and Organized Crime and Policing Act 2005.

13 Delays with the review of PACE were caused because Home Office staff were diverted to deal with the ruling in the ECtHR about the retention of DNA (Zander, 2010).

14 One variation was that in the RCCP it was recommended that detention reviews be conducted after 4 and 24 hours, but in PACE they take place more frequently after 6, 15 and 24 hours.

15 There were studies of police malpractice in the police station prior to the RCCP such as Baldwin and McConville (1979) and Bottoms and McClean (1976: 115–17), but the RCCP seemed to focus attention on the issues.

16 See the debate between Smith (1997), McConville *et al.* (1997) and Duff (1998).

17 Bucke and Brown (1997) collected data in 1996, in 25 police stations in ten police service areas, using observation, custody records and a questionnaire. Phillips and Brown (1998) collected data in ten police stations in six police service areas from 4,250 suspects using a mixture of observation, documentary sources and questionnaires.

18 McLaughlin *et al.* (2001) conceptualize the term in the context of New Labour, while McLaughlin and Murji (2001) argue that the connection between neo-liberalism and managerialism has been overstated.

19 Sullivan (2001) argues that there remains a moralistic dimension to neo-liberalism, which is neglected by commentators such as Garland (1996, 2000) and evident in exclusionary policies which coexist alongside the responsibilization of the middle classes.

20 A search of the electronic ProQuest/CSA Illumina database (accessed 6 February 2009) in both the social science and arts and humanities subject areas showed that were 1,099 references to managerialism in peer-reviewed journal articles dating back to 1958, the first of which was Hood (1990b, cited in Hood, 1991).

21 Hough (2007) defines privatization as 'the transfer of services from the public sector to the private sector, as happened with British public utilities' in the 1980s (p. 81).

22 Non-intimate samples are 'a sample of hair other than pubic hair, a sample taken from a nail or from under a nail, a swab taken from any part of a person's body other than an orifice, and a skin impression (except dental impressions)' (Liberty, 2008).

23 See, for example, Padfield (2006) and Harding (2001).

24 See Genders (2002), Harding (2001), Liebling (2004: 26), McClean and Liebling (2007), Padfield (2006). Alison Liebling has recently undertaken an ESRC-funded study comparing public and private prisons. Shefer and Liebling (2008) appeared to be the only output from the study, based on a search of CSA/Illumina on 15 February 2010 under the terms 'Liebling' and 'prison'.

25 There are three types of legal advisors that can be requested: first, a nominated solicitor of the suspect's choosing, who is mostly paid for through legal aid and likely to be someone that they have used before; second, the duty solicitor who is on-call at the time of the suspect's detention and whose services are publicly funded; third, CDS Direct who provide free telephone legal advice, but only for less serious offences such as drink-driving.

Chapter 2

Governance and legitimacy in multi-professional police custody areas

The purpose of this chapter is to set out the theories that form the backdrop to the book. It is necessary to explore the relationship between police custody and theories about constitutional and institutional forms of governance, what I call relational governance and legitimacy, because this helps to place the micro-world of the police custody process within its meso- and macro-social context. Before turning to the main body of the chapter, first I define and critically assess values relevant to the police custody process to give a sense of the norms that shape its operation.

Police custody values

Four main sets of values are of relevance to police custody in England and Wales. These are: the tension between due process and crime control; the emphasis on adversarialism, which is contrasted with the emphasis on inquisitorialism in mainland Europe; a growing concern with human rights driven in part by the ratification of the Human Rights Act 1998; and procedural justice (which has some similarities with due process) and the legitimacy of the police and other legal authorities. Here, I critically explore each of them in turn. First, the criminal justice process can be understood in terms of what should be the appropriate balance between crime control and due process values. Crime control values refer to 'the system's capacity to apprehend, try, convict, and dispose of a high proportion of criminal offenders whose offences become known' (Packer, 1968: 158).[1] Yet the criminal justice process operates in the context of high volumes of crime and limited resources, meaning there must be a premium placed on speed and finality. Packer goes on to say that this presupposes 'an administrative, almost managerial model', akin to a conveyor belt on an assembly line, involving a series of routinized operations and hurdles, with success being gauged by whether the case reaches the end of the line (1968: 159–60).

By contrast, due process refers to the idea that there should be a set of rules, often written in law, which are publicly known and embody values – such as the presumption of innocence and equal access to defence counsel – that emphasize fairness (Packer, 1968: 165–6). In the crime control/due process model, the idea is that due process acts as a brake on the crime control 'conveyor belt'; it limits and constrains crime control values and helps to reduce mistakes being made in the determination of guilt (Packer, 1968: 164–5; McConville *et al.*, 1998; Smith, 1997, 1998). However, in practice, it is argued that the tendency is for crime control values to trump due process values (e.g. McConville *et al.*, 1998). Indeed, it may be that these tendencies are deepened by managerialist pressures on the criminal justice process to efficiently suppress criminal conduct.

In relation to police custody, PACE and the Codes of Practice can be seen as the set of rules around which due process turns, while arrest and detention, as well as the collection of biometric data and the police interview, among other things, are used to fulfil crime control values to convict as many suspects as possible. Outwardly, it would seem that due process is of crucial significance to the police custody process.

Crime control and due process, however, cannot fully model the police custody process because it falls into what Tyler and Huo (2002: 11–12) call a social control or deterrent model of compliance in which people are pressured into accepting decisions made by the police or court through the threat or use of sanctions. By contrast, the process-based model of regulation, encompassing ideas about procedural justice and legitimacy, secures compliance with decisions because people view the procedure as fair and they trust the motives of those who are making the decisions.[2] In the police custody process, there are likely to be some decisions, such as the decision about whether to charge, which suspects must accept not because of the use of or threat of sanction, rather because of procedural fairness, which I discuss shortly. At the same time, there may be other decisions – for example, the decision that they must go back to their cell – which they accept because of the use of or threat of sanction, such as the use of force. Therefore both due process and procedural justice are useful for understanding suspect behaviour in police custody.

Second, the criminal justice process has been conceptualized in terms of adversarialism. Put simply, adversarialism is when the prosecution and defence build competing cases to either support the innocence or guilt of the defendant, which is contrasted with inquisitorialism, where both the defence and the prosecution search for the 'truth' (Hodgson, 2004: 174). In the adversarial system that is the foundation of English criminal justice, an outcome is determined through the clash of opposing parties. It is also assumed that there is a separation between the investigative, prosecutorial, adjudicative and penal functions of the process. In practice, this so-called separation is illusory. For example, the police do not conduct interviews with suspects as a neutral fact-finding exercise; rather they use them as an opportunity to build a case against the suspect (Leo, 2008: 17). The police acting in partisan ways, so Leo (2008) argues, also has the effect of undermining suspects' legal rights and the search for the truth, as well as contributing to unfair procedures and unreliable outcomes that undermine the legitimacy of the entire process.

While adversarialism may offer a way of understanding suspects' relationships with the police in police interviews, and police–solicitor relationships, on its own, it is unlikely to shed light on the broader spectrum of working relationships in the custody area and on other aspects of the police custody process, which are only indirectly connected to the building of a case against the suspect, such as the custody environment. Furthermore, the cross-fertilization of practices between the inquisitorial and adversarial systems means that few would argue that they function as entirely one or the other (Spencer, 2005: 1). This further complicates the use of advsersarialism to understand the findings from present research.

Third, the concept of human rights offers another way of exploring how the criminal justice process should be conceptualized. The human rights perspective in the twenty-first century focuses primarily on the relationship between citizens and the nation-state, which has largely been expressed in legalistic terms, the Human Rights Act 1998 (HRA) being one example of this. The Act concerns mainly civil and political rights and its main articles include the right to life, freedom from torture or inhuman or degrading treatment, freedom from slavery or forced labour, personal freedom, the right to a fair trial, no punishment without law, the right to a private life and family, freedom of belief, freedom of expression, free assembly and association, the right to marriage and the right to freedom from discrimination (Gearty, 2007: 24–5; Newburn, 2007: 887). The main thrust of the HRA is that the police and the courts should be mindful of it when interpreting existing laws. Yet it is also precarious in that it can be removed from the statute books or rights within it can be 'restricted or truncated where the interests of the democratic system itself demand' (Gearty, 2007: 27). Nevertheless, the HRA offers some protection against authoritarianism; it provides the means for individuals to challenge what they regard as unacceptable infringements of their human rights by the state, after the event. At the same time, there are few proactive methods for guarding against systemic abuses, with the exception of the UN Subcommittee on Prevention of Torture and other Cruel, Inhuman or Degrading Treatment or Punishment (SPT) (Sanders and Young, 2006: 34).

In relation to police custody, there are numerous examples of how the HRA and the European Convention on Human Rights (ECHR) have been used to challenge unacceptable practices in police custody areas, such as those described above in relation to the retention of DNA from suspects who were neither charged or convicted. Similarly, Rosemary Pattenden and I have explored how human rights provisions – such as Article 6 of the ECHR, which concerns the right to a fair trial – are being breached by the lack of privacy afforded to suspects in police stations when consulting with their legal advisor (Pattenden and Skinns, 2010). While such challenges may not entirely succeed, a clear statement of human rights can, in principal, act as a brake on the pursuit of crime control.

Aside from individual claims brought under the HRA after the event, a more proactive approach has been taken with the introduction of an official inspection process for designated police custody areas, albeit that it was forced upon the police following the ratification of the optional protocol for the UN Convention Against Torture, known as OPCAT, in December 2003. OPCAT was created as a result of the work of the UN SPT, which is one of the UN mechanisms used to prevent torture and other forms of ill-treatment (OHCHR, 2009). Up until 2003, only HMIC regularly inspected police custody facilities. It took until 2008 before inspection arrangements were underway, being shared by HMIC and HMIP. These shared inspection teams are due to visit 76 designated police custody facilities in England and Wales over a period of six years.

However, the human rights language has yet to percolate through to PACE and the associated Codes of Practice, albeit that its provisions should be interpreted with the HRA in mind. There are no explicit mentions of human rights in the 2008 Codes of Practice. This contrasts markedly with the equivalent document in Ireland, for example, where mention is made at the outset of the importance of promoting 'respect for, and observance of human rights and fundamental freedoms' (An Garda Síochána, 2008: 3). However, it may be that human rights values will begin to influence PACE in the future, as one of the purposes of the board set up to review the legislation is said to be ensuring that measures are compatible with human rights requirements (Home Office, 2008b: 54). Given the limited explicit focus on human rights in police custody in England and Wales, it is too early in its development to warrant including it as a framework for the book.

Fourth, the concept of legitimacy has also grown in importance in debates about policing, although discourses on legitimacy are not routinely incorporated into discussions about policing in England and Wales; for example, legitimacy was referred to only in passing in the recent review of policing by Sir Ronnie Flanagan.[3] This suggests that legitimacy offers an original way of examining and defining police practices, including in relation to police custody.

At its simplest, legitimacy refers to whether or not an action is perceived as valid and acceptable (Tankebe and Gelsthorpe, 2007). Sparks and Bottoms say that legitimacy

> refers to the claim by the more powerful party in a social relationship (a decision-maker, a public official, an office-holder of some kind, but also on occasion a parent, for example) to exercise whatever power they hold in a justified manner. It also refers to their success, or otherwise, in having this claim acknowledged by others, and especially by the people over whom power is deployed. (2008: 95)

Sparks and Bottoms (2008) derive this definition from Beetham's (1991: 20) three-dimensional conceptualization of legitimacy, which suggests that authority is only legitimate if it is exercised in ways that conform with the rules of society, if those rules are rooted in a common framework of beliefs that further the collective good rather than individual interests and if the public consent to this power relationship. For example, Beetham says that 'a given power relationship is not legitimate because people believe in its legitimacy, but because it can be *justified in terms* of their beliefs' (1991: 11). According to Sparks and Bottoms (2008), this means that people in authority, such as police officers in a custody suite, have a better chance of their authority being regarded as legitimate if they follow the rules prescribed for their own behaviour and act in accordance with widely accepted moral standards in society.

The conceptualization of legitimacy has also been influenced by extensive social psychological empirical research by Tyler and others. Tyler (2003) argues that the most important factor shaping the legitimacy of legal authorities is procedural fairness (measured by the quality of decision-making and interpersonal treatment), and that this factor is more important than the favourability of the outcome or the effectiveness of the police.

The sociological take on legitimacy by Beetham (1991) and Sparks and Bottoms (2008) and the social psychological perspective of Tyler (2003) are not incompatible. Rather, they emphasize different aspects of legitimacy. Beetham (1991: 11) emphasizes that those in authority cannot afford to ignore the need for a kind legitimacy which fits with societal conceptions of it, while Tyler (2003) emphasizes that claims to legitimacy are at stake during routine encounters as a result of procedural and interpersonal factors (Sparks and Bottoms, 1995). Together this means that citizens do not comply with legal authorities because they are coerced. They comply because those legal authorities act in ways which fit with societal conceptions of procedural fairness, providing citizens with a moral reason to obey. This suggests that in police custody whether staff respond appropriately and swiftly to suspects' requests, for example for a drink or for a legal advisor, and whether staff keep suspects informed about why they are waiting and how long they are likely to wait will impact on how suspects behave while they are in police custody. That is, these procedural elements of the police custody process may impact on whether suspects comply with the police in both the shorter and longer term.

Constitutional and institutional arrangements: the rules governing the police

As noted in Chapter 1, police governance is partly concerned with constitutional and institutional arrangements, such as policies or the law. The public police are held to account in a variety of ways but via three main methods. Firstly, the police are accountable through some notion of democratic governance. Since the Police Act 1964, the first aspect of this is represented by the tripartite system involving chief constables, police authorities (involving nine councillors and eight independent members, as a result of the Police and Justice Act 2006, which eliminated magistrates as members (Jones, 2008: 701)) and the Home Secretary. However, this has been found to be an imperfect system; even after the Police and Magistrates Act 1984 tried to strengthen the role of the police authority, they still have less power than chief constables and increasingly the Home Secretary (Jones, 2008). A further aspect of democratic accountability is linked to various attempts to introduce more grounded community-based accountability mechanisms including the police-community consultation groups (PCCGs) or community engagement groups (CEGs) introduced by PACE; community consultations on localized concerns about crime and disorder introduced by the Crime and Disorder Act 1998; and more recently, the introduction throughout England and Wales of neighbourhood policing teams.

Second, the police are held to account by what may be called organizational governance which has three aspects: internal governance whereby police personnel are held accountable to force orders, policies and discipline by their managers; managerial accountability where individual forces are subjected to various Home Office introduced targets and key performance indicators enforced by HMIC, the Audit Commission and, since 2008, an assessment framework shared with other partner agencies such as the local authority, which are known as Assessment of Policing and Community Safety (APAC); and finally, investigation of the police by the Independent Police Complaints Commission, which acts as a transition point from organizational governance to legal accountability.

The third form of governance of the police is rooted in and derived from the English criminal law as police officers may be pursued through both criminal and civil courts because of their actions (Jones, 2008). The involvement of private security companies in police custody facilities raises the possibility of further forms of legal accountability through the contract between them. It also probably muddies the water thus making it difficult to identify who to pursue through the courts and rendering the public sector in a precarious position if contracts are badly drafted (Johnston *et al.*, 2008).

These constitutional and institutional forms of governance are suggestive of vertical relationships in which central government and chief officers lay down the rules, for example by setting targets, drafting legislation and issuing policy while the police implement them and chief officers enforce the rules. According to Dixon (1997: 1–8), this understanding of police governance emerged in early legalistic–bureaucratic accounts of the police in the 1960s and have a modern-day equivalent in what he calls 'police science'. In these accounts, the rules (including the law) are viewed as the major determinant of police activity and it is assumed that to change police practices it is simply necessary to change the rules. However, Dixon (1997: 3) notes that modern academic research on policing began with the 'discovery' of police discretion and therefore the idea that police practice may not be entirely in accordance with the rules. Consequently, there was growing recognition that the implementation of the rules, as well as their effectiveness in governing the police, is influenced by factors, such as police culture, the structural positioning of the police and the agency of individual officers.

Police culture refers to the 'values, norms, perspectives and craft rules of the police', which help them to cope with and adjust to the demands of the job (Reiner, 2010: 117–18). A series of common characteristics has been identified which includes: a sense of mission, action-orientated behaviour and cynicism; suspicion, isolation, solidarity, pragmatism and authority; machismo, prejudice and conservatism (Reiner, 2010: 119–32). These commonalities arise because of the unique but enduring pressures that they face, such as having to deal with dangerous situations (Loftus, 2010). In spite of these commonalities, it has been increasingly recognized that police culture varies within police organizations (e.g. by rank, role, shifts) and between police organizations (e.g. between different police services or jurisdictions) (Foster, 2003; Reiner, 2010: 132–7). For example, Reiner (2010) says that police culture is

> neither monolithic, universal nor unchanging. There are differences of outlook within police forces, according to such individual variables as personality, generation or career trajectory, and structured variations according to rank, assignment and specialization. The organizational styles and cultures of police forces vary between different places and periods. (pp. 117–18)

Therefore it may be that staff in police custody areas interpret and put these core characteristics into practice in ways which are shaped by the pressures of the custody environment and this, in turn, affects how they implement the law therein. Since the police officers in custody areas are of the same rank as patrol officers and also spend some of their time out on patrol, it is expected that they would exhibit some of the same occupational characteristics as officers on the street, who have been the focus of much of the research on police culture. It is also likely, though, that other practitioners in the custody area have their own set of occupational characteristics, some of which may conflict with those of the police. For example, Reiner (2010: 124) says that one of the key groups regarded as 'other' by the police are what he calls 'challengers'. This group includes people like doctors, legal advisors and appropriate adults, who are able to influence how the police treat their clients.

There is much debate about how and whether police culture(s) impacts on police practices (e.g. Foster, 2003; Waddington, 1999). However, there is evidence to suggest that police culture(s) can inhibit observance of the rules. For example, the diversity agenda, including diversity training and diversification of the workforce, has had a mixed impact on police culture and police practices. In a study of patrol officers, Loftus (2008) argues that the diversity agenda has only 'interrupted' aspects of the dominant white, heterosexual, male culture, changing behaviour but not attitudes, so that officers overtly abide by the rules, while racism is pushed underground into the recesses of exclusionary 'white spaces', making it more subtle and hidden rather than eradicating it. This study provides a clear and recent example of how the governance of the police through laws or policies can be undermined, and even subverted, by police culture(s). In custody areas, it is expected, however, that the police would more closely observe the rules because their behaviour is more visible than when they are on the street as a result of the widespread use of CCTV and the presence of other criminal justice practitioners in the custody area.

The governance of the police through the law is also affected by the structural position of the police in the criminal justice process, as well as their wider position in society. For example, McConville *et al.* (1997: 182) argue that case construction takes place within the structural context of capitalism which requires a strong state, and which is enabled by an ideology of crime control. Within this ideology, the police are the dominant party over other institutions in the adversarial system and over suspects, which makes case construction a partial and partisan process. McConville *et al.* say:

> The case is a product of a) low-level officers operating under conditions of low visibility, enforcing b) particular socio-economic and political policies, through c) socially (rather than legally) constructed criteria which incorporate and produce structural bias within d) a permissive institutional and legal framework riddled with contradictions, in which e) rule breaking is sanctioned in a graded manner, allowing a large amount of rule breaking when the law is insufficiently permissive to the police. (1997: 182)

However, this interpretation expresses a political position, which leads them to overstate the impact of structural factors on police practices. It is more likely that police culture(s), structural factors, as well as officers' agency interact in ways that can both support and undermine the implementation of the rules and, therefore, support or undermine the effectiveness of constitutional and institutional arrangements in governing the police.

This is precisely what is argued by Chan (1997: 71–5), drawing on organizational theorists such as Sackmann (1991) and Schein (1985), as well as Bourdieu's (1990) theory of culture. She distinguishes between structural conditions (known as the field) and cultural knowledge (known as habitus). The former refers to the historical relations between the police and certain social groups and the anchoring of these relations in legal powers and discretion, as well as the distribution of power and material resources in society. The latter refers to 'the collective construction of reality' (Sackmann, 1991: 21, cited in Chan, 1997: 71), which occurs through shared organizational knowledge. However, she also notes the importance of police officers' agency and thus the non-deterministic influence of culture and structure. Chan says:

> [S]tructural conditions do not completely determine cultural knowledge, and cultural knowledge does not totally dictate practice. Working within structural conditions of policing, members have an active role to play in developing, reinforcing, resisting or transforming cultural knowledge. They are not passive carriers of police culture ... The relationships between the elements are neither uni-directional nor deterministic. (1997: 74–5)

While the present research was not intended as a study of police culture, it is inevitable that in police custody areas this interplay of structure, police culture and individual agency is likely to be manifest in the treatment of suspects and explain the extent of observance of the PACE Codes of Practice.

Relational forms of governance

My argument so far is that constitutional and institutional arrangements contribute to the formal rules that govern police practices, but that the effectiveness of these rules in governing the police can be undermined by the interplay between structural, cultural and individual factors. As noted in Chapter 1, governance is also connected to the regulation and ordering of contemporary societies in which various social actors, including citizens and the police, are engaged in policing. This form of governance is not so much about governing the police as about governing a range of actors engaged in policing and thereby 'governing' crime. Henceforth, I shall refer to this as relational governance, since it is concerned with how relationships between citizens, non-state organizations, criminal justice actors and the government are used to govern each other and to alter the multiple causes of crime and contribute to security. This aspect of governance emphasizes the importance of horizontal relationships between local actors and organizations, and to a lesser extent vertical relationships (e.g. between local actors and central government).

In what follows next, my argument is, first, that since the birth of the modern professional police in the form of the Metropolitan Police Service in 1829, the governance of crime was *perceived* – whether it was or not, in reality, is a contentious matter – as being primarily the responsibility of the state (which can be read as the police). However, recently a variety of theorists, in reflecting on contemporary patterns of policing, have begun to explore whether and how the role of the police in policing has and should change. The state has been either regarded as an equal player in a security network of equals, or as the primary provider of policing, or as playing a variety of equal and more prominent roles than other policing providers, depending on contextual exigencies. It is important to examine these different strands of the debate because police custody areas, which involve both police and police staff and other criminal justice practitioners, are places where the dynamics of these multi-professional relationships can be observed, enabling a comparison of relational theories of governance with empirical reality. As this book shows, the third strand of this debate – that the state plays a variety of equal and more prominent roles – provides the best model of multi-professional relationships in police custody areas.

My second argument, however, is that these relational theories of governance tend not to explore the role of the law in governing policing providers, which thus differentiates them from constitutional and institutional forms of governance. Relational theories of governance also neglect other important matters, namely the legitimacy of the various actors and organizations engaged in policing. This is a surprising omission, given so-called 'police fetishism', that is, the popular myth of the police as the primary provider of policing without whom social order would collapse, and as largely 'crime-fighters' and law enforcers (Reiner, 2010: 3–4). In theory, relational theories of governance imply a need for a reworking of the ideologies about the police, as well as a reconceptualization of police legitimacy. This is a matter that is addressed below in the discussion of police legitimacy.

Nevertheless, these relational theories of governance add important insights into multi-professional police custody areas. In what follows here, I answer two key questions, the first of which is particularly important for multi-professional police custody areas: (1) What are the origins of relational theories of governance? (2) Where is the locus of power in these theories of governance? To answer these questions I compare and contrast Johnston and Shearing (2003), Loader and Walker (2006, 2007), Garland (2001) and Crawford (2006).

What are the origins of relational theories of governance?

Relational theories of governance arose in order to understand perceived shifts in the patterns of policing. These included the growth of the private security industry (Johnston, 2007) as well as the policing of quasi-public places such as Disneyworld (the focus of Shearing and Stenning's (1983) classic article), and, furthermore, multi-agency crime prevention partnerships (e.g. Crawford, 1997) and the way that policing is delivered in conjunction with populist punitive forms of punishment (Garland, 2001). It is also possible to trace the themes in these relational theories of governance to Foucault (1991) and Cohen (1985); one of the key ideas in *Discipline and Punish* is that authority does not rest solely with the state. Instead, authority (or discipline as Foucault calls it) is dispersed in society through actors and organizations implicated in a growing 'carceral archipelago' and web of social control that extends beyond the prison walls and into society (Foucault, 1991: 293–308).

However, relational theories of governance, particularly Johnston and Shearing (2003), have tended to overstate the epochal nature of these shifts in the patterns of policing. In fact, the public police never had a monopoly over policing and there is a growing recognition that this idea is a myth, albeit a powerful one (Jones and Newburn, 2002).[4] Moreover, there are clear parallels between contemporary patterns of policing and those prior to 1829 when the state began to assume a more prominent role in the delivery of security. For example, Zedner (2006) compares the private 'thief-takers' that were the precursors to the Bow Street Runners in the early nineteenth century and the security markets of today in which policing services are contracted out and the public can buy additional security patrols from global providers. Consequently, the pluralization of policing, including that in police custody areas, cannot be regarded as a new phenomenon. Rather, it is suggestive of a return to policing patterns which are equivalent to the privately remunerated or unpaid non-professionalized public officials of old, such as parish constables, night-watchmen and thief-takers.[5] Late modern societies are in the midst of a slow return to private forms of policing in which the responsibility for policing is spread throughout society rather than being perceived as solely the responsibility of the police.

Where is the locus of power?

Firstly, the state has been regarded as an equal player in a security network of equals. This is the position taken by Johnston and Shearing (2003: 25–6), who argue for an understanding of the role of the state in the governance of security which does not give analytical preference to any organization or actor. Rather, their concept of nodal governance conveys that the state is one of a number of potentially equal players involved in the delivery of security, i.e. they refuse to prioritize any particular locus of power. Essentially, Johnston (2007) asks us to keep an open mind about which, if any, of those involved in the governance of security play a dominant role, leaving the matter to be assessed through empirical enquiry, which recognizes variations across space and time. This implies that, potentially, in a multi-professional setting like a police custody area the locus of control could rest with any one of the criminal justice practitioners therein. As we shall see, this hypothesis was not supported by the present research, which found that the police played a dominant role.

This first strand of the debate about the role of the police in policing can also be critiqued on a number of levels. Johnston and Shearing's (2003: 25–6) ambivalence about the role of the state in the governance of security is empirically and morally troubling. In empirical terms, they use the crime and disorder reduction partnerships in Middlesbrough to illustrate their arguments but their analysis is largely derived from policy documents rather than other kinds of data. Such policy documents are more of a 'wish list' than a reflection of practices on the ground. Their analysis is also at odds with other research on crime and disorder partnerships, which was not based on policy documents and which found that the locus of control tends to rest with the police (Skinns, 2005: 317; Jamel and Mair, 2003; Phillips, 2002; Crawford and Jones, 1995; Liddle and Gelsthorpe, 1994; Sampson *et al.*, 1988).

By understating these inter-agency differences and by regarding the role of the state in nodal governance as analytically equal to others in the network Johnston and Shearing (2003) treat power relations within such networks as benign. Reiner (2010: 30) says that this is the main explanatory deficit of the new policing theories; they 'bracket out' the significance of political economy in shaping the context and problems that police organizations, cultures and officers face. In particular, Reiner (2010: 30) argues that pluralization in policing can be regarded as the symptom not the solution to the current predicaments faced by the police, which were set in motion by economic neo-liberal policies of the Conservatives in the 1970s and which were later endorsed by New Labour. It is within this wider context, that relationships between the police and police staff in police custody areas must be seen.

By contrast, the second strand of the debate about the role of the police in policing argues that the state *should* have the primary responsibility for policing; this is the position taken by Loader and Walker (2006, 2007: 170). The starting point for their thesis is the concept of security as a public good (Loader and Walker, 2006, 2007: 192–4); by this they mean that public services, opportunities and justice should be fairly distributed in society. They outline and dismiss four types of scepticism in policing and security studies about the role of the state, which they largely take to mean as the police:

1. The state as a meddler – the state meddles with the interests of some of its citizens in order to protect the interests of all, albeit this is a situation grudgingly accepted as part of the social contract.
2. The state as partisan – a position associated with the Left, in which the state acts to protect the interests of the socially and economically powerful to the detriment of the rest of society and the state is therefore seen as unwelcome and evil.
3. The state as idiot – a position associated with Johnston and Shearing and others, in which, because of a lack of knowledge and capacity, the state is only one of multiple providers of security.
4. The state as cultural monolith – a position associated with Johnston and Shearing and others in which the state fails to act in ways which are contextually-specific, thereby trampling over local diversity.

These four vices of the state are dismissed by Loader and Walker (2006), saying that they could be reined in through legislation and that they are an unavoidable downside of state involvement in security, which is counterbalanced by the virtues of the state. Through their concept of 'anchored pluralism', they argue that the state *should* retain the most prominent role in governing security to enable it to act, for example, as an arbiter in decisions about public security, and that this is in the interests of ensuring that security remains a public good for all to enjoy equally. However, this role is not just about the ordering of social practices; more fundamentally it acts to constitute social meanings about what is 'the public' or 'the social', thereby contributing to the important task of altering the public's perceptions of security, that is of 'civilizing security'. According to Loader and Walker (2007: 7) civilizing security is a vitally important task in a neo-liberal climate where civil liberties are being eroded by widespread fear and anxiety about security.

Loader and Walker's (2007: 192–4) account is persuasive, but it remains unclear what was meant by 'civilizing' security; they do not specify precisely which aspects of security are in need of modification. Moreover, it may be that the state (which can be read as the police, in their account) *should* be given a primary role in decisions about security, but what about decisions about other social problems such as social welfare? For example, should the police decide what is best for a suspect when concerns about welfare and security are in conflict? Finally, in relation to police custody areas, can the state be read as the police when the police employ civilians or private security staff as detention officers, who are not officially police officers and yet who do the bulk of the work therein?

The strong state thesis, which gives the primary responsibility for policing to the police, is also advanced by Garland (2001). Unlike Loader and Walker (2006, 2007), however, Garland (2001: 124–7) does not specify how the state ought to govern policing providers and thereby crime; rather he explores how it *is* governing crime in late modern society. He argues that through the process of responsibilization the state has divested itself of its responsibilities for crime control and has deliberately activated action and built strategic alliances with non-state actors and organizations. In contrast to Johnston and Shearing's (2003) concept of a security network, the fact that the state is directing this action suggests that such strategic alliances are not partnerships of equals. Moreover, Garland (2001: 124–7) regards the offloading of troublesome state functions as a positive by-product of a deeper concern with 'governing at a distance' in which the state cajoles and persuades non-state actors and organizations to do its bidding. Garland says:

> The state's new strategy is not to command and control but rather to persuade and align, to organize, to ensure that other actors play their part. Property owners, residents, retailers, manufacturers, town planners, school authorities, transport managers, employers, parents, individual citizens . . . the list is endless . . . must all be made to recognize that they have a responsibility in this regard. They must be persuaded to exert their informal powers of social control, and if necessary, to modify their usual practices, in order to help reduce criminal opportunities and enhance crime control. (2001: 126)

Responsibilization is one of many adaptive responses to the 'crime complex' – that is, the politicized nature of crime and fear of crime in late modern societies – and that it is made manifest in preventative partnerships or a 'network of more or less directed, more or less informal crime control, complementing and extending the formal controls of the criminal justice state'.[6] In police custody areas, citizens acting as appropriate adults and independent custody visitors (who were formerly known as lay visitors) appear to be obvious examples of responsibilization. Of course, responsibilization may be rhetoric and may not reflect empirical reality, not least because appropriate adults have been found to be ineffective and so may not do that much governing of crime, even indirectly by looking after the welfare of suspects (Jacobson, 2008: 31).[7]

The third strand of the debate about the role of the state in policing suggests that the state may play a variety of roles, depending on the context of policing. This is what is conveyed by Crawford's (2006: 466) series of models of the relationships between the state and other policing providers:

- The *monopolistic* model whereby forms of policing are integrated within the hierarchical state police organization. The state retains primary responsibility for policing. This is illustrated by the proliferation of police community support officers, who are non-warranted civilian staff, but who are paid and directed by the police.

- The *steering* model whereby the police seek to 'govern at a distance' the policing activities of others. This involves state agencies mobilizing and making use of non-state resources, such as individual citizens or private security officers, who may become accredited by the state. These third parties then act as a 'junior partner' of the police. Garland's (2001: 124–37) concept of responsibilization would fit here in Crawford's model.
- The *networked* or *nodal* model whereby policing providers link in horizontal partnerships in the co-production of security. This is in line with Johnston and Shearing's (2003) conceptual model, although Crawford (2006) argues that his variant of this presupposes an element of coordination by the state.
- The *market* model is founded on competition (and conflict), which structure relations between different providers. As is necessary, the police might contract out their services (e.g. for the policing of football matches) or buy in services from private organizations (e.g. detention officers in police custody areas).
- The *private government* model means that state policing is shut out of providing policing (e.g. this might happen in gated communities which employ their own security guards) or has relinquished its responsibilities, leaving tasks to private organizations and individuals.

The flexibility of Crawford's (2006) models of the role of the state in policing is an advantage. Of the three strands in the debate, Crawford's (2006) models are the most useful for understanding the variations in the relationships between the police and other criminal justice practitioners in police custody areas. Indeed, the present research showed that Crawford's (2006) models coexisted alongside each other in the police custody areas; some relationships were best characterized by the monopolistic model (e.g. relationships between the police and appropriate adults), and others were best characterized by the steering model (e.g. relationships between the police and doctors). For the purposes of this book, therefore, the state can be regarded as playing a variety of equal and more prominent roles in the delivery of policing.

Police authority and legitimacy

I now move on to consider how the police and other criminal justice practitioners – either in partnerships or on their own – use their authority to secure compliance. Compliance with the law has been thought of either in terms of utilitarian or process-based models. Much of the existing research on police custody can be regarded as loosely premised on the former. Research on police custody has noted the tension between due process – that is the need for rules that are publicly known, which value things such as the presumption of innocence and equal access to defence counsel – and crime control values – that is the need for a case to reach a successful conclusion, namely conviction – with the criminal justice scales being seen as tipping in favour of crime control (e.g. McConville *et al.*, 1997; McConville *et al.*, 1994: 273). This model assumes that suspects are coerced into complying with the decisions of criminal justice actors. It is premised on the idea that, as rational actors, suspects comply with the police out of a utilitarian need to minimize costs and increase any potential benefits; for example, suspects might agree to be interviewed because they are promised a cigarette at the end of it.

By contrast, the process-based model of regulation, encompassing ideas about procedural justice and police legitimacy, secures compliance through cooperation because people view the procedure as fair and trust the motives of those who are making the decision (Tyler and Huo, 2002: 11–12), and also because decisions are based on accepted and shared norms (Beetham, 1991: 11). Since the birth of the modern police, policing has largely been regarded as a state-led activity meaning that legitimacy is conferred on the state. The long-held view of the police as the spearhead of policing means that it is difficult to see how policing by a variety of actors and organizations can secure legitimacy if it is decoupled from the police (and the state). The main aim of this section is to answer the question of how legitimacy can be secured if policing is decoupled from the state, a question that has received scant attention in theories of relational governance. In order to answer this question, it is first necessary to critically explore the growing body of evidence about police legitimacy and its implications for research on police custody.

How is legitimacy secured by the police?

Legitimacy is concerned with whether or not those in positions of power, such as the police, use their power in a justified and accepted manner which is acknowledged by those who are subjected to power being exercised over them, as well as by other members of society. For the use of power by the police to be viewed as legitimate, citizens must also believe in the moral rightness of the police to act in the ways that they do, and this belief must stem from police behaviour being in accordance with rules which are widely known and accepted in society. Of course, there are also other reasons why suspects comply with the police, for example out of 'dull compulsion' when they go through the motions of obeying the police not because they share the same moral values as them, but rather because they feel they have little other choice (Carrabine, 2004: 180–1).

There is a growing body of empirical evidence which is focused on the social psychology of police legitimacy, with Tom Tyler being one of the key researchers in the area. There are two key findings from research spanning North America, Asia and Europe (MacCoun, 2005). First, the key determinant of police legitimacy is how the police treat the public, which is known as procedural justice, which Tyler (2003) categorizes into the quality of the decision-making by the police (i.e. whether it is neutral, unbiased and based on objective indicators) and the quality of interpersonal treatment (i.e. whether people are treated with dignity and respect). However, Leventhal (1976, 1980, cited in Paternoster *et al.*, 1997) provides a more comprehensive framework of procedural justice, identifying six constituent components. These are as follows:

1. Representation, so that citizens feel that they can take part in the decision-making process.
2. Consistency in how people are treated, so that citizens feel that they are treated no differently to other people and no differently to how they were treated in the past.
3. Impartiality or neutrality of the police, so that the police suppress any biases they have about citizens or about the outcome.
4. Accuracy, so that the police make competent high-quality decisions based on valid information.
5. Correctability, meaning that there are mechanisms in place to ensure that unfair or incorrect decisions can be put right.
6. Ethicality, which is concerned with treating citizens politely, with dignity and with respect for their rights.

The second key finding is that procedural justice is a more important influence on police legitimacy than other instrumental considerations such as outcome favourability, police effectiveness in combating crime or distributive justice (e.g. how the police distribute their resources) (Tyler, 2003). These two key findings are summarized in Figure 2.1. Furthermore, it is important to note that research on the legitimacy of the police and legal authorities has contributed to theories about why it is that people comply with the law at all.

The importance of fairness in the process of justice originated from the empirical work of Thibault and Walker (1975, cited in MacCoun, 2005) who found that the majority of American college students, who were asked to assess hypothetical conflicts and mechanisms for resolving them (avoiding labels such as lawyers, judges or references to legal systems), identified the adversarial system as the fairest mechanism.[8] Since then, there has been a growing body of evidence which has converged on the importance of procedural fairness as an antecedent to police legitimacy and police legitimacy as an influence on cooperation with the police and compliance with the law. For example, in the Milwaukee domestic

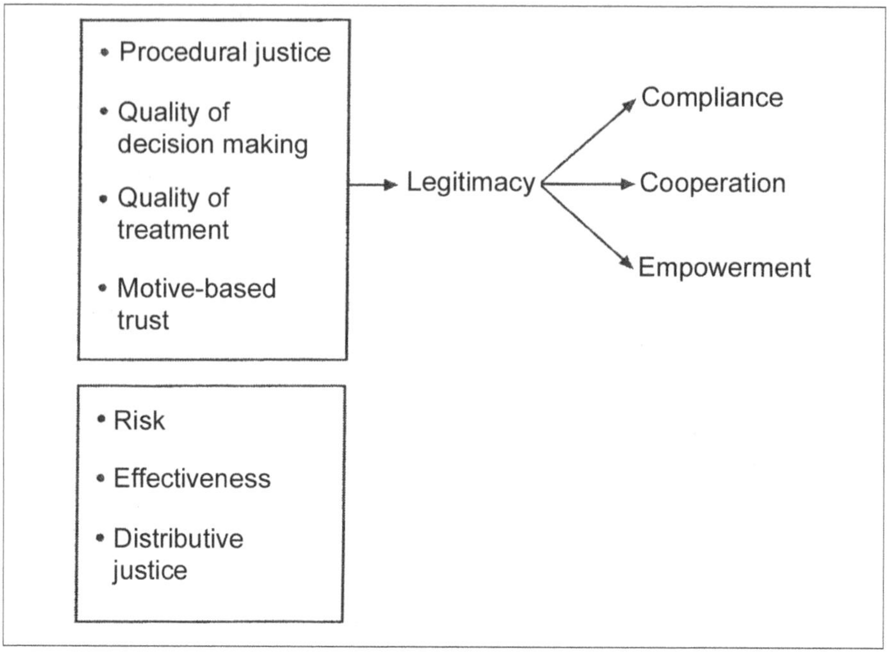

Figure 2.1 Conceptual view of the process-based model of regulation (Tyler, 2003: 307).

violence experiment Paternoster *et al.* (1997) found that procedural fairness lowered the likelihood of subsequent violence, regardless of whether the outcome of the case was favourable or not. More recently, Tyler and Huo (2002: 175–6) found that acceptance of outcomes in encounters between citizens and legal authorities (as a proxy measure of immediate compliance with the law) was best predicted by perceptions of trustworthiness of legal authorities and whether or not citizens felt that they were fairly treated rather than by perceptions of the fairness of the outcome. Furthermore, Sunshine and Tyler (2003) found among a sample at two points in time of residents of New York City that legitimacy influenced compliance with the law independently of distributive fairness, police effectiveness and the risk of being sanctioned and that, importantly, the key antecedent of legitimacy was procedural fairness.

The implication of the research by Tyler and others is that suspects in police custody are most likely to view the police as legitimate, then cooperate with the police and later comply with the law, if suspects are fairly treated. By fairly treated this might mean:

- being given an opportunity to make requests of the police when in the cells or to have legal representation so that they or their legal advisor can participate in decisions about their case (e.g. about police bail);

- being treated in a similar manner as other people in the custody area or in similar ways to how they have been treated in the past by the police (e.g. being given adequate access to refreshments, fresh air or shower facilities);
- perceiving that the police are neutral and unbiased in how the police treat them while they are in police custody;
- providing their version of events in a police interview so that the police can competently make decisions about any charge;
- having an opportunity to complain either to the police or through the Independent Police Complaints Commission about the way they were treated in police custody if they feel that it was unfair or the decisions taken were incorrect;
- finally, being spoken to politely and being informed of, as well having the opportunity to make use of, their rights and entitlements (e.g. to things like legal advice).

Of course, Tyler's conceptualization of the links between procedural justice and legitimacy is not without its critics. A key criticism is that it cannot provide an insight into the origins of legitimacy; rather, it is a theory about how, once established, citizens' sense of the legitimacy of legal authorities can be diminished and to a lesser extent, if at all, enhanced by their direct dealings with legal authorities, and how this affects the likelihood that they will cooperate with the police and comply with the law.[9] In this sense, Tyler's account is only partial as it does not fully consider the origins of legitimacy, as rooted in social life. In particular, Smith (2007a) argues that he does not consider all the factors that influence the legitimacy of the police; his account only deals with legitimacy at the individual rather than the collective level; he focuses only on direct rather than vicarious experiences influencing legitimacy; his account does not fully examine spirals in legitimacy in which previous experiences impact on current feelings; and his account may not apply equally to other points in time or to other cultures.[10]

The idea that legitimacy is rooted in social life is part of what Tankebe (2007: 48–56) means by the mass legitimation of power. Following Beetham (1991: 20), he argues that mass legitimation of power is partly accomplished through legal means. The ruled assess whether or not the behaviour of the rulers conforms to established rules prescribed by custom or by law. Furthermore, he argues that this legalistic approach to mass legitimation requires, first, that the law is exercised for the greater good of society rather than in the interests of the powerful, second, that there is a moral consensus about how the rulers are to use their authority (e.g. by not taking bribes) and, third, that the law is an expression of the recognized, accepted and shared norms of society. Furthermore, following

Coicaud (2002), Tankebe argues that mass legitimation also depends on the ruled expressing consent to being ruled and being willing to exchange infringements on their liberty for enhanced security.

This criticism that Tyler's conceptualization of legitimacy cannot fully assess the origins of police legitimacy as rooted in social life may appear tangential to a book about police custody; after all, the bounded nature of police custody means that it is likely that present research has little to say about the mass legitimation of power. I note this criticism of Tyler's work, however, to demonstrate that how suspects respond to the police in police custody may not entirely be a product of their immediate circumstances, and their perceptions of the legitimacy of their treatment and of legislation such as PACE depends on whether it expresses norms that are recognized by suspects and by the wider society. I am arguing, therefore, for a more sociologically informed understanding of police custody and of police legitimacy therein, which recognizes that the law, the police and suspects are all part of a wider socio-political environment. The danger with research on police custody is that this wider context could easily be forgotten or surpassed by focusing on the minutiae of the police custody environment.

Second, Tyler (2003) reviews research which focuses largely on relationships between citizens and legal authorities; consequently, he says little about how legal authorities, such as the police, cultivate their own sense of legitimacy in which they justify the rightness of their authority and develop a sense of their own identity. Tankebe (2007: 56–63) calls this the 'endogenous legitimation of power'. He says that the police cultivate a sense of their own legitimacy by engaging in public actions, such as speeches, rituals and displays. Police uniforms are another obvious way of signalling their legitimacy and their unique identity. These self-legitimation activities contribute to self-confidence among the rulers and the administrative agents, without which the stability and the effectiveness of their authority would suffer.

This conceptualization of the internal machinations of police legitimacy could be one reason, alongside the demands of the job (e.g. having to face danger), why 'authority' has remained a stubborn feature of police culture (Loftus, 2009: 190; 2010): it is a ritual and a display which enhances police officers' belief in their own legitimacy. Loftus (2010: 10) found that police officers liked to maintain control over members of the public; anyone who was impolite or challenged their authority, even though this is not unlawful, provoked a 'repertoire of reactions', including the 'attitude test', which if the member of the public failed led to arrest. Interestingly, this so-called 'contempt of cop' was invoked mostly when officers were in the company of other officers. In part, this was because they did not want to lose face, but it might also have been because being spoken to impolitely, in front of an audience, is likely to have damaged the process of self-legitimation and the self-confidence accrued by the officer. Theories about endogenous forms of legitimation also help to explain another of Loftus' (2010) findings. She observed that some of the older and more experienced officers appeared better able to 'rise above' impoliteness from the public; this may have been because these longer-serving officers had already developed sufficient belief in their own legitimacy. As argued in Chapter 4, similar flashpoints about the impoliteness of suspects occurred over the use of buzzers in the cells in the custody blocks.

Furthermore, questions have to be asked about why someone would accept an unfavourable outcome, even if they perceived the process by which the decision was reached as fair. The implication is that legal authorities and ideas about the legal system (including procedural justice) might serve as an ideology which persuades and even hoodwinks citizens into believing that they are being treated fairly, while also giving them outcomes which are substantively unfair. MacCoun (2005) calls this the 'dark side' of procedural justice, which he explains using the notion of false consciousness – originally a Marxist concept used to explain why the proletariat remains exactly that – to suggest that those who receive unfavourable outcomes do not realize that they are unfair.[11] This ideology might also have the effect of ensuring that those social groups who already disproportionately receive unfavourable outcomes, both from the criminal justice process and in other aspects of life, remain in a disadvantaged position. From this perspective, procedural justice is also the antithesis of social justice because it means that there is no need to confront persistent and large-scale social inequalities (Haney, 1991, cited in MacCoun, 2005).

Therefore MacCoun (2005) is right to conclude that procedural justice is a double-edged sword which can, on the one hand, give those in the criminal justice process a voice and allow them to be treated with dignity and respect as well as encourage them to comply with the law, and, on the other hand, could contribute to further inequality in the distribution of outcomes in the criminal justice process and in society. Consequently, in this book, I reflect on the meaning of these malevolent and benevolent aspects of procedural justice for suspects in police custody. For example, in Chapter 8, I examine the possibility that the rules about the fair treatment of suspects can be manipulated by both suspects and the police. To an extent they both appeared to engage in strategic forms of compliance, paying lip-service to the rules, so that, for each, it led to a satisfactory outcome.

In sum, police legitimacy, for the purposes of this book, is to be thought about as being conferred on the police through procedural justice and by the police acting in accordance with rules which are known and accepted by suspects and by the wider society. The bulk of the evidence suggests that if legitimacy is conferred on the police by suspects in the way I have just described, then suspects are more likely to cooperate with the police and, later, comply with the law. In addition, police officers cultivate a sense of their own legitimacy in using their authority through public actions (such as displays of their authority) and uniforms.

How can legitimacy be secured when policing is decoupled from the state?

Having outlined the main research findings on police legitimacy and their limitations as well as the implications for research on police custody, here I return to the central question about how legitimacy can be secured when policing is decoupled from the police. This question is important because it has not been addressed in relational theories of governance, but also because of the multi-professional nature of police custody areas in the present study.

For some of the criminal justice practitioners in the custody process, legitimacy is likely to be conferred by citizens on (civilian non-sworn) police staff in the same way as for the police, that is through procedural justice and through the police staff, like the police, acting in accordance with rules (such as the PACE Codes of Practice) that are widely known and accepted by citizens. This process may also be aided by police staff being readily associated with the police, and perhaps even being thought of as being the same, if not, similar to the police by sharing similar uniforms and tasks. In this sense, the police might, through association, indirectly lend police staff legitimacy. This possibility is also noted by Crawford (2008: 175–6) who says that the 'police might lend legitimacy to non-police providers through accreditation schemes and partnership arrangements', although he also says that 'the transfer of legitimacy to other providers might undermine [the police's] own legitimate basis of authority'. In addition, the uniforms and tasks that police staff share in common with the police can be regarded as rituals and displays which are important to the endogenous forms of legitimation described above. They may give police staff self-confidence to use their authority. In sum, for police staff, we might expect that mass legitimation and endogenous forms of legitimation, using Tankebe's (2007: 48–56) terms, are conferred in the same way as for the police.

While the police may 'lend' police staff legitimacy it may be that one of these groups of policing providers has more legitimacy, in the eyes of suspects, than the other. It may be that civilians – whether police staff or medical staff, legal advisors, drug workers or legal advisors – act as a buffer in the sometimes strained relationships between suspects and the police, which suggests that police staff, not the police, are likely to be more legitimate. By lending legitimacy to police staff, this might also undermine the legitimacy of the police in the way that Crawford (2008) suggests.

As for the other criminal justice practitioners who work in the custody area – that is, legal advisors, doctors, drug workers and appropriate adults – it is more difficult to judge how and the extent to which legitimacy is likely to be conferred on them relative to the police. Unlike the police, their actions are not underscored by the threat of or use of force. Consequently, legal advisors, medical staff, drug workers and appropriate adults are likely to wield less power over suspects than the police and police staff. This is not to say that power is not an issue in their relationship with the suspect; rather it is more likely that legitimacy would be conferred on them through acting in fair rather than coercive ways. For instance, medical staff, drug workers and legal advisors try to find ways of establishing a trusting working relationship with their clients by reminding them of the confidential nature of their discussions. Like police staff, therefore, these other kinds of criminal justice practitioners might be regarded as more legitimate than the police.

Conclusion

To conclude, there are two main points to be made. First, there is a need to integrate theories about governance with theories about procedural justice and legitimacy. Relational theories of governance assume but do not fully discuss that those in authority are legitimate and that the law is part of the context in which governance takes place. Theories about legitimacy, however, have focused on the law and on legal authorities as the main source of authority in society, but neglect the idea that the divesting of power from the police to other social actors means that it is not just legal authorities that need be concerned with legitimacy. This need for practitioners other than the police to be legitimate is all too apparent in police custody areas where the police work alongside non-warranted police staff; as I discuss in Chapter 6, police staff may be the 'deputies' of the police, but they also have a different and perhaps more legitimate relationship with the suspects than the police do, although this was not because the police 'lent' them legitimacy in the way that Crawford (2008) argues. To the contrary, the police staff deliberately distanced themselves from the police.

Secondly, theories of governance and legitimacy provide an important backdrop to the present research. The growing body of work on what I have called relational governance emphasizes that it is important to critically examine the relationship between the police and others involved in policing. One of the objectives of this book, therefore, is to explore these relationships within the confines of the police custody process, critically assessing the roles played by the police, non-warranted police staff, legal advisors, doctors, appropriate adults and drug workers. These are discussed in Chapters 6 and 7. Similarly, the growing body of research on procedural justice and legitimacy has also yet to be fully explored specifically in relation to suspects or the police custody process or the differences between police and police staff. One of the objectives of this book is to explore in Chapters 4 and 5 suspects' experiences of procedural fairness, in terms of the custody environment and how they are treated by staff while detained in police custody and in terms of access to their rights and entitlements.

In sum, this chapter has outlined values and theories relevant to the custody process and which provide the 'glue' that brings the chapters in the book together. However, in Chapter 3, these theories and normative ideas are largely left to one side while I describe the roles and responsibilities of practitioners in the custody area and the nature of the suspect population. The aim of this third chapter is to provide a firm foundation for the analysis in the remainder of the book.

Notes

1 Crime control values are different to the goal of crime control, which refers to the suppression of criminal conduct (Duff, 1998).

2 Tyler (2003) argues that people do not obey the law because of the fear of punishment; rather, they obey the law because acting in procedurally just ways causes citizens to recognize the legitimacy of legal authorities.

3 In the Flanagan report (2008: 88) democratic legitimacy is mentioned; however, this refers only to how the police could increase accountability to citizens in a democratic way.

4 For example, in the 1950 census there were 85,000 public police compared to 66,000 private security officers (Jones and Newburn, 2002).

5 See Elmsley (1991: 8–15) for an examination of the role of these public officials in policing.

6 Garland (2001: 124) also argues that, by contrast, responsibilization of state and non-state actors has been accompanied by highly-visible displays of sovereign might, as evidenced by populist punitive policies resulting in mass imprisonment in the 1980s and 1990s.

7 In other settings, however, such as the crime and disorder reduction partnerships (CDRPs), responsibilization was more symbolic than real; responsibility for crime and disorder reduction appeared to have been dispersed to local actors and organizations, but the reality was that the CDRPs rarely involved citizens, and central government tended to micro-manage the CDRPs from afar through performance monitoring and funding arrangements (Skinns, 2005: 317).

8 This finding was later replicated among students in European countries employing the inquisitorial system, suggesting that the findings were not simply a result of familiarity with the adversarial system (Anderson and Otto, 2003, cited in MacCoun, 2005).

9 For example, in a recent study of interactions between the police and citizens, Skogan (2006, cited in Smith, 2007a) found that by treating citizens badly, the police can diminish their legitimacy in the eyes of citizens, but by treating them well it makes little difference to how citizens view the police and is unlikely to enhance their legitimacy.

10 Tankebe (2010), for example, found that the Sunshine and Tyler (2003) scale used to measure legitimacy could not be replicated in Ghana, making it

difficult to determine whether the links between procedural justice, police legitimacy and cooperation and compliance can be replicated in other cultural contexts.

11 MacCoun (2005) is careful to point out that the concept of false consciousness implies that true consciousness is possible. The concept of false consciousness is also problematic because it creates a vacuum which can be filled by academic interpretations, regardless of the expressed views of research participants.

Chapter 3

Cops, docs, 'DPs' and others: staff and suspects in the custody process

The purpose of this chapter is to explore the roles and responsibilities of those working in the custody area, including police, police staff, medical practitioners, legal advisors, appropriate adults and drug workers, and the characteristics of the suspect population.[1] This information is important to enable a balanced understanding of relationships within the custody area, as well as the implications for conceptual and theoretical issues. This chapter is also concerned with what it is like in police custody and what it feels like for suspects. This contextualized information about the two custody areas in this and Chapter 4 will also help practitioners to explore the extent to which the findings apply or otherwise to their own working environment.

Since the 1980s, the increasing involvement of a range of criminal justice practitioners has led to much informal negotiation of roles within police custody areas. However, in the light of workforce modernization described in Chapter 1 in which civilianization has given way to privatization (meaning that public and private police staff are employed to perform tasks traditionally performed by the police alone), it is possible to describe police custody areas as multi-professional settings. Of course, this begs the question of the meaning of the term 'professional' and whether in fact some practitioners might be regarded as professionals (e.g. doctors and legal advisors) and others might not (e.g. police officers, drug workers, police staff). It also begs the question of the significance of the concept; Sir Bernard Shaw suggests that 'all professionals are conspiracies against the laity' (1911: Act 1). Therefore coming from a profession might be a means of commanding respect, particularly for practitioners who find themselves in a custody area which is regarded as police territory. These are matters that I return to in Chapter 7.

Roles and responsibilities

The police and police staff

Inspector

The inspector's role in both sites revolved around PACE duties (such as detention reviews and authorizing searches of suspects' houses), staffing, line management and performance management. However, inspectors in Sunnyside had an additional role, managing the contract and their relationship with Security Ltd, especially when systems and processes broke down (SNS8).[2] In addition, their performance management roles also varied. In Sunnyside, inspectors ensured that the custody process, such as booking-in times, operated as efficiently as possible, whereas in Gormiston they ensured efficiency in relation to completion of drug tests (for which there was a performance target), charging and prosecutions, especially of suspects who were 'bailed to return'. GMS8 went on to say that while his role was not 'sexy', it was important as without it there would be financial costs to the police, human costs to suspects and costs to public perceptions of the police.

Security Ltd manager

There was also a Security Ltd manager in Sunnyside who sat in the same office as the inspectors and who organized the staffing rota and stock for the custody area, although some police officers were sceptical about how much he contributed to the custody area, as they felt that his job did not appear demanding.

Custody officers and detention supervisors

PACE introduced the role of the custody officer, who is supposed to be of the rank of sergeant or above, whose remit is to ensure that staff comply with the PACE Codes of Practice. They are there to ensure that suspects are fairly treated and have access to their due process rights.[3] In theory, custody officers are supposed to provide independent oversight of the custody process, but in the past there were limitations on the extent of their independence. McConville *et al.* (1991: 55) noted that custody officers tended to be facilitators rather than guardians or gatekeepers of the custody process; for example, they shared the cultural values of the arresting officers, meaning that they were emotionally committed to believing the arresting officer's version of events and authorized detention regardless of the circumstances and whether it was lawful. Similarly, Choongh (1997: 173–7) found little evidence of independence and some evidence of custody officers failing to safeguard suspects' rights (e.g. they failed to prevent investigating officers from interviewing suspects off the record, and they failed to protect suspects from excessive use of force or the use of belittling or humiliating language or behaviour).

In the present research, custody officers booked in suspects (including authorizing detention, reading suspects their rights and conducting a risk assessment), managed the detention of suspects, advised and managed the more junior members of staff or police staff in the custody area, a matter that was also noted by Choongh (1997: 173), made decisions about the necessity of an interpreter or an appropriate adult and made decisions about bail. In Sunnyside they also had a 'whiteboarding' sergeant who 'controlled the board', meaning that when a number of sergeants were working the 'whiteboarding' sergeant had overall responsibility for coordinating the treatment of suspects, for example ensuring that the appropriate agencies were contacted or that detention reviews were conducted on time, and ultimately that the maximum length of detention without charge (known as the 'PACE clock') was not exceeded. For custody officers, like GMS11, the complex needs of some suspects meant there were a number of responsibilities that they had to juggle at once which, in combination with the ambience of the custody area and shift work, explained why it was an unpopular job for some, albeit one where the stress ended with the end of the shift. However, custody officers also lamented that their role had changed in that they had been mostly divested of the responsibility for charging suspects, which was largely done by the Crown Prosecution Service following the introduction of 'statutory charging' in 2003.[4]

In Sunnyside, in addition to there being custody officers, there were also detention supervisors who were employed by Security Ltd and who performed a similar role to the custody officer. This role had only recently arisen to free up custody officers' time, to speed up the booking-in process and to provide opportunities for career progression for Security Ltd staff. This detention supervisor described his role:

> [B]asically I supervise the Security Ltd staff, that's the custody assistants, the janitors, and the custody administrators, and I book in the suspects, and basically I am responsible for any other issues to do with the building while we're working, should any damages or breakages occur, because the buildings are Security Ltd buildings. (SNS1)

The main difference between detention supervisors and custody officers was that detention supervisors were not responsible for key parts of the booking-in process, including the authorization of detention, the reading of suspects' rights, informing suspects of charges (decided on by the Crown Prosecution Service) or making decisions about bail. But as SNS6, a Security Ltd manager, said, 'PACE says that the custody officer has to ensure that the rights and entitlements are done, it doesn't actually say he has to give them himself, he just has to ensure that they've been done.' While the booking in of suspects was done by custody officers, not civilians, in Gormiston, the possibility of civilians doing it met with mixed views among staff. Some interviewees (e.g. GMS1) felt that it was a waste of resources to have custody officers booking in suspects when in fact the role could be performed equally well by police staff. However, this view was not shared by other staff members (e.g. GMS10) who felt that the stressful nature of the job would limit its appeal to civilians, especially if civilians were to be paid less than custody officers.

While detention supervisors were not supposed to authorize suspects' detention or read them their rights, in practice they *did*, for example when custody officers were too busy to help. Even when custody officers were free to help, detention supervisors were observed to authorize detention and read suspects their rights without asking anyone until after they had done it, at which time they would enter a sergeant's lapel number on the computer system (SNPO7).[5] These deviations from the rules reflected the feeling that some detention supervisors saw them as unnecessarily bureaucratic. One detention supervisor thought it nonsensical that he was not allowed to authorize detention and some custody officers agreed with him, whereas other custody officers abided by the rules (e.g. SNPO1). Even when detention supervisors did request a custody officer to authorize detention or read someone their rights this was done with no more than a cursory nod of the head and without the sergeant checking the details (SNPO2, SNPO7). This is a clear example of what Crawford *et al.* (2005: 42) have called 'power creep' in which police staff necessitate new powers as they are drawn into new roles, as well as 'mission creep' in which police staff move away from their original purpose by taking on additional roles. As well as overstepping their role and powers, these arrangements added to the already routinized way in which suspects' detention was authorized in which decisions were only rubber-stamped rather than carefully considered by gatekeepers like custody officers and detention supervisors.

Jailors, designated detention officers and custody assistants

In Gormiston, custody officers were assisted by jailors who were police constables and designated detention officers (DDOs) who were civilians employed by the police, while in Sunnyside custody officers and detention supervisors were assisted by custody assistants and a custody administrator who were both employed by Security Ltd. The jailors, DDOs and custody assistants appeared to do virtually the same tasks as each other, which were to collect biometric data, carry out cell checks, look after the welfare of suspects in the cells (e.g. responding to their requests) and accompany suspects to and from their cells. A jailor (GMS4), a custody assistant (SNS4) and a DDO (GMS3) all described their roles in similar terms. This jailor's views encapsulate what they did in the custody area, albeit that he was more sympathetic than the others about suspect needs:

> [T]he key thing is to ensure that all suspects are regularly checked to make sure that they're breathing, if they have any needs, that they're met as well, because obviously they have rights, they may want to make phone calls to let somebody know that they're there, contact their solicitors. Also it's about making sure that the environment that they're in is reasonably tidy, protecting their welfare, because there are some suspects, particularly once they've realized that they're maybe going to court, and they may be detained, and it's possible that they're going to prison, can become very negative, very suicidal, so it's actually reading their body language, trying to offer that support as well. It's also about making sure . . . that they see the doctor if required, so it's making an assessment of their immediate medical, physical, state, as well as looking at their emotional state . . . it's about facilitating their needs as well as balancing it against the fact that they're in custody, and maintaining security. (GMS4)

In Gormiston, the reason that the jailors and DDOs performed similar roles was because the role of the DDO in Gormiston had expanded to encompass some of the tasks that had been performed by police constable jailors. DDOs had originally been employed through Home Office funds to drug-test suspects, but their permanence in the custody area and the need for them to 'muck in' meant that they had gradually incorporated other tasks, such as cell checks, into their role, as well as training the police constable jailors who had limited experience of working in the custody area (GMS10, GMS2, GMS4, GMS5). Therefore, as with the detention supervisors, there was evidence of 'mission creep' among the DDOs (Crawford *et al.*, 2005: 42).

By contrast, the custody assistants in Sunnyside divided the tasks between them, partly because it was a large custody block; for example, one would be allotted the role of fingerprinting, another cell checks and so on. This separation of roles for police staff in Sunnyside had some unintended consequences, however; the custody assistants would only perform their allotted role. Those fingerprinting, for example, refused to answer the telephone or do the cell checks in order to help out their colleagues. This inspector explained:

> Because everybody knows what their role is . . . they allocate a role to the custody assistants, so we'll have a custody assistant who's on fingerprints, and that's all they'll do for that day, which is great if he's got enough to keep him busy, if they haven't, they'll sit and play computer games, or something like that, and the phone can be ringing on the desk but they'll not think about answering it because it's not

> their job for the day. You will have people who are on checks and you say, can I have some prints done, they say, I'm on checks, who's on prints, oh Fred is, where's he, he's on lunch, I need some prints done, and in some cases people will resist. (SNS8)

This suggests that the police staff in Sunnyside adopted a more instrumental, routinized and bureaucratic approach to their job than the police staff in Gormiston. That is, they focused on the means not the ends whereas in Gormiston the police staff appeared to focus on the ends not the means.

All the same, DDOs and custody assistants had come to be seen as invaluable to the police custody process simply because they possessed specialist skills (e.g. at collecting biometric data), which police officers no longer had (e.g. SNS6) and because they knew the job better than probationer police constables called on to act as jailors. Consequently, one interviewee, GMS5, described the DDOs as 'an absolute Godsend, they're worth their weight in gold'.

There was one important difference between the police staff in Sunnyside and Gormiston, which was that the police staff in Sunnyside did not have designated powers. Under the Police Reform Act 2002 police staff working in custody areas (as detention officers or custody assistants) can be designated to have the power to:

- take fingerprints;
- conduct intimate and non-intimate searches, the latter with or without consent;
- conduct a search to find relevant marks or features to ascertain identity;
- take photographs;
- take a footwear impression.

Since chief officers decide on the designation of powers they can vary between police forces, hence the variation between Gormiston and Sunnyside. SNS5, a Security Ltd manager, and SNS9, a police officer, said that the chief constable was opposed to designation and that this was because of concerns that the police would have to train the police staff rather than the training being provided in partnership with Security Ltd, as was the case at the time of the research.

While Security Ltd police staff did not have designated powers, in practice, this made little difference to their work as they still performed many of the tasks above but first had to ask suspects for their consent (SNS1, SNS6) and if they did not give consent or withdrew it then the police might need to assist them (e.g. by restraining the suspect while the police staff operated the fingerprint machine). A further and perhaps more important difficulty arose if a suspect could not give their consent, for example because they were mentally ill, intellectually impaired or intoxicated. In SNPO5, a female custody assistant was asked to search a mentally ill female suspect because there were no female police officers available. The custody assistant could not obtain the suspect's consent because she did not understand what was being asked of her and so the custody assistant reluctantly performed the search, requesting that a note was made on the custody record of what had happened as she was concerned about negative repercussions. This is perhaps why two police officers in Sunnyside (SNS8 and SNS9) were in favour of police staff being designated with powers, including the power to search suspects as well as to use pepper spray.

In neither site did police staff have powers to use force other than the common-law power that all citizens have to defend themselves. Police staff also reported that they should only use force when assisting police officers (SNS5). Police staff received similar training to the police on this, although they did not carry the same equipment, such as pepper spray and a baton. When police staff did assist police officers, a custody assistant commented that rank and role were forgotten and that police officers and police staff became equally respected (SNPO3). However, certain situations – for instance, if police staff went alone to a suspect's cell – put pressure on police staff to deviate from the rules, as this Security Ltd interviewee explained:

> [I]f a DP [detained person] tries to run out the door, they [Security Ltd employees] have actually got no powers to stop them, so if they try to grab them, or take them down, they are leaving themselves . . . open for an assault charge. If they're there with a sergeant or a police officer, and the police officer lays on hands first, then that's fine . . . I'd say eighty percent of [Security Ltd] staff have actually laid on hands first, because it's just a natural reaction, you see somebody running out the door, your gut reaction is to stop them. (SNS6)

This quotation illustrates how practices can vary from the rules laid down to safeguard suspects from inappropriate use of force and is another indication of 'power creep'. It also shows that there has been a shift in the modus operandi of the police, as contrary to what Bittner (1970: 122) has argued, police monopoly over the unrestricted use of force has been broken, at least in practice. In theory, since police staff were not designated with the power to use force, it maintained an illusion that this power rested solely with the police. This matter is discussed in more detail in Chapter 6.

Custody administrators

Finally, there were also custody administrators in Sunnyside, but not in Gormiston, who were employed to answer the phones and to contact practitioners, such as legal advisors, appropriate adults and medical practitioners, and the people nominated by suspects to be notified of their arrest. They also remotely opened and closed the doors into the custody area, although this was a task that was shared with the booking-in staff. By contrast, in Gormiston, these administrative tasks were mainly performed by the custody officers, albeit not as effectively, given that some interviewees complained that telephone lines to the custody area were either engaged, answered and then immediately put down or answered but left unattended (e.g. GMS12). Since the research was conducted, some of the burden on the police of contacting legal advisors may have been alleviated by the introduction of the Defence Solicitor Call Centre (DSCC). Since January 2008, all requests for legal advice are now routed through the DSCC.

Level of staffing

Table 3.1 shows the average number of staff per shift in each of the custody areas. These data were collected during participant-observation as the researchers kept a note of who worked on each shift. The table shows that, on average, Sunnyside had around three extra staff per shift compared to Gormiston, meaning that in spite of them processing more suspects, they had a lower staff to suspect ratio in Sunnyside. The extra staff were largely due to an extra detention supervisor and custody administrator, as Gormiston did not have anyone in equivalent roles. Coupled with the fact that they had ten less cells in Gormiston, it was unsurprising to find that staff repeatedly described the custody area in Gormiston as busy.

Another fundamental difference between Sunnyside and Gormiston was that Sunnyside was staffed by a permanent team of inspectors,

Table 3.1 Average number of staff per shift

Police and police staff roles		*Sunnyside*	*Gormiston*
Police	Inspectors	0.4	0.3
	Custody officers	3.1	3.1
	Jailors	n/a	2.0
Police staff	Custody manager	0.5	n/a
	Detention supervisor	0.9	n/a
	Custody assistants	3.2	n/a
	Custody administrators	1.0	n/a
	DDOs	n/a	0.9
Total staff per shift		9.1	6.3
No. of suspects during participant observation		234	217
Av. staff to suspect ratio per shift		1:1.2	1:1.6

sergeants, detention supervisors, custody assistants and custody administrators. In Gormiston, however, only designated detention officers were permanent, while custody officers and jailors would spend five weeks at a time working in the custody area. At the time of the research, the Metropolitan Police Service were discussing the introduction of a permanent team of custody officers and jailors. Some interviewees were opposed to the idea of working permanently in the custody area because of concerns about 'burn-out', reduced front-line capacity, staff becoming desensitized because of the regularity of their contact with suspects, divisions between front-line and custody-based staff and personality clashes between those permanently based in the custody area, as well as a lack of financial incentive (e.g. GMS8). Others were in favour of a permanent team because it would increase ownership of the custody area and what happened in it; there would be a specialized workforce who knew the job well and performed consistently; it would increase the independence of custody officers who were no longer working on the street; and altogether it would make police custody safer and more efficient. However, those in favour of a permanent custody team in Gormiston also felt that it should be a team of civilians, not police officers, who should perform the job.

Medical practitioners

According to PACE, suspects are entitled to request medical attention and this request must be met as soon as is practicable (PACE code C, 2008: 9.8). Indeed, it is recommended that information about this entitlement must be included in the rights and entitlements provided to suspects. In addition, a suitably qualified medical practitioner must be called to assess someone as quickly as possible if they are detained under the mental health legislation, although it was only in Sunnyside that police custody was used as a place of safety as the Metropolitan Police Service had a policy of taking the mentally ill to hospital.

As Table 3.2 shows overall requests were made for a doctor for 42 per cent of suspects, which is a similar proportion to the 45 per cent noted by Newburn and Hayman (2002: 46). In addition, only 5 per cent of suspects for whom a doctor was requested did not consult with the doctor. This figure was more than the proportion of requests for intimation (i.e. suspects' requests to have someone informed of their arrest) and legal advice that went unmet, which are discussed in Chapter 5. This is perhaps because of the gravity of the concerns of custody staff about the welfare of suspects, while legal advice and intimation were regarded as more dispensable because the consequences of not having them were not a 'life and death' matter. Similarly, Newburn and Hayman (2002: 135) concluded that police officers were inclined towards being overzealous in requesting a doctor, even if it proved unnecessary, rather than risk making the wrong decision.

Table 3.2 Requests for and consultations with a doctor

Site	*Sunnyside*	*Gormiston*	*All*
Requests for a doctor of all suspects (%)	34	51	42
Consulted with a doctor of all suspects (%)	32	50	40
Requests unmet, of those suspects for whom a request was made (%)	6	2	5

The provision of forensic medical services varied between Sunnyside and Gormiston. In Gormiston, services were provided by a principal forensic medical examiner who managed 14 other forensic medical examiners, henceforth referred to as doctors. On each 12-hour shift, one doctor simultaneously covered five police stations, although two of these were overspill police stations, which were only used if the other three were full. Requests for the doctor were paged directly to the person on-call who would then telephone the custody area to discuss the details of the request. Since the doctor simultaneously covered five police stations, this could mean that occasionally there were requests for them to be in different places at once. On these occasions the doctor had to decide, based on the urgency of the case, where to go first, deciding between medical emergencies and 'PACE clock emergencies'. The latter was when the police wanted the doctor to assess fitness for detention or interview because the maximum time that the police could detain a suspect was running out. The length of time it took the doctor to attend the police station depended on how far away they were and/or how many other suspects they had to see. However, in Gormiston, the police complained that there were frequently delays with the doctor if they were dealing with matters at a different police station, prolonging detention, for example, if they were waiting for the doctor to certify a suspect fit for interview.

Furthermore, there were no financial incentives for doctors to arrive at a specified time. Doctors, in this area, were paid a fee per shift, per call out and per patient and thus were a considerable cost to the police, especially given that one suspect might consult with the doctor on numerous occasions. Indeed, Jones and Newburn (2002: 140) argue that police officers in their research were resentful of doctors benefitting from the call-out system, which also led to them having too many calls to deal with. The majority of suspects in both sites had only one consultation with the doctor; the figures were 69 per cent in Gormiston and 65 per cent in Sunnyside, with χ^2 analysis showing that there was no significant association between the area and the number of consultations suspects received. However, the two areas did vary in terms of the maximum number of consultations received, which was seven in Gormiston but only four in Sunnyside, and in terms of the total number of consultations received, which was 309 in Gormiston compared to 213 in Sunnyside. This is interesting given that there were more suspects in Sunnyside than Gormiston and that the two custody areas were dealing with a similar proportion of suspects identified as being at risk. Perhaps the difference arose because, as I describe below, there were more requests for the doctor to assess the fitness of suspects in Gormiston than in Sunnyside. Alternatively, the difference may have been related to the different remuneration processes in the two sites.

In contrast to Gormiston, in Sunnyside medical services were provided by a team of doctors and nurses who also covered four custody areas in the police service area. However, the team were employed by a private company called Sunnyside Forensic Medical Services, which had been set up by a former principal forensic medical examiner and which was subcontracted by Security Ltd to work in the custody areas of Sunnyside Police. The company was paid based on the number of consultations with suspects, but staff were paid per shift, which may in part explain why staff in Gormiston conducted more consultations than in Sunnyside. However, consultations with suspects brought to police custody as a place of safety were charged separately and provided a financial buffer for the company. Interestingly, the company were also fined £120 per case when they were late for an arranged consultation. Hence, if they were late for a pre-arranged appointment, the medical staff would note on the custody record the reason they were late (e.g. if custody staff forgot to inform them of all the people they needed to see) (SNS2).

The roles and responsibilities of medical staff in the two areas were broadly similar, except that there were no nurses in Gormiston, unlike in Sunnyside. Medical staff were responsible for assessing the fitness of suspects (for detention, interview and charge) and making recommendations to the police about when someone was likely to become fit. The medical staff also recommended whether suspects required an appropriate adult and took intimate samples from suspects (e.g. penile swabs in rape cases). Generally, the medical staff were there to 'take any medical responsibility for the people in police care, and to avoid deaths in custody' (GMS9). However, as Newburn and Hayman (2002: 135–6) note, the role is more complex and contradictory than this. They argue that conflicts of interest arose in doctors' working relationships with the police and their patients; for example, it was unclear what the doctor should do if they heard or saw information of interest to the police during the course of an examination, as the British Medical Association says that doctors should protect client confidentiality – yet they are paid by the police. Moreover, this conflicting role may not be understood by the suspect. While some consultations in their research took place in a private room, the rest took place in the cells, in the presence of a police officer and within sight and earshot of the CCTV.

The forensic medical staff also assessed suspects for a wide variety of ailments including medical problems (such as cuts, epilepsy, diabetes, heart problems, head injuries), drug and alcohol withdrawal and mental health problems (such as depression, self-harm, suicidal intentions). Overall, the custody records showed that the most common reason for requesting a doctor on the first occasion was to assess fitness for detention, interview and/or charge, which is similar to the finding in Newburn and Hayman (2002: 46) that 44 per cent of suspects saw a doctor because they were unfit through drink or drugs. In Gormiston, doctors were primarily requested to assess fitness (57 per cent); but, in Sunnyside, it was to deal with medical problems (35 per cent) followed by assessments of fitness (25 per cent), and there was a significant relationship between the area and the reason for requesting a doctor for the first time ($\chi^2 = 56.6$, $p < 0.05$). This suggests that in Gormiston there was a larger number of suspects who were intoxicated as a result of alcohol or illicit drugs and, therefore, requiring a doctor to assess their fitness.

After consultations, doctors rarely prescribed medication and any medication that was given was only to make suspects comfortable and fit for detention, interview and charge. Consequently, mostly they only prescribed paracetemol for pain relief, dihydrochloride (or DFs as they were commonly known) for heroin withdrawal and, in special circumstances, benzodiazapenes such as diazepam (valium), for example, if someone was known to be addicted to them or to those suspected of murder, but they were generally not given to problematic drug-users because of concerns about not being able to rouse suspects if they needed to evacuate the custody area (e.g. SNS2). DFs were used in Sunnyside and Gormiston because they were 'safe and simple, straightforward' (GMS9) and made suspects fit for four to six hours. However, heroin users would normally have to wait a period of time before they were given DFs. In Sunnyside, even if someone had positive signs of withdrawing from heroin they would normally only be prescribed DFs once they had spent eight hours in custody to allow any drugs they had consumed prior to entering custody to be processed by the body and in order to minimize the risk of death in custody (SNS8).

Both sites had similar policies on prescription drugs already in the possession of the suspects. In accordance with PACE code C (2008: 9.9), suspects who were not dependent drug users were only allowed to take prescription drugs in their possession which were clearly labelled as their own, once this situation had been reviewed by the doctor. Drug-dependent suspects, however, were not allowed to bring with them to custody prescription drugs (such as methadone and subutex), even if they were labelled with the suspect's name, because of fears of overdose and death in custody (GMS9). This was also in accordance with PACE, which says that no police officer can administer or supervise the self-administration of drugs listed in the Misuse of Drugs Act 2001 (PACE code C, 2008:

9.10). Yet there were exceptions to this: one interviewee (GMS7) said that occasionally police officers took drug-dependent suspects, for whom they had a 'soft spot', via the chemist to collect their prescription on the way to the police station. Given that this practice violated PACE, it raises questions about why police officers might do this, other than out of goodwill. Perhaps police officers used this as a bargaining tool to encourage compliance. At the same time GMS7 and GMS9 said that it was not unheard of for custody staff to think it appropriate for problematic drug users to suffer the pains of withdrawal as a kind of punishment which might help them reconsider their actions, especially if they had been difficult with staff. It would seem, therefore, that overall 'cold turkey' was the norm for drug-dependent suspects in both sites.

Legal advisors

According to PACE, all suspects are entitled to request free and independent legal advice from a solicitor or accredited legal practitioner while they are in police detention, and they are informed of this right when they are booked into the custody area if not before. Once a suspect has requested legal advice this request should be met as soon as is practicable and in any case within 36 hours. If suspects change their mind about consulting with a legal advisor, a record must be made of this and it must be authorized by someone of the rank of Inspector or above. The shift towards a qualified right to silence as a result of the Criminal Justice and Public Order Act 1994 means that the need for legal advice is all the more essential. This is because refusing to answer police questions could harm someone's defence, as adverse inferences could be drawn from this silence later in court. In theory, only a legal advisor is in a position to clarify whether it is sensible to remain silent.

Custodial legal advice is provided by a legal advisor nominated by the suspect or by the duty solicitor if their nominated legal advisor is unavailable or if suspects do not have a legal advisor to nominate. Since October 2007, for a limited number of offences,[6] legal advice is also provided by the Criminal Defence Service (CDS) Direct. Furthermore, in the light of the changes wrought by the Carter Review, since 14 January 2008 all requests for legal advice are to be made via the Defence Solicitor Call Centre (DSCC) rather than directly to the Duty Solicitor Scheme, CDS Direct or nominated firms as was the case during the course of the research. The Defence Solicitor Call Centre is staffed by employees from First Assist Ltd.

At its most simplistic, the role of the legal advisor in the police station is:

> to protect and advance the legal rights of clients. On occasions this may require the solicitor to give advice which has the effect of the client avoiding giving evidence which strengthens a prosecution case.

> The legal advisor may intervene in order to seek clarification, challenge an improper question to their client or the manner in which it is put, advise their client not to reply to particular questions, or if they wish to give their client further legal advice. (PACE Codes of Practice, 2006: 6D)

As this solicitor explained, part of protecting and advancing the rights of clients is to act as a check on the police to ensure that PACE is observed:

> The solicitor's role is to protect and enhance the rights of the suspect, so under the Police and Criminal Evidence Act the suspect has a right to free legal advice. So initially it's to provide telephone advice to the person detained and then, when and where appropriate, to attend the police station to give advice about the interview process, and particularly whether to answer questions or not, but also to ensure that the person's basic rights are being observed under the PACE, to make sure that they've had a proper rest period, that they've been fed and watered, and that they've been allowed to make a phone call and have someone contacted to let them know that they're there. And of course, if the person is charged, to try and get them bail. (GMS12)

As I explore in Chapter 7, the role of the legal advisor, not least because of the predominantly adversarial system within which they operate, can place them at odds with the police contributing to tensions in their working relationships.

PACE also states that consultations with legal advisors should take place in private either over the telephone or in person. Yet in practice there were opportunities for the privacy of telephone legal advice to be compromised; for example, in Sunnyside, telephone legal advice took place in the suspect's cell over an intercom with a loudspeaker which meant that the entire conversation between the suspect and the legal advisor could, in theory, be heard by anyone within earshot of their cell. As a colleague and I have argued elsewhere, such practices are unlawful (Pattenden and Skinns, 2010).

In addition, if consultations took place in person, concerns about suspects escaping meant that the police employed the dubious practice of locking legal advisors and suspects into consultation rooms together, which was a source of antagonism. While the rooms had panic alarms on the wall, legal advisors would remain locked in the room until the police responded to the alarm. One solicitor complained about the risks that this posed to his safety; for example, he had refused to be locked into a consultation room with a mentally ill suspect until he had been permitted to view the police risk assessment of the suspect (GMS12). By contrast, a police officer, GMS3, said that it was OK to lock solicitors in consultation rooms with their clients because by the time solicitors arrived at the custody area the police already knew about the likely risks posed by the detainee and would inform solicitors of these risks and/or not even bring suspects out of their cells in the first place.

Indeed, the safety of legal advisors in custody areas has been the subject of a recent Home Office Circular (34/2007), which suggested that consultation rooms should be fitted with panic alarms which release the locked door and, failing this, police officers should stand near to the door during the consultation. These recommendations may alleviate solicitors' concerns but their success depends on how quick police forces are to make the necessary changes to their consultation rooms. Given that custody staff are already overstretched, it seems unrealistic to expect officers to stand guard outside consultation rooms in the interim period until appropriate door releases and alarms are installed. Furthermore, having a police officer visibly standing outside the consultation room may inhibit the discussion between the solicitor and their client, not to mention increasing the opportunities for eavesdropping on the conversation. Moreover, it is curious that doctors and drug workers are not mentioned in the recommendations, which have as much relevance to their safety at work as to legal advisors'.

Appropriate adults

According to PACE, appropriate adults (AAs) are called when suspects are juveniles (under 17 years of age) and/or mentally disordered or otherwise mentally vulnerable (e.g. if they have learning difficulties). The idea for AAs originated from the 'Confait Case' which highlighted that vulnerable suspects can be pressured into falsely confessing to murder (Dixon *et al.*, 1990). This led to AAs being given the role of advising suspects, observing whether interviews are conducted fairly and properly and facilitating communication between the suspect and the police, although Jacobson (2008: 31) found that the input from AAs can be ineffective because of uncertainties about their role.

The Youth Offending Service has a statutory duty to provide AAs for suspects under the age of 17, but there is no similar statutory duty for vulnerable adults. Custody officers are responsible for deciding whether a suspect requires an AA, although this depends on them recognizing, in conjunction with the doctor, difficult-to-identify mental health or intellectual impairments. These difficulties are compounded by the fact that suspects may be embarrassed to admit they have problems (Kemp and Balmer, 2008: 13). The AA might be a parent or guardian or responsible adult over 18 years of age or a social worker who knows the suspect. If such a person is unavailable then most areas have an AA service staffed by volunteers, paid staff or a mixture of both. Volunteering to be an AA is not an enticing prospect, particularly for those in full-time employment, given the possibility of being on-call at night-time.

There were variations between Sunnyside and Gormiston in terms of the staffing and funding of the AA services. In Sunnyside, the AA service was coordinated by two employees from the Youth Offending Service. During office hours they could be contacted directly and out of office hours requests were communicated to their on-call volunteers via the Carelink service provided by the local authority. The volunteers staffing the AA service in Sunnyside were unpaid, a fact that was reportedly forgotten by the police (SNS15). This interviewee went on to say that one of the reasons that the police forgot that the AAs were mostly volunteers was because they were focused on their investigatory role, which meant that they were only concerned with whether an AA attended so that they could proceed with the interview. An AA, who was a trained social worker, also felt that the volunteer AAs should be shown greater respect by the police (GMS14). At the same time, there was some awareness that AAs were unpaid among the private police staff, as one commented that she tried to be particularly nice to the AAs because of their volunteer status (e.g. SNS7).

In Gormiston, the AA service did not have the same kind of visibility in the custody area as in Sunnyside, and staff seemed unsure about who they should contact for suspects with mental health problems. Interestingly, the researchers from the present study were asked three times to act as AAs during the course of one week of participation observation in Gormiston. Therefore it is not surprising that Medford *et al.* concluded that, among custody officers in the Metropolitan Police Service, there was confusion about the existence of AA schemes (Medford *et al.*, 2000: 19). In Gormiston, there was a mental health team of social workers who were represented in the custody area during office hours. However, their role was to assess and divert mentally ill offenders from the criminal justice process, rather than acting as an AA, although occasionally they would take on this role, for example for someone they had assessed (GMD10). In addition, key workers for adults with learning disabilities and learning difficulties also acted as AAs, including out of office hours, but only for their clients (GMS14).

In spite of the use of volunteers, there were suggestions that there was a lack of available AAs particularly at weekends, as the custody area was short staffed (SNS6). Similarly, it was reported that, on occasions, AAs had been sought from a local supermarket or from the street, something that was also observed by Newburn and Hayman (2002: 132). Presumably this was because there were none available or because the police were afraid that without one they would have had to let the suspect go, as this solicitor explained: 'If they can't get an AA they have to let them out . . . because you can't progress the case without an AA, and the longer you keep them there, the closer the police know that the clock's running out' (SNS11). SNS12 felt that the availability of AAs had decreased, particularly at night-time when there was only one person from social services covering the county which prolonged suspects' detention. Indeed, these difficulties with attendance, particularly out of hours, have long been noted in research which has also pointed to the under-resourcing of social services (e.g. Dixon *et al.*, 1990). At the same time a representative from the AA service said that there was a 'canteen culture' in the police of moaning about the lack of AAs.

The role of the AA was variously described by interviewees. An AA was required when a suspect was read their rights, interviewed or asked to provide or sign a written statement or during identification procedures or in interview or when they were charged or cautioned and when they were intimately searched. GMS14, a social worker who acted as an AA, said that her role was not only to ensure that the suspect understood their rights, but also to ensure that if they had committed a crime that they understood they had done something wrong and understood the likely penalty for their actions. To fulfil their role, an AA could consult the suspect's custody record, consult in private with the suspect, provide advice about key decisions (e.g. whether to consult with a legal advisor) and make representations to the reviewing officer about their continued detention. In addition, one suspect, GMD13, who had an AA because he had bipolar disorder, said that the AA was there to 'listen in on the interview' and to answer his questions (of the AA), if he was unsure of what the police said to him. The AA for GMD13 thus appeared to view their role as being about checking comprehension. However, a solicitor (SNS11) viewed the AA as being there not to only aid comprehension (given the common usage of 'legal speak'), but also to safeguard suspects from undue pressure from the police or even legal advisors. According to Pierpoint (2006), these ambiguities in the role of the AA stem from a clash of due process, crime control and welfarist ideals that underpin the job.

These uncertainties about the role of AAs devalued their work among suspects and custody staff. In addition, as this solicitor explained, their volunteer status also compromised the quality of the service delivered: 'I think there are a couple of whacky ones [AAs], because it is voluntary and I suspect beggars can't be choosers, so you do get some weird people' (SNS11). Consequently, AAs were not viewed in an altogether favourable light by suspects or staff. Suspects, whose views perhaps matter the most, expressed mixed opinions about the value of AAs. GMD13 above and SNS4 were ambivalent about the work of their AAs, whereas GMD6 (who was a diagnosed schizophrenic) said that AAs had made no difference to his many experiences of police custody and that they were not very useful and were only 'there for the sake of it' because they were expected to be there by law.

Some staff recognized the invaluable service provided by AAs, for example when parents refused to attend the police station (GMS10, GMS4), while others (including legal advisors) failed to recognize their training or acknowledge the importance of their work (GMS10). Even worse, some interviewees questioned the value added to the police custody process by AAs, especially when they were parents rather than trained volunteers and also when a legal advisor was present as well. Newburn and Hayman (2002: 132) also noted that AAs felt undervalued. One police officer (SNS9) in the present study argued that AAs might have made sense when they were introduced with PACE to curb the extraction of false confessions, but questioned whether they were still needed given how little value they added to the custody process. This solicitor also remarked that AAs did not add anything and that they were a hindrance, particularly for juvenile suspects who had a poor relationship either with their parents or with social services:

> They don't add anything to me having to deal with my clients . . . If anything, I have to wait, and it causes delay . . . so it doesn't really help me as a solicitor, because 99 times out of 100, you know, I've got a good rapport with my client anyway, and I don't need an AA. However, it is a fundamental human right to have an AA, but they don't actually add anything to what I'm doing. (SNS11)

Police officers, one from each site, also believed that AAs prolonged detention because there were few available out of hours, meaning that vulnerable suspects had to spend the night in the cells as the police could not fully process them (SNS12, SNS9 and GMS5). Similarly, Jacobson (2008: 31) cites research by Medford *et al.* (1996) which found that on average, a vulnerable adult spends over 4.5 hours in custody prior to the AA's arrival, with some waiting more than 20 hours. Staff in the present research were frustrated by these perceived delays. One police officer, SNS9, felt that the prolonging of detention was particularly problematic given the limited amount that AAs added, other than 'sitting in the chair' during interviews. By contrast, a legal advisor was concerned about the impact of prolonged detention on juvenile suspects, who may be arrested for minor matters such as theft or being carried in a car at 4 p.m. but might spend 24 hours in custody waiting for an AA.

However, multivariate analysis of the factors that predict the length of detention without charge showed no significant association between the involvement of the AA and the length of detention (Skinns, 2010). At the same time, this finding also needs treating with caution: the data were possibly skewed because not all suspects who required an AA consulted with one. For example, 19 per cent of suspects were identified as at risk either because they were a juvenile and/or because they were mentally ill or intellectually impaired, but only 13 per cent of all suspects consulted with an AA, meaning that approximately 32 per cent of vulnerable suspects who were potentially in need of an AA assessment did not consult with one. Newburn and Hayman (2002: 48, 131) also found that not all suspects assessed as requiring an AA saw one. The reasons for this were that some AAs, often parents, did not attend, some suspects refused to see the AA, but in one tenth of cases it was unclear why suspects did not see the AA. They also found that 56 per cent of those who saw an AA had to wait 4–7 hours for the AA to arrive with the rest waiting longer. This may have been because the police were seeking help, for example from a social worker, after a parent or guardian refused or could not attend the police station. However, this meant that suspects requiring an AA could be held for lengthier periods relative to those that did not while the police sought an AA. This was problematic given that they were vulnerable and given that the police had to provide care appropriate to their age and level of distress (Jones and Newburn, 2002: 131).

In the present study, there was a variety of explanations for the 32 per cent of suspects identified as vulnerable who did not consult with an AA, although the small absolute number of consultations with an AA (N = 108) ruled out the possibility of using multivariate analysis to explore these factors. One possibility is that information about whether an AA was consulted was not routinely recorded on the custody record. Alternatively, it might have been that the police were overzealous in their initial risk assessment and, in fact, the custody officer later decided that suspects were not as vulnerable as first noted on the custody record and were, therefore, not in need of an AA. A third explanation of the data is that AAs were not made available to all the suspects that needed one. Certainly the observational research suggested that this did happen on occasions.

During participant observation (GMPO2), a man suspected of shoplifting, who had mental health and drug problems as well as difficulties understanding English (as he was of Moroccan origin) did not have a legal advisor, an AA or an interpreter. He had seen the doctor who had, presumably, certified him fit and did not recommend an AA. Yet staff observed him rocking in his cell and described him as 'not being the full ticket' but still no AA was sought. Furthermore, he was repeatedly asked by one sergeant to consent to a drug test as he had committed a trigger offence and which, if he refused, was an imprisonable offence. After considerable pressure being put on him by the sergeant, he consented to the drug test, but not without refusing first and appearing distracted as if he had not understood what was being asked of him. However, he later changed his mind and refused the drug test and was charged with failure to supply a specimen for a drug test.

Concerns about delays and the lack of availability of AAs meant that the need for an AA could be ignored by the police, particularly if they were short of time on the 'PACE clock'. However, in the case of vulnerable adults it may be that staff miss the signs of mental illness or intellectual impairment. Jacobson (2008: 28–9) argues that this is because there is a lack of routine screening and a tendency to rely on health professionals to identify those in need and because police officers receive limited training on how to recognize mental disorder. However, it is also perhaps because mental illness and intellectual impairment are difficult to spot and it is unreasonable to expect the police to do so. Gudjonsson *et al.* (1992: 25, cited in Choongh, 1997: 165) found that even clinical psychologists struggled to identify impairments over the short periods for which suspects were detained and that the police only identified 4 per cent of a possible 20 per cent of suspects as in need of an AA.

Regardless of the reasons, the lack of safeguards for suspects may have grave consequences. For example, Medford *et al.* (2003) found that the absence of an AA increased the likelihood that the police interrupted vulnerable adults' versions of events, which can have implications for the accuracy of the accounts provided.

Drug workers

The primary role of the drug workers in both sites was to identify potential clients, assess them and refer them to a case manager in their local criminal justice integrated team (CJIT), who would then engage them in treatment (such as substitute prescriptions), as well as tackling some of the wider issues affecting their lives including difficulties with housing, benefits, employment and education. If suspects were already in touch with the CJIT then they would be referred to their case manager. The role of the drug workers in Sunnyside and Gormiston differed in that Gormiston was regarded as having a high number of problematic drug users, which meant that suspects suspected of trigger offences were drug-tested on arrest. This meant that in Gormiston there was an extra referral route for suspects to the drug workers; if suspects tested positive for cocaine or opiates they were legally obliged to see the drug worker for an assessment and to attend follow-up appointment(s) through the 'Tough Choices' initiative. In both sites, clients were also identified by drug workers either by name, for example because they were known to them, or because suspects requested to see a drug worker. In Sunnyside, one of the drug workers said that the police kept a note of the people who requested a drug worker and even called him when he was not in the custody area to inform him of potential clients.

In Sunnyside, there were two drug workers who covered the custody area; they were not permanently based there, but either one of them was present in the custody area four days per week (SNPO2). In Gormiston, there was a drug worker in the custody area between the hours of 8 a.m. and 10 p.m. In both sites, drug workers had access to the paper custody records, which helped the drug workers to identify known clients. In Sunnyside, the drug workers were also allowed to view the custody records on the computer, sitting in the same area as the police staff if a desk was available. However, in Gormiston the drug workers sat separate from the police as they had their own room where they could conduct assessments with clients in private. In Sunnyside, the drug workers could only speak to suspects privately in the cells or in the exercise yard.

The suspects

Throughput and busyness

The custody areas in Gormiston and Sunnyside had similar numbers of suspects during the two weeks that data were collected (N=466 in Sunnyside, N=417 in Gormiston). However, the custody area in Sunnyside had a larger capacity, having 36 cells compared to Gormiston's 26. This meant that the ratio of suspects to cells each day was 1.2:1 in Gormiston and 0.93:1 in Gormiston; that is, each day Gormiston had more suspects than there were cells which, along with the PACE clock, may have contributed to additional pressures on staff to process suspects as quickly as possible to make space for new suspects. In addition to the fewer cells in Gormiston, there were also fewer staff; as already noted the staff-to-suspect ratio was higher in Gormiston (1:1.6) than in Sunnyside (1:1.2). Therefore, since Gormiston had fewer cells, fewer staff, yet roughly the same number of suspects as Sunnyside over the two-week period of data collection, this suggests that the Gormiston custody area was busier than that of Sunnyside.

The busyness of the custody areas was observed in both sites, with staff frequently multi-tasking, for example answering the phone and releasing the gates while booking in suspects (SNPO5). The busyness of the custody area was also acknowledged by staff in interviews. A solicitor said that part of his role in a busy custody area like Gormiston was to remind the police of the need to deal with suspects expeditiously, as he felt that they interpreted this liberally. When reflecting on the busyness of the custody area, police and police staff complained about the lack of opportunities to take breaks, citing the fact that they were too busy (e.g. SNS7). When GMS10 was asked why he did not take a break he said 'because it's too busy' and because he was conscientious about his job. Similarly, another police officer, GMS8, said that sergeants took pride in being busy partly because it made their shift pass quickly but also because it showed that they were able to cope under pressure. Another police officer, GMS5, went even further saying that he enjoyed the 'frantic work conditions' and that if he took a break, especially while the custody area was busy, he would feel as if he was letting his colleagues down. This explains why management directives to take breaks were ignored by staff in both sites.

The willingness of staff to rise to the challenge of a busy custody area was linked to an occupational culture which valued officers' ability to thrive under pressure and to demonstrate commitment, which was reminiscent of the occupational cultural characteristics of solidarity and

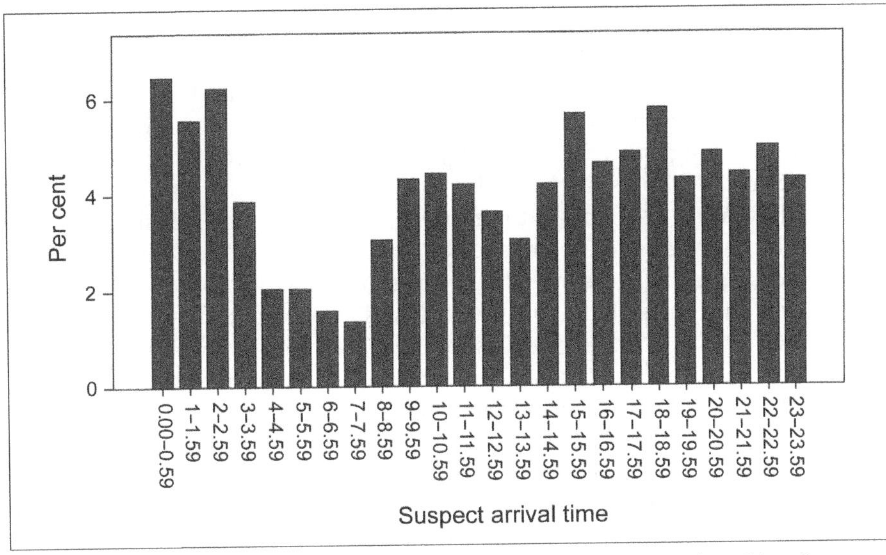

Figure 3.1 Frequencies for suspect arrival times in both sites (combined)

efficiency described in other research (Reiner, 2010: 119, 122–3). However, the busyness of the custody areas also suggests a shortage of staff which, as I discuss later, impacted on stress and the quality of service provision in terms of staff responsiveness to suspects. For example, during participant observation, a group of sergeants commented that staff were 'so busy looking after the human rights of suspects that they don't look after themselves' in terms of taking breaks, going outside for ten minutes or eating food, and that management failed to appreciate this aspect of their job. Yet perhaps this was a matter that not even management could do anything about; after all, managerialist pressures to do more with less are the likely source of understaffing and the concomitant busyness of the custody areas.

At the same time, the custody area oscillated between peaks and troughs in terms of the busyness of staff, as shown in Figure 3.1.[7] There were periods of 'downtime' when staff were able to go and get coffee or eat a meal – some even switched the lights down and went to sleep. There were also occasions in both sites when suspects and arresting officers had to queue either in the custody area, holding bays and/or the car park. This meant an uncomfortable wait for suspects, for example on a hard wooden bench while wearing handcuffs, unless the arresting officers agreed to take these off, as this suspect noted: 'They wanted to leave the cuffs on at first, I said, look, come on, I'm in custody, I can't go anywhere, so they took the cuffs off in the end' (GMD14). However, there was a sense of teamwork among the staff, particularly in Gormiston; officers on street patrol would sometimes step behind the desk and start booking in suspects to ease the long queues and the congestion in the custody area. This willingness to step behind the custody desk was also a consequence of the Gormiston officers rotating between custody and street patrol; it appeared that the arresting officers were empathetic as it could easily have been them struggling with a lengthy queue of suspects to be booked in.

As Figure 3.1 shows, arrivals did not occur at random in the two sites; rather, they fitted around shift patterns and pub and club closing times. In Gormiston, suspects were most likely to arrive on Mondays, while in Sunnyside, suspects were most likely to arrive on Saturdays and there was a significant difference between the police stations in terms of the day of arrival ($\chi^2=15.4$, $p<0.05$). Similarly, there was a highly significant difference between the police stations in terms of the time of arrival ($\chi^2=43.1$, $p<0.01$). In Gormiston, suspects were most likely to arrive between 3 and 4 p.m. (7.4 per cent), whereas in Sunnyside suspects were most likely to arrive between 2 and 3 a.m. (6.9 per cent). These peaks occurred in the hour or two immediately after shift-changes at 6 a.m., 2 p.m. and 10 p.m., perhaps because the incumbent staff got straight to work in arresting people, with their work tailing off towards the end of their shift. In these busy periods staff booked in over thirty suspects per hour. Bottlenecks like this have also been identified in previous research. Maguire (1988) found that in the busiest city centre custody area in his research, there were eleven occasions over a three-week period when there were more than six custody records to complete per hour and that this was generally on Friday and Saturday nights between 11 p.m. and 2 a.m. Similarly, Brown (1989) found 'log-jams' of suspects, which he defined as seven or more to book in per hour at weekends. The staff in the present research were booking in more suspects than mentioned in the existing research.

Suspect characteristics

Table 3.3 summarizes the composition of suspects in the custody areas. The two sites had similar levels of throughput, similar proportions of suspects identified as being at risk, but differed significantly in terms of the sex, age and ethnicity of suspects, the reason for arrest, the reason for the identified risks and case disposal. Sunnyside had a much higher proportion of juveniles and lower proportion of males compared to Gormiston. Sunnyside also had a larger proportion of white suspects in custody than Gormiston, which was in keeping with the ethnic make-up of the areas in which the police stations were situated. At the last census in 2001, the proportion of white people in the relevant census area for Gormiston was 75.4 per cent and in Sunnyside it was 94.3 per cent. Therefore in both areas there was a disproportionate number of minority ethnic suspects in police custody, which may reflect policing practices, such as stop and search, which differentially impact on minority ethnic citizens (e.g. Bowling *et al.*, 2008).

Table 3.3 Composition of suspects in custody

Variable		*Sunnyside*	*Gormiston*	*All*	χ^2
Sex	% male	81	86	83	3.56*
Age	% juveniles (17 or under)	19	16	18	2.11 (p=0.086)
Ethnicity	% white	87	52	71	131.41**
Reason for arrest	Sexual/violent offences (%)	33	25	29	10.53*
	Property offences (%)	23	22	23	
	Disorder (%)	15	19	17	
	Drug offences, fraud and other offences (%)	20	22	21	
	Breaches, recalls, warrants (%)	8	12	10	
Identified risk	% at risk	66	67	67	No association
Reason for risk	Mental illness or impairment (%)	15	18	16	41.98**
	Drugs or alcohol (%)	50	29	40	
	Medical (%)	12	20	16	
	Juvenile (%)	12	8	10	
	Other including risk of violence or escape (%)	11	26	18	
Case disposal	Charged	41	45	43	12.16*
	No further action	27	18	23	
	Cautioned	14	18	16	
	Bailed to return	15	16	15	
	Other (e.g. taken to hospital)	3	4	3	
N		466	417	883	

*$p<0.05$
**$p<0.01$

In the present research, suspects' long-term relationships with the police led some suspects to be angry and resentful about how they were treated. For example, GMD7 complained bitterly about being harassed by the police because his 'face was known to them', having been arrested on previous occasions. This also reflects Choongh's (1997: 76) view that the frequency with which some individuals find themselves stopped, arrested and detained is not coincidental; rather those who find themselves in the category of the 'policed' end up in a long-term relationship imposed on them by the police in their pursuit of deference and authority.

There was also a significant difference between sites in terms of the reason for arrest with Sunnyside having more arrests than Gormiston for sexual and violent offences and Gormiston having slightly more arrests for breaches, warrants and recalls, and disorder. This is a surprising finding given that, as Table 3.4 shows, all crimes were committed at a higher rate in Gormiston than in Sunnyside, including violent offences. However, based on the two weeks of custody data it is possible to estimate the crime rate for 2007 for violent and sexual offences and property offences per 1,000 of the population. For Sunnyside the violent and sexual crime rate was 25.8 compared to 32.6 in Gormiston, and the property crime rate was 18.3 and 28.8 respectively. Therefore in fact the custody record data were broadly representative of the underlying crime trends in the two areas.

Table 3.3 shows a significant difference between areas in terms of the reason for someone being identified as at risk, with drugs/alcohol being a much more important reason in Sunnyside than in Gormiston, and other reasons being of more importance in Gormiston compared to Sunnyside. This difference, however, was an artefact of different recording practices as there was no 'other' box for staff to tick in Sunnyside.

Furthermore, there were also differences between areas in terms of case disposal, with Gormiston charging and diverting slightly more suspects

Table 3.4 Crime rates per 1,000 of the population 2006/7

	Sunnyside	*Gormiston*	*National average*
Population	255,000	183,000	
Violence	29.9	34.4	16.7
Robbery	1.6	8.2	1.2
Theft of a vehicle	3.2	6.5	2.9
Sexual offences	1.3	1.6	0.9
Burglary dwelling	4.0	13.4	4.3
Theft from a vehicle	7.0	19.6	7.6
All sexual and violent	31.2	36.0	17.6
All property	15.8	47.7	16.0

Source: UpMyStreet.com

than Sunnyside and Sunnyside taking no further action against a higher proportion of suspects than Gormiston. This is an interesting finding as it suggests that perhaps staff in Gormiston were arresting and detaining more of the 'right' people and that they were also more efficient at collecting sufficient evidence to divert or to charge suspects. This interpretation of this finding is all the more convincing in view of the fact that Gormiston was also a busier police station (with fewer cells and fewer staff) and detained suspects for significantly less time than Sunnyside.

Staff perceptions of suspects

As Table 3.3 shows, staff regularly dealt with suspects with complex social needs, some of whom could be difficult and resource intensive. For example, 15–18 per cent of suspects were identified as at risk as a result of mental disorder or intellectual impairments. Yet there was evidence that staff could become desensitized to the needs of suspects. During participant observation in Gormiston a woman in her thirties with drug, alcohol and mental health problems was arrested for a breach of her bail conditions, which meant she had to be detained until the next available court which was the following morning. When she was informed of this decision she became upset and had to be restrained after she repeatedly attempted and succeeded in headbutting the wall. She was later taken to hospital with suspected concussion, accompanied by one of the jailors, leaving them one short in the custody area (GMPO5). Staff appeared unperturbed by these events, unlike the researcher. Even so, they showed professionalism in how they dealt with this suspect, but this was not always the case. In SNPO5, a woman arrived at the custody area being restrained by a large number of police officers. Most of the staff (police staff and police) gathered round to watch her and all laughed loudly when she fell and banged her head on the wall.

Staff attitudes seemed to be rooted in stereotypes about suspects. Stereotyping occurs when probably false attributions about a whole group are unproblematically generalized to particular individuals. This tendency towards a 'them' and 'us' outlook is characteristic of police cultures which emphasize isolation and solidarity. Reiner (2010: 123–4) distils the research on the categories employed by the police down to seven key groups including 'good-class villains' (e.g. professional or experienced criminals), 'police property' (e.g. drug users, the unemployed, ethnic minorities, visible youth subcultures, sex workers), 'rubbish' (e.g. couples repeatedly involved in domestic disputes), 'challengers' (e.g. doctors or lawyers who have the power to challenge the police), 'disarmers' (e.g. vulnerable suspects who require additional support), 'do-gooders' (e.g. lobby groups such as Liberty) and 'politicians'.

In the present study, stereotypes were manifest in how the police discussed suspects who might be regarded as 'police property'.[8]

Problematic drug users, or 'fucking junkies' as some officers described them (e.g. GMPO6), were stereotyped as liars, dirty and lazy. One drug worker (GMS6) said that while police attitudes towards problematic drug users had improved, they continued to use stereotypes: 'I think it's got a lot better in the police force, the training generally is a little bit different than it used to be, but kind of generally speaking, a crackhead's a dirty crackhead, so he just can't help but theive, you know, that's the analysis [by the police].' The following conversation between a suspect observed in GMPO6, who was brought from his cell to be released, and two sergeants also conveyed that officers held stereotypes about suspects as being stupid:

Custody officer: Good morning.
Suspect: What's good about it?
Custody officer: If you are going to be like that you can go back in your cell.
Suspect: Alright then. [He goes to his cell followed by a jailor who locks him back up.]
Custody officer: What is wrong with people?
Custody officer 2: Stupid, aren't they. That's why they get arrested.

Gender stereotypes and sexist attitudes were also observed. For example, in SNPO4, an 18-year-old woman was brought into the custody area for being drunk and disorderly. She was not read her rights as she was too drunk and was taken directly to a cell by two female officers and a male rather than a female detention supervisor. The detention supervisor later said that this was against protocol yet there was no attempt to find a third female member of staff. In the cell, her jewellery was removed by the detention supervisor and he then held her down while female officers removed her top. As this happened, the suspect described herself as a 'fat slag'. Later the detention supervisor commented to the researcher that 'she said it [that she was a fat slag] and she was!' This incident showed a disregard for the rules and a lack of respect towards this female suspect. This suspect was later interviewed for the research; she acknowledged that she was 'drunk and mouthy' in the custody area but did not remember being stripped in her cell. However, when asked how satisfied she was with how she was treated in custody she said some of the staff had been 'rude' and 'arrogant' and that she would have liked the staff to have been more polite to her (SNS7). This incident was not representative of how all female suspects were treated, yet it still raises questions about the likelihood that legal authorities will be regarded as legitimate by the minority of suspects who are treated like this.

The case of Christopher Alder described briefly in the introduction shows that stereotyping can also lead to lethal consequences. An indication of how this might happen became apparent during participant observation in Gormiston, although thankfully without any lethal consequences. Some staff held the view that illegal immigrants acted up (e.g. 'gently' banging their head against the wall and/or feigning illness) because they thought it meant that they were more likely to be released from custody and less likely to be deported. On day two of participant observation, a Chinese suspect arrested for fare evasion and for selling counterfeit DVDs – who complained of stomach pains via an interpreter on the telephone – was regarded in this way. Consequently, staff were impatient with him. For example, he was slouched against the custody desk due to his stomach pains and intermittently he was hauled to his feet by a member of staff on the other side of the desk. One of the custody officers kept telling him to stand up and that they did not want him 'slobbering all over my custody desk'. Later, the suspect was permitted to see the doctor who concluded that he was hungry at which point staff's impatience turned to derision. Had this suspect been seriously ill, the stereotype about illegal immigrants feigning illness might have meant officers missed the signs of serious illness. The racially prejudiced undertones of this incident illustrate the subtle way in which prejudice can influence police practices.

Conclusion

This chapter has described the roles and responsibilities of staff, suspect characteristics and staff perceptions of suspects. For police staff there was clear evidence of Crawford *et al.*'s (2005: 42) 'power creep' and 'mission creep' in that police staff had begun to overstep their intended roles, taking on new roles and powers. For example, in practice, they authorized suspects' detention, read them their rights and used force when they were not supposed to. The latter is perhaps the most troubling and also challenges Bittner's (1970: 122) idea that the police have a monopoly over the unrestricted use of force.

Medical staff were shared between a number of police stations and were provided by forensic medical practitioners in Gormiston, who were paid by the police, and by a combination of forensic medical practitioners and nurses in Sunnyside, who were subcontracted by Security Ltd. Medical staff were largely involved in assessing a suspect's fitness for detention, interview and/or charge. Legal advisors' role was to advance the rights of their clients, albeit that this could be hampered, for example, by a lack of privacy during telephone consultations. The role of appropriate adults was uncertain and they were perceived to be unavailable and as prolonging detention. This contributed to mixed views about their value in the custody process. Finally, drug workers were either permanently or partially based in the custody area in either their own office or in the same area as the police staff. They were there to engage with problematic drug users, who were known to them, referred themselves to the drug workers or who tested positive for cocaine or opiates.

In terms of the suspect population, there were more suspects per police staff member in Gormiston and Gormiston also had fewer cells, suggesting that the staff there were under pressure to process suspects more quickly than in Sunnyside. In both sites, suspects were largely white, adult males, although the proportion of minority ethnic suspects was disproportionate to the composition of those residing in the police service area. Suspects were mostly arrested for sexual/violent offences with a large proportion of them being identified as being at risk because of alcohol or drugs. Most suspects were also charged at the end of the custody process. The police sometimes acted in ways that suggested that they were desensitized to the complex needs of suspects, as well using negative stereotypes particularly about 'police property', such as illegal immigrants and drug users.

By setting out these important parameters of the police custody process, this chapter is intended as a platform on which to build the rest of the book. An understanding of the roles and responsibilities of staff is vital to exploring the relationships between them, which are critically assessed in Chapters 6 and 7. An understanding of suspect characteristics and staff perceptions of them is not only vital to an appreciation of suspect experiences of the custody environment, which is explored, next, in Chapter 4, but also to grasp some of the reasons why suspects do not fully access their rights and entitlements, which are examined in Chapter 5.

Notes

1 Data were not systematically collected about the role of the Crown Prosecution Service as they were not based in the custody area but rather in rooms elsewhere in the police station.

2 Henceforth all interviewees are referred to with a subject code, where SN refers to Sunnyside and GM refers to Gormiston. This is followed either by S denoting staff member or D denoting detainee which is also followed by a number which refers to the number of the interview. In this case, SNS8 refers to the eighth staff member interviewed in Sunnyside.

3 In 2005, as a result of the Serious and Organized Crime and Police Act, there were provisions to civilianize the role of custody officer, which were later repealed during the review of PACE because of the important role they were believed to play in custody areas (Home Office, 2008).

4 'Statutory Charging' means that the Crown Prosecution Service (CPS), who are based in police stations (or CPS Direct who are contactable over the telephone), make decisions about whether and what to charge in all but the most minor of cases. However, on 20 May 2010, the incumbent Home Secretary, Theresa May, announced plans to return much of this decision-making to custody officers (O'Neill, 2010).

5 Henceforth data from the participant observation are referred to using codes, where SN refers to Sunnyside and GM refers to Gormiston. PO refers to the fact that the data were drawn from participant observation rather than an interview, and the number denotes on which day, of seven, the data were collected.
6 Cases include those under the Road Traffic Act 1988 such as driving with excess alcohol, driving while unfit through drink or drugs, drunk in charge and failing to provide a specimen; cases in relation to non-imprisonable offences; cases of warrants for failing to appear at court or failing to pay court fines; cases of breaches of police or court bail conditions (Legal Services Commission, 2007).
7 This tendency for peaks and troughs was also noted by Newburn and Hayman (2002: 38–9).
8 Talk about 'police property' may not be translated into police practices (Waddington, 1999).

Chapter 4

'Down the block': the custody environment for staff and suspects

On arrival at the police station, suspects were normally booked in first. While being booked in suspects were accompanied to the desk by two arresting officers. In theory, there were five stages to this process, which mostly occurred one after the other depending on the suspect's compliance,[1] their level of intoxication and the busyness of the custody area.[2]

1. *Details of arrest and the suspect.* The officer booking in the suspect normally asked 'do you know why you are here?' The reasons for arrest, however, including location and the suspect's personal details were normally provided by the arresting officer. The booking-in officer would then clarify with the suspect if they understood why they had been arrested, which could provoke an argument if the suspect disagreed with the reasons and circumstances of their arrest.
2. *Risk assessment.* Suspects were questioned about their physical and mental health, including drug problems, previous suicide attempts, whether they attended a special school and/or if they had trouble reading or writing. At this stage the booking-in officer sometimes decided whether or not they needed a doctor and/or an appropriate adult. They were also asked whether they would like to see a drug worker.
3. *Reading of rights.* The booking-in officer explained verbally and in writing to suspects that they had the right to free and independent legal advice, to have someone informed of their arrest and to view the PACE Codes of Practice. They were asked to sign to say they had been informed of their rights and to confirm their decisions about their rights and entitlements.

4. *Search and removal of property*. Next suspects were searched and their property removed, primarily to prevent them from harming themselves while they were in the cells. Suspects were normally searched by the arresting officer, unless they were of a different sex. They were asked to remove their outer clothes and personal property, and to take off their shoes. Property was listed and bagged to be taken to the property store. Suspects were then patted down and searched with a metal detector wand. If necessary, they were taken to a private room to be strip-searched.
5. *Biometric data*. Suspects were taken to have fingerprints, a DNA sample and a photograph taken. And in Gormiston, offenders who committed trigger offences were tested for opiates and cocaine.

For suspects who were intoxicated and/or non-compliant, at the bare minimum, they were searched and had their property removed, sometimes by force. This involved five or six staff assisting one another; three restrained the suspect, while the others removed the suspect's property. This normally took place in a cell with staff exiting in a carefully orchestrated manner, so that the last person out of the cell managed to shut the door before the suspect could stand up and move towards the cell door. In these circumstances, the rest of the booking-in process was completed later, for example when the suspect was sober or 'better behaved'. Even where force was not used, the volume of information requested, if not demanded, from the suspect meant it was possible to see why Choongh (1997: 81) concluded that the booking-in process is used to establish control over suspects and to assert that police custody is police territory. The drug-testing of suspects through coercive means can also be seen in this light. Therefore obedience and deference to the police seemed to be the 'path of least resistance', but also a means of, later, easing access to things like cigarettes, drinks, showers and fresh air, as well as to other rights and entitlements discussed in Chapter 5.

After booking in suspects were taken to the cells. Unlike in other jurisdictions, suspects are nearly always placed in a cell by themselves while they are in police custody in England and Wales. In other jurisdictions, such as in the US and in Australia, the police deliberately place more than one suspect in a cell together, believing that multiple-occupancy protects suspects from self-harming, as well as providing them with some much-needed company (AUI6 and USI5).[3] This is in spite of there often being only one communal toilet and sometimes not enough bench space for suspects to all lie down during the night-time, meaning that some of them have to lie or sit on the floor. By contrast, in England and Wales, the police tend to house suspects separately so as to protect them from each other.

Even so, police custody can be unpleasant for all concerned. For some suspects, police detention can be uncertain, uncomfortable and stressful where even small things, such as staff forgetting to bring them a drink of water, can matter a great deal. And while in detention they are expected to cope not only with the uncertainties about what is going to happen, but also a lengthy period of solitary confinement. Equally, staff in custody areas continually have to deal with a wide variety of suspects, a large proportion of whom are identified as being at risk as a result of their multiple needs including addictions to alcohol or illicit drugs, mental illness and intellectual impairment and/or serious medical ailments such as epilepsy and heart problems which have to be carefully monitored. Not only that, while suspects are arrested mostly for mundane crimes, a few are arrested for very serious and unpleasant offences. In addition, the staff mostly work shifts in a custody environment that can be airless and without much natural light. Furthermore, staff work in a rapidly changing organizational context and in a multi-professional setting alongside colleagues who may not share their aims and objectives, occupational culture or performance indicators. This means that police custody areas can be tough, stressful environments for workers and suspects.

What is also apparent is that the stressful nature of the police custody environment has changed little over the last decade. For example, Newburn and Hayman noted in their research conducted in 2000 that 'officers are expected to adhere to high standards of professionalism, while coping with staff shortages, working in an ill-designed custody suite, facing distressed and sometimes abusive suspects, as well as coping with the professional demands of others such as solicitors and doctors' (2002: 58). They also noted the range of tasks that custody staff were expected to perform from clearing up vomit to calming a claustrophobic suspect to checking cells and responding to suspect requests for a solicitor or toilet paper, which meant they were constantly negotiating a complex set of 'demands, requests, needs and rights' (2002: 61).

The purpose of this chapter is to explore suspect and staff experiences of the police custody environment and of being in the cells. As with Chapter 3, this chapter is primarily descriptive, thereby providing a basis for the rest of the book. There are two parts to this chapter. The first examines the police custody environment, describing the facilities (e.g. the rooms in the custody suite and what they were used for), the CCTV, the materials and procedure used to log information about suspects, the cells themselves and how the building was maintained. In the second section I describe suspect experiences in the cells and the buzzer and intercom system used to relay their requests to police officers and police staff, documenting how this could be a frustrating and upsetting experience.

The police custody environment

The facilities

The custody environments in Sunnyside and Gormiston had similarities and differences. Both were purpose-built custody areas, although Gormiston was refurbished in the 1990s while Sunnyside was refurbished in 2001 as part of a public finance initiative, meaning that Security Ltd had become responsible for the refurbishment and then the upkeep of the building as well as providing the majority of the staff in the custody area. The Gormiston custody area was on the ground floor of a fully operational police station which was in the heart of the borough of Gormiston not far from a street known for its bars and restaurants. Like most police stations, the entrance to the custody area was at the back of the police station; suspects were delivered by police cars and entered the custody area through the car park. While the custody area was not underground it felt as if it was, as there were no windows letting in natural light. The custody area was also poorly ventilated with a few air conditioning units placed sporadically behind the booking-in desk. Some of these broke down during the participant observation in summer much to the dismay of the staff (e.g. GMPO1).

Similarly, the custody area in Sunnyside had a subterranean feel to it, although there was more natural light than in Gormiston as a result of two windows in one corner of the custody area. The ventilation of the custody area was also better as the whole of the custody area was air conditioned. Like Gormiston, the Sunnyside custody area was on the ground floor of a police station, though this station was largely used for administrative rather than operational matters. Unlike in Gormiston, the Sunnyside custody suite was four miles outside of the city centre on an industrial estate. The location of the custody area caused problems for suspects on release and/or if they were bailed to return. One suspect (SND9) noted that release from custody was hard, as the custody area 'is in the middle of nowhere'. However, the police did issue taxi/bus vouchers depending on need (e.g. if someone was disabled) and on the time of their release. Nonetheless, even if you did have money for a taxi (as the all-female research team did), waiting outside was unnerving, particularly at odd times of the day when there was not much passing traffic.

For the police, the location of the custody area was problematic because of the traffic and also because of the increased journey time, especially if suspects were being aggressive. The decision to move the custody area outside the city centre had also disgruntled some of the other practitioners working in the custody area (e.g. appropriate adults and legal advisors) because they were not consulted and the location added to their journey times.

As with Gormiston, suspects in Sunnyside were delivered to the police station in cars, which arrived at the back of the main building and entered via two holding areas. In the custody areas, Sunnyside had 36 cells while Gormiston had 26. Both also had different cell wings for male, female and juvenile suspects with shower facilities at the end of each. Both custody areas could be loosely described as 'hub and spoke' designs; in Gormiston the booking-in area was the hub, which was connected to three corridors as the spokes, whereas in Sunnyside the booking-in area was connected to eight corridors. For the most part, these corridors led to the cell block areas. The cells themselves were sparse and varied in size. Most had an integral toilet and sink. The doors were solid, heavy and metal with a hatch in them, known as the wicket, which could be opened allowing the jailors to observe or speak to the suspect. The wicket was never left open because it could be used as a ligature point. For the same reason, the walls between the cells were also solid and there were no bars anywhere, unlike the police custody cells in other jurisdictions.

In Sunnyside, other than the cells, there were approximately 17 rooms, the majority of which opened directly into the custody area. The rooms were as follows:

- eight interview and consultation rooms;
- two secure waiting areas;
- an office for the Inspector(s) and custody manager from Security Ltd;
- a doctor's room;
- a room for legal advisors;
- a room containing the equipment used to collect biometric data;
- a room containing the equipment used to breathalyse suspects;
- a tea room;
- two toilets – one for suspects and one for staff.

In Gormiston, there were only 11 rooms, which included:

- four interview and consultation rooms;[4]
- a doctor's room;
- a room for the drug workers;
- an inspectors' office which doubled up as an office for the mental health workers;
- a room containing the equipment used to collect biometric data and breathalyse suspects;
- two toilets;
- a tea room.

Not only were there more rooms in the custody area in Sunnyside, the actual custody area was more spacious. In Sunnyside, the booking-in area comprised a large room at the centre of which was an elevated platform which was known by staff as 'the bridge'. One suspect, SND9, described it as 'an island in the middle of a big room'. On 'the bridge' there were six computer terminals used to book in suspects. The design of 'the bridge' meant that staff were approximately one to two metres above suspects, who had to look up at staff as they were booked in. This was not the case in Gormiston where staff sat behind a custody desk that was slightly above the eye level of suspects and their computers were protected by a toughened plastic casing. Unlike the booking-in area in Sunnyside, the custody area in Gormiston felt cramped as four computers were placed on top of the booking-in desk, which took up two-thirds of a narrow corridor. Paper custody records were stored behind the custody desk. Consequently, there was a constant flow of staff behind the custody desk, as they collected or returned custody records. Further down the corridor and out of view from the main custody desk, there was another terminal that was used to deal with suspects bailed to return.

Sunnyside custody area may have been more spacious, but the design of 'the bridge' was problematic for non-police custody workers and suspects. The height of the bridge was reportedly to protect staff from potentially violent suspects, although the symbolism of power and control that it conveyed was not lost on suspects or other practitioners. A solicitor (GMS11) said that the bridge was a psychological tool used to intimidate suspects and ensure they were 'in awe' of the police. This suspect described the bridge as:

> [L]ike a spaceship, and you feel inferior because they're all up there, and you're down here, so you're having to look up . . . You're actually looking up at them like that and speaking to them, and they're looking down like that at you, so it does make you feel inferior a little bit, yes, it's quite intimidating if you're not used to it. (SND2)

Similarly, SND4 and SND7 disliked being looked down on by staff as they booked them in, as did SND6, who commented on the 'psychology' of the booking-in desk which she described as the police being 'high behind this castle affair, in the turret, and you're down there at ground level having to look up to them'. SND9 felt that the staff were looking down on him while booking him in and that the staff 'think they're all high and mighty, like the power goes to some of their heads sometimes'. However, he felt that this would only be intimidating for people who had not been in police or prison custody before. This suggests that the physical environment implicitly exerted control over suspects, as did other parts of the custody area, such as the cell buzzers described below.

CCTV

In part, the growing use of CCTV in police custody areas was driven by the Royal Commission on Criminal Justice in 1993, which recommended their use in custody areas, and in 1999 the Police Complaints Authority recommending their expansion not only into custody areas, but also into designated cells, as a means of reducing the number of deaths in police custody, particularly of minority ethnic suspects (Newburn and Hayman, 2002: 13–14). In 1999, the Metropolitan Police Service, where Gormiston is located, had installed CCTV in their custody suites and planned to have CCTV in designated cells, while Sunnyside police service had CCTV in some custody areas but not all and were planning to introduce CCTV in designated cells. Nearly eight years later, both sites had CCTV which covered all parts of the custody area such as the booking-in area, the holding areas and the corridors, as well as all of the cells in Sunnyside and 10 of the 26 cells in Gormiston. The in-cell cameras in Gormiston were reserved for vulnerable suspects who were in need of 15-minute cell checks, as it meant that if for whatever reason the jailors were unable to check on someone the custody officers could do so instead by looking at the monitor on their desk.

At the booking-in desks, at least, the cameras recorded audio and visual material in both sites, which meant they could capture interactions between staff members and between staff and suspects. These data were recorded, although the researchers never directly asked how long they were kept. One interviewee, SNS6, described how the cameras were used to protect staff from (racial) abuse by suspects. The cameras were also regarded as being there to protect staff from unfounded allegations; a detention supervisor in Sunnyside explained that he had been falsely accused of trying to drown a mentally ill suspect but the CCTV evidence was used to successfully refute the allegation. One of the Security Ltd managers described the CCTV cameras as a 'godsend'. None of the staff expressed concerns about the cameras invading their privacy, preferring to think of them in terms of protecting them as well as suspects. Similarly, Newburn and Hayman (2002: 69–70) noted a consensus among staff about the advantages of the cameras in the custody area (e.g. in terms of protecting staff against unfounded allegations) outweighing the disadvantages (e.g. in terms of intruding on their personal conversations).

Something that the staff in Newburn and Hayman's (2002) study did not note was the potential for the cameras to be used to monitor their performance and to hold them to account. Yet this was precisely how they were used in Sunnyside, although not in Gormiston. In Sunnyside, footage was used by managers to monitor the performance of Security Ltd staff (e.g. when carrying out cell checks) and hold them to account, as this Security Ltd worker explained:

> [I]f they're saying we're down in the cell blocks, and they're constantly getting their checks late, we can actually go and look on CCTV to see if they were actually in the cell block at the time that they said ... if they have said they were in the block and they weren't, they end up getting disciplined for it. It is the case that they can lose their job. It's that severe. (SNS6)

In Gormiston, the cameras were not described as a tool for monitoring staff performance, but they were described by an inspector (GMS4) as an accountability mechanism used to monitor events in certain areas of the custody area if issues came to light after the event.

Unlike staff, suspects expressed mixed views about the use of in-cell cameras. SND6 felt uncomfortable using the toilet in her cell knowing that it could be viewed on CCTV monitors and so asked to use a toilet outside her cell, where there were no cameras. Suspects in Newburn and Hayman's (2002: 110) study also expressed similar concerns about the privacy implications of in-cell cameras. Unbeknown to SND6, most of the monitors for the in-cell cameras had a greyed-out rectangle over the toilet area to protect suspects' privacy, albeit that this could be removed by staff if they had concerns about what a suspect was doing. By contrast, a suspect, SND9, endorsed the use of the cameras because they made him feel safer in the knowledge that if something were to happen to him, there would be an immediate response by staff.

However, the cameras were only as good as the people monitoring them. SND9 appeared unaware that staff were not monitoring the cameras all of the time and thus the cameras lulled him into a false sense of security. Interestingly, this lack of continuous monitoring was predicted by staff interviewed prior to the implementation of in-cell cameras in Newburn and Hayman's (2002: 70) research. Norris and Armstrong (1999: 59, 199) also refer to this fallibility; in town-centre CCTV systems, responses depended on operators interacting effectively with technology and on the integration of different systems. Norris and Armstrong (1999: 59, 199) note two particular failings: firstly, the fallibility of reaction – even when individuals are seen, the reaction to them may not be swift; secondly, the fallibility of completeness – even though CCTV systems seem to provide widespread coverage, it is only superficial.

The cameras were not continuously monitored in Sunnyside or Gormiston either because staff were occupied with other matters or because the staff that could continuously monitor the cameras did not have monitors on their desks. In Sunnyside, for example, the custody assistants did not have monitors at their desks for the in-cell cameras (SNPO7). They had to ask the staff sitting at the booking-in desk to switch the monitor to focus on relevant cells and then the booking-in staff, rather than the custody assistants, had to monitor the suspect. Furthermore, while there was CCTV covering all the cells in Sunnyside, only a few cameras could be viewed at once on the monitors at the booking-in desk. This was also the case in Gormiston. This meant that the 'CCTV cells' were reserved for those that were considered to be at risk by the police, whether that was because they had been aggressive or were mentally ill or intoxicated. It was normally the person booking in the suspect that decided at the end of the risk assessment whether or not to place them in one of the 'CCTV cells'. However, during busy periods it was possible, especially given that 67 per cent were identified as being at risk, that CCTV cells were not available in Gormiston or that staff could misjudge who was vulnerable, albeit that the regular physical cell-checks could be used to address such mistakes.

Overall, the CCTV cameras in Sunnyside and Gormiston accorded with the dichotomy that Newburn and Hayman (2002: 88–9) draw between care and control. On the one hand, they enabled staff to better monitor vulnerable suspects, as well as protecting staff against false allegations. On the other hand, at least in Sunnyside, they were used to surreptitiously monitor staff performance and had the potential to intrude on the privacy of staff, but to a greater extent suspects, albeit that few suspects complained about such matters, except about the filming of the toilet area. Yet, as I have argued with a colleague, the positioning of cameras which capture audio and visual information close to telephones used by suspects to speak with their legal advisors may amount to an unlawful infringement of their right to private consultation (Pattenden and Skinns, 2010). A similar concern was also raised by Newburn and Hayman (2002: 130, 178–9) but to little avail as their suggestions that legal advice take place in telephone booths had not impacted on the sites in the present research.

Logging information about suspects

At the time of the research, Sunnyside had an electronic system for logging information about suspects, rather than the paper records used in Gormiston. During participant observation in Sunnyside, a detention supervisor reported that the electronic system was lengthier and more complicated to use than the old paper records, but that they were harder to fabricate. However, the software that they were using was due to be replaced with a different kind of software in July 2007 in a roll-out across police forces of the National Strategy for Police Information Systems (NSPIS). There was resistance to this change among the staff in Sunnyside as it meant further training, and also those who had tested NSPIS felt it was inferior to the current system.

Similarly, in Gormiston staff expressed resistance to the NSPIS roll-out planned for September 2007, albeit they expressed different reasons. One staff member (GMS1) was concerned that delays would be caused to the custody process because only a limited number of trained custody staff would be able to input information, which had previously been recorded by a range of staff including the jailors, DDOs and arresting officers. Similarly an interviewee (GMS11) noted that the soon-to-arrive electronic system was likely to be faster but problematic for the large number of police officers who were not computer literate. Doctors expressed different concerns about the use of NSPIS which had already arrived in other custody areas that they attended; they argued that the new system was about measuring how quickly they arrived rather than the quality of the service they provided, and that they could not record confidential information about clients as that information could be viewed across the Metropolitan Police Service. In addition, GMS9 complained that the software was unnecessarily bureaucratic as it was a series of questions in which you could not proceed to the next until the previous one was complete, leading him to misrecord information simply to enable him to proceed to the next.

Despite their different formats, both systems contained similar information about suspects which included:

- risk assessment information such as information about medical and mental health and drug use;
- personal details such as name, age, date of birth, next of kin and nominated person to be contacted;
- details about why they were arrested, such as the circumstances of the arrest, charges and outcomes, and whether they required a legal advisor;
- biometric data such as fingerprints, DNA and in Gormiston drug-test results;
- logs of everything that happened to suspects while they were in police custody such as which practitioners they saw, what they ate/drank, phone calls, reviews of detention, interviews, etc.

The main difference between the two systems was that the electronic system was able to flag when cell checks and detention reviews were needed or overdue. In fact, random 'dip-checks' of the custody records were used to monitor the performance of individual staff members from Security Ltd, particularly as the company was fined if cell checks were not conducted on time. This was not the case in Gormiston. To the contrary, it seemed that little was done with the information on the custody records, aside from them being used in court, although perhaps this changed after the introduction of NSPIS. However, one of the unintended consequences of the electronic custody record system was that it made cell checks bureaucratic: after doing the cell checks, staff prioritized logging that they had performed the cell check rather than responding to suspects' requests such as for water or for a legal advisor.

The cells – 'dead dirty, dingy little things' (GMD6)?

Some suspects were ambivalent about the cleanliness and temperature of the custody environment because they viewed it as of less importance relative to the other aspects of the custody process or their desire to leave custody. As this suspect explained: 'I've been arrested, and I just want to fucking get it over and done with really . . . it could just be an old barn and I wouldn't care' (SND3). However, for some people the cleanliness and warmth of the cells mattered to them and could affect the level of stress they felt when they were in custody. In Sunnyside, suspects mostly described the custody area as clean, which was unsurprising given that the building had only recently been refurbished. For example, SND9 said that the custody area was better than others he had been to because it was modern, clean, fresh, if a little far out of the city centre. There were complaints, though, about the cleanliness of blankets. During participant observation, staff complained that clean blankets were not delivered regularly enough, which meant that they had to re-use some of them by spraying them with lavender spray and that they sometimes ran out of blankets during busy periods.

Some suspects in Gormiston also described it as reasonably clean (GMD5, GMD13 and GMD9) and even very clean (GMD14). For example, GMD12 said 'it's just basically a cell . . . it's not like you'd want your house to be, is it? But I suppose it's a punishment room, isn't it really. It wasn't dirty, and there wasn't any dirt like sticking out, but you see what I mean, it wasn't nice either obviously'. However, there were a number of suspects that described the cells in Gormiston as dirty, having blood, dirt and worse on the walls, having unclean toilets and because the cells smelled (GMD3, GMD6, GMD7 and GMD10). As this suspect explained:

> It's horrible in there, you've just got a blue blanket, that they don't wash, a hard blue mattress, a metal bed thing, a dirty toilet that no-one comes to clean . . . some people get toilet roll I don't know how they manage to wet it, throw it up in the thing like that, some people write all over the walls, some people piss and shit on there, you've just got to be lucky to be honest . . . (GMD8)

Another suspect (GMD2) asked to move cells because his was unclean, although his request was not met immediately and staff eventually only cleaned his cell rather than putting him in a different one. He said that this only happened after he asked to be moved in front of one of the researchers. Staff in Gormiston who were not permanently based in the custody area also considered it to be dirty, for example, a doctor GMS2, complained that cleaners only mopped the custody area, but never hoovered or power cleaned it so that the dirt dried as dust, causing allergic reactions among staff.

It was not just the cleanliness of cells that affected suspects. The lack of daylight could also be distressing (SND4, GMS13), as could the temperature of the cell, if it was too cold or too hot and if suspects did not know that they could ask for a blanket. In February, SND6 said that she was cold during the night and so put her leather jacket over herself as a blanket. She said she was later woken by a jailor opening the door and 'chucking a blanket' at her, even though she hadn't asked for one, which she thought 'was quite nice of them'. However, later when she felt hot, anxious and claustrophobic, having spent ten hours in the cells, she wanted the wicket – that is, the small hatch in the cell door – left open so she could have some air, but this was not allowed because the wicket could be used as a ligature point. Similarly, SND5 reported feeling 'freezing cold' in his cell during the night, but seeing as he had not been in police custody before he did not realize he could ask for a blanket. SND7 requested two blankets because he was cold, but his request for the second blanket was refused because they had run out as 'there were too many people in there' and as a result he was 'freezing'.

In Gormiston, during a muggy and warm week in July, suspects were still reportedly cold when they were in the cells. GMD1, GMD5 and GMD6 were cold enough to ask for blankets. For example, GMD5 also said that 'it was a bit cold' and that he asked for a blanket and was brought one straightaway. GMD2 also said that he was cold in his cell, but that he had not wanted to ask for a blanket for fear of becoming more annoyed by being given a dirty blanket. He was already annoyed because his cell was dirty and his request to move to a different cell had been forgotten. Experienced suspects such as GMD4, GMD11 and GMD12 said that the temperature depended on the weather outside: in the winter it was 'freezing' and in the summer they were 'sweating' in 'horrible', 'sticky' and 'airless' cells.

Building maintenance and equipment

Aside from the matter of the cleanliness of the custody area, discussions about building maintenance did not arise in Gormiston, although this is not to say that issues did not exist, rather that they were more pressing in Sunnyside and connected to the relationship between the police and Security Ltd as a result of the PFI contract. Sunnyside may have had a new custody area, which was an improvement on the old custody area, but essential maintenance work was not being done because of a dispute about who should do it. The problems identified by SNS1 and SNS4, who were Security Ltd employees, included a shower that did not drain properly and which could not be used; ledges in the low-bench cells reserved for the intoxicated, which were a health and safety hazard for suspects; nesting pigeons; no safety alarm in the exercise yard; a room that smelled of sewage; and poor heating in the cell block. There was also a lack of necessary equipment such as safety blankets, paper towels, sporks (which are the cutlery given to suspects with self-harm issues) and staff alarms; staff radios and other kinds of equipment were reportedly cheap, ineffective and unsafe, including a paper shredder without a safety guard and rubber gloves which easily split.

A number of staff were disgruntled by these inadequacies which they attributed firstly to poor management. For example, SNS4 said that managers failed to order sufficient equipment of a high enough quality. The difficulties also arose because there were uncertainties about whether the police or Security Ltd were responsible for addressing the problems, such as that with the shower (SNPO1). Moreover, the relationship between police and Security Ltd provided opportunities for buck-passing responsibility for problems with the building and equipment and this relationship could be used as an excuse for inaction. Security Ltd's reluctance to fix the problems was attributed by Security Ltd employees and police officers, such as SNS1 and SNS7, to their need to make a profit for shareholders. Aside from the risks to the health and safety of suspects and staff, these difficulties were also having an impact on the morale of staff. They were upset that Security Ltd was unwilling to do anything to make their jobs easier (SNS1). The implication was that Security Ltd managers were not taking seriously the complaints made by operational staff and that the operational staff had little or no recourse for resolving matters.

In the cells

Staff experiences

Working in police custody areas can be stressful because of their busyness, especially in Gormiston, given the wide-ranging nature of suspects' needs, as well as the threats to staff safety as this custody officer explained: 'People that come in here usually aren't very hygienic, they've got various illnesses, . . . the people that come here are violent sometimes, and in law we take on a lot of risk, and if something goes wrong, then it's our [head on the] block' (SNS3).

Police custody areas could also be noisy, with suspects sometimes constantly banging and shouting on the cells doors, as was the case in SNPO6 when there was a group of young men who had been arrested together for robbery and who spent much of their time in custody conducting shouted conversations in spite of staff trying to separate them. The constant noise could bubble over into annoyance among the staff; for example, one of the custody assistants expressed annoyance at one of the researchers who accidentally left the door open between the custody area and the cells, which made the shouting and banging from the cells more audible.

Moreover, the lack of natural light in the building combined with shift-work meant that some staff did not see any natural light in the winter time (SNS7). In Gormiston, it was also the lack of space in the custody area that made it 'horrible'; one staff member, GMS11, noted: 'There's no little friendly chatting area, you're either lined up to be booked in, and you're trying to be booked in when there's people pushing and shoving, and police officers trying to do things . . . There's no space.'

Consequently, from the police point of view, working in a police custody area was unpopular relative to working on the streets; it was viewed as a punishment, pasturing or promotion posting. For example, in Sunnyside, one detention supervisor commented that some police officers only ended up working in the custody area as a form of punishment. As for 'pasturing', it was noticeable, in both sites, that around one or two custody officers on any shift were close to retirement. As for being a promotion posting, in Gormiston, a stint working in the custody area was a necessity, particularly for probationary PCs or police staff wishing to join the police. As GMS4 explained 'if you take the jailor's role . . . which you have to perform, and it's not necessarily seen as a pleasant posting, some officers may like it, but generally people want to be out there dealing with issues'. He later said:

> Not a lot of people choose to do a jailor posting, they're told that they're doing a jailor posting . . . so I might turn up for duty and I'm here, and I'm jailor on Friday, I'm jailor on Thursday, it's not like you've applied to do the job of a jailor because it's something that interests you.

During participant observation (GMPO1 and GMPO5), one jailor said that he did not join the police to work as a jailor and that he did not like being at the beck and call of suspects, fetching them cups of tea or water when they rang the bell. Duties in the custody area, even if they secured promotion, did not match up with beliefs that 'real' police work was about crime-fighting and action (Reiner, 2010: 119–21).

Suspect experiences in the cells

Police custody can be intolerable, distressing, boring, scary, unpleasant and uncertain, as well as isolating, disorienting and humiliating (Choongh, 1997: 97; Sanders and Young, 2006: 188). One suspect said of her time in the cells:

> [I]t's horrible, it's like a dungeon. Imagine spending two nights in there, you've got to be a good sleeper like me . . . Yes, it was very depressing, very, very depressing . . . There's no routine at all, no fresh air, no water tap, no sink, they've got nothing, imagine as a

> human you've got nothing. Come on now, this is England; they're spending millions on everything. Prisoners are still people, they treat you like shit. (GMD8)

The main themes in the data were that police custody could be stressful, depressing, isolating and boring. Suspects found police custody stressful because they were nervous and worried about the uncertainties of what was going to happen to them (GMD1). Suspects also described how they were too nervous to eat (GMD10 and GMD3), and how they asked for a Bible to read not because they were religious, rather to take their mind off thinking the worst (GMD13). GMD4 also described his time in the cells as 'sitting there constantly worrying, when am I being interviewed? Am I being charged? Am I getting out? It's a lot of stress.'

Suspects also experienced a loss of control. This was partly because they were deprived of their liberty. As this suspect said: 'I'm not used to being locked up in one place . . . you need your freedom, I'm not used to it, so it was a different experience' (GMD3). Similarly, GMD6 also said that police custody was an awful experience, not because of the staff, but because of being deprived of his liberty. Consequently, GMD4 and GMD7 said that they thought police custody was worse than prison because suspects were 'constantly banged up' and there was no routine around which suspects could orientate themselves and which could help the time pass or give them something to look forward to.

However, suspects also felt a loss of control because they were reliant on staff to respond to their requests for things that would be taken for granted in the outside world. Making these requests could be humiliating as well as an invasion of their privacy. For example, suspects depended on the police to inform them of the time (as watches were routinely removed), provide warmth, food, drinks, toilet paper, sanitary towels, even to take them to the toilet if there was no integral sanitation if they wanted some privacy away from the CCTV cameras. As GMD7 noted, requests were not always responded to swiftly, if at all. He said:

> I didn't get any water, silly things, but in those places they're not silly things, because when you're in there with a dry throat, and you're just being a bit annoyed. I just wanted a drink of water, that's not hard for them to pour a tap and say, there you go, I didn't even get a drink that day. (GMD7)

This loss of control was underscored by an imbalance in power relations between suspects and staff, albeit that it may have been mitigated somewhat by the existence of CCTV, meaning that the police were simultaneously the watchers and the watched.

Some suspects felt depressed in police custody. One suspect said: 'Depression, that's the worst thing in police custody, you're put in a cell and you're just left there' (GMD14). And since there was nothing for suspects to do in the cells they found that time passed slowly and that they were bored. 'You're basically in a room with nothing in it, and I was in there for a long time . . . the time wasn't going fast' (GMD5). The lack of human contact including with family and friends also meant that the isolation could seriously impact on suspects' mental health as this suspect explained: 'You feel . . . really isolated, the first few days are the worst, the isolation you feel, it can make you seriously suicidal, and by the time you get put into custody in prison, you're virtually on the brink of taking your life, that's the worst thing, that needs to be sorted out' (GMD14).

Suspects' time in the cells was also punctuated by cell checks by staff. The frequency of the cell checks ranged from suspects being put on constant watch to being put on 15, 30 or 60 minute checks. However, like Newburn and Hayman (2002: 45), I found it was difficult to examine the frequency or consistency with which these checks were performed. They found that if a check was missed, the suspect's next check would be delayed until all the cells were inspected, meaning that the main imperative was to have uniform checks rather than to check suspects individually at the time actually required. In the present research, there was also a distinction made between staff simply observing them breathing and staff physically rousing them either by banging on the door or shouting at them until they woke up. The latter was necessary for the intoxicated and the doctor would usually provide instructions about this. However, normally, the type and frequency of the cell checks was determined by whoever booked them in who would take into account the information from the risk assessment. After the cell check, information about the physical state of the suspect (e.g. if they were awake) was transferred from a clipboard to the custody record.

For some staff, a busy shift might be entirely comprised of nothing other than performing and writing up cell checks. Once one set of checks were complete, it was time to set off on the next round, which could be tedious (GMS4). Some suspects were aware of regular cell checks taking place (e.g. SND9, GMD5 and GMD13). Similarly, GMD9 said that he was checked on every hour through the 'little sneaky window'. SND2 said that he was checked on a few times, with an eye appearing in the hatch, but that staff did not put their head through the door and ask if he was alright, which he would have preferred. SND3 said that during the day-time she was checked every 15 minutes, but that during the night-time the checks were less frequent. She was also told that staff did not check suspects as often as they were supposed to at night-time, although she could not verify this as she had been asleep overnight. Similarly, GMD2 felt that there were discrepancies between the checks that he observed staff perform and what appeared on his custody record, which fits with Newburn and Hayman's (2002: 45) assessment of cell checks noted above. He said that staff had recorded on his custody record that he was asleep when, in fact, he had not slept at all. However, one cannot discount that perhaps suspects were checked and were not aware that they had been checked, as SND5 and GMD2 acknowledged.

Responding to cell buzzers and intercoms

In Sunnyside, all cells were fitted with buzzers *and* intercoms which allowed suspects to converse with staff to make a request, for example, for a drink of water or to find out when their legal advisor was likely to arrive or to let them know if they were feeling unwell. In addition, these intercoms were used to receive phone calls, for example from their legal advisor or friends or family. As discussed in Chapter 3, cell intercoms, where the entire conversation could be heard by anyone within earshot of the cell, could increase opportunities for unwanted intrusions into suspects' conversations with their legal advisor. The buzzers in the cells in Sunnyside could be pressed repeatedly by suspects, making a sound at the desks where the custody assistants sat until they answered the buzzer. In Gormiston, however, there were cell buzzers but not intercoms; when a cell buzzer was pressed it registered on a screen monitored by the DDOs and jailors in the 'goldfish bowl', which was the room where they sat. When the buzzer was pressed there was no sound in the cell or the 'goldfish bowl' and the staff had to physically walk to the cell to find out why the suspect had pressed the bell. On occasions (e.g. GMPO3), the DDOs and jailors were occupied with other matters rather than watching the screen and responding to buzzers.

Cell buzzers appeared to create resentment and friction between staff and suspects. At face value, staff did not want to be at the beck and call of suspects and found ways to prevent this from happening, but perhaps there was also a broader issue of power and control at stake. There was evidence that staff behaviour had a negative impact on suspects; being in solitary confinement and feeling as if no one would respond to you, even in an emergency, was a terrifying prospect for some. Furthermore, the buzzers, especially in Sunnyside where no human contact was required, were dehumanizing. SND4 disliked the buzzer system for precisely this reason as she felt that staff could only properly judge someone's needs by speaking to them in person. The buzzer system may have saved staff resources by limiting the time spent walking around the cell block, but at the cost of dehumanizing suspects, antagonizing them (e.g. by switching them off mid-sentence) and increasing their sense of isolation (e.g. if staff did not respond promptly).

Staff responses to buzzers were on a continuum. Buzzers were either switched off or the staff threatened to switch them off, due to them not responding to the buzzers when they were pressed or being slow to respond to the buzzers. At the other end of the continuum, they responded to them promptly and efficiently. In Sunnyside, suspects

(SND2, SND4 and SND7) reported that their buzzers had been switched off. SND7 said that she had been frustrated rather than upset by her buzzer being switched off and that the reason for it was because she had annoyed staff by repeatedly asking for water as she was drunk when she arrived in the custody area. In SNPO2, one of the custody assistants was observed having an altercation with a suspect over the intercom. The suspect asked if staff could telephone his mum to request that she bring in some trousers for his court appearance the next morning. The suspect was insistent and so the custody assistant reminded him that he had already used his 'phone call' and that it was 'extra' for him to deal with this request. At this point, the suspect remonstrated, saying to the custody assistant that he could help him if he wanted to. The custody assistant responded by saying 'if you continue to shout, I will switch off your buzzer'. SND4 also said that:

> [T]here's about two or three [staff] up that [custody area] that are alright, but the rest of them are horrible, really unhelpful, especially the one who answers the buzzers to you. She or he keeps you waiting on that buzzer, and then they just cut you off without you even finishing, and you ain't got nowhere to turn to. You press it again and they just ignore the buzzer. I find them really not helpful at all.

Another vulnerable suspect (with mental health and drug problems) arrested for shoplifting and assaulting a police officer and who was very distressed for most of her detention said that staff ignored her pressing the buzzer and her request to talk to someone when she was feeling down and panicky in the cells on her own. By ignoring this request, it suggests that staff had become desensitized to the suffering of suspects. By contrast a drug worker suggested that it was not that buzzers were switched off, rather that staff occasionally ignored them and instead checked on the CCTV monitor to make sure that suspects were OK. This may be true, but regardless of whether the buzzer was switched off or ignored it had the same isolating and frightening consequences for suspects, as well as it being annoyingly loud. Indeed, one suspect, SND9, thought that she had pressed a panic alarm rather than the cell intercom.

Suspects in Gormiston also reported that buzzers appeared to be switched off. GMD8 said that 'the buggers turn it off . . . If they get pissed off with you they turn it off . . . some people keep buzzing them, and then they know which door to turn off, so obviously that's when they start the kicking and the banging'. Similarly, GMD2 said that he went a bit 'nutty' in the cell after he banged on the door and pressed the buzzer but no one came'. GMD3 and GMD7 also said that they repeatedly pressed the buzzer to no avail. An independent custody visitor (GMS11) also said that on her last visit to the custody area at least one suspect had reported that their buzzer did not work. GMD11 said that there had been occasions when he had his buzzer switched off in Gormiston, but only when he was drunk, abusive and aggressive. He said that mostly staff were responsive to his buzzer because 'they have to go and get whatever you ask them for'.

Other suspects reported that it was not that buzzers were switched off, rather that staff were slow to respond to them. For example, SND3, SND8 and SND9 reported waiting for approximately twenty to forty minutes for someone to respond to their buzzers. In Gormiston, GMD10 said that staff were so bad at responding to his buzzer he was unsure if it worked. Another said that staff took an hour to come to his cell:

> [Y]ou press the bells . . . they don't work, you press it, you can't hear anything, you press it, press it, press it, and no one, it might take them about half an hour, or an hour, to come to the cell like, it's just pathetic, say if you're dying . . . I'm surprised a few people haven't like died in there. (GMD8)

Similarly, GMD9, GMD12 and GMD13 said that it took 30–60 minutes for staff to respond to the buzzer, although GMD13 accepted and GMD12 acknowledged that this was probably just because they were busy with the suspects who were aggressively banging on their cell doors and that this was because the noise from the banging was irritating for staff and suspects.

The lack of responsiveness to cell buzzers either wilfully to exert power and control or because staff were too busy is worrying. As Leigh *et al.* (1998) found, a quick response to calls for help may be one way of preventing deaths in custody, although they also found that staff took thirty minutes or more to respond and immobilized cell buzzers. Non-response to cell buzzers is likely to add to the stress that suspects experience in police custody. Indeed, SND8 said that it was frightening when staff did not respond to the cell buzzer, since she was aware that staff were not always monitoring the CCTV cameras in the cells.

Dealing with suspect requests

The buzzer system and the way staff responded to the buzzer are two separate but connected issues. For example, a suspect could be unhappy with the buzzer system by which they made their request, but happy with the response that they got once the buzzer was answered. This was the case for SND9 who felt that staff were slow to answer the overly loud buzzer, taking 20–40 minutes on occasions, but once he made his request the staff were very good at dealing with it. In particular, he liked the attitude of the staff who brought him tea: 'They weren't just like, here you are. You can have a chat with them. They seemed decent'. SND6 and SND7 were reasonably happy with how staff dealt with their requests for water, although they also felt the cups were too small, which meant that they were constantly asking for more. Similarly, some suspects in SNPO2 and SNPO5 were happy with how they were treated by the police and police staff in that their requests were met and they were talked to politely.

In Gormiston, GMD13 was happy with how his requests were dealt with. He informed staff at the outset of his detention that he drank a lot of fluids and so they were bringing him four cups of water at a time. Similarly, GMD12 and GMD14 described how responsive staff were to them. GMD12 said, '[i]t couldn't have been any better, on that occasion, it was really good, they were helpful and they showed concern, they sort of asked whether I was hungry, or thirsty, or whatever.' GMD4, GMD5 and GMD6 also described how staff willingly brought them cups of tea and blankets on request and acted in a professional manner. GMD4 even knew the DDOs by name to ask them for things. A more experienced suspect noted, however, that staff were responsive to suspects' requests provided they were compliant:

> At Gormiston police station it's OK . . . if I've asked for a cup of tea, or I ask for something to eat, or I ask for a cigarette, you know, they're quite good . . . if you're pleasant to them, they'll be pleasant to you. I mean, if you're rude to them, they won't let you out for a cigarette basically, I mean, I can't really say anything about them, at Gormiston they've been quite good . . . But, I mean, I've had a couple of troubles in Gormiston police station, but it's been my own fault, when I've been stupid, I've kicked the doors and all that, but I mean, it's OK, I've been to worse places. (GMD4)

Perhaps not all suspects were compliant all of the time, which may in part explain why some of their requests were refused or 'forgotten'. GMD7 described how his request for water was forgotten, which he believed to be on purpose as he felt he had a poor relationship with the police having been in police custody on a number of previous occasions. By contrast, GMD3, GMD6 and GMD9 noted that their requests for water were genuinely forgotten by staff. For GMD3, eventually his legal advisor sorted it out for him, but by that time he said he was 'dying' for a drink of water after waiting what he estimated to be about five hours. However, it was also likely that some requests could simply not be met, as was the case for SND6 who wanted the wicket left open to her cell so that she could have some air.

Requests were also neglected because staff were genuinely too busy, particularly in Gormiston where there were fewer staff per suspect. For example, an independent custody visitor said that staff in Gormiston did not have time to meet multiple requests from suspects for water, although it was important that they did meet these requests for intoxicated suspects. At the same time, as GMD9 hinted, busyness could also be used as an excuse as suspects were none the wiser about what was going on beyond the walls of their cell, meaning 'it was difficult to argue with staff' about what they should or should not be doing to help them.

Another explanation of why suspects' requests were not met was that staff did not like having to meet suspects' requests because this did not fit with their expectations of the job. For example, this GMS4, a police officer jailor, expressed some discomfort at dealing with suspects' requests, but was reasonably sympathetic, recognizing that the stakes were high. He said that it was part of the role of the jailor to look after suspects' welfare and to prevent deaths in custody, but that sometimes it felt like 'you're running a hotel service because every minute the bell's ringing. Can I have food? Can I have tea? Some of the suspects can be quite rude, aggressive'. By contrast, in GMPO1 one jailor said that working in the custody area was not the reason why he joined the police and that he resented having to make prisoners tea and be at their beck and call every time they rang the bell. Similarly, SNS6, a Security Ltd employee, said of suspects that 'they think it's their goddamn right that they can go out for a fag, they've got enough rights as it is'.

The view offered by SNS6 suggests that part of the reason why suspects' requests were not always met was because they demanded 'too much' of staff and because there was a finite number of requests that a suspect could make. At best, this suggests a lack of professionalism and integrity and at worst that staff engaged in a 'power struggle' with suspects; denying requests was a way of exerting control over them. As GMD8 explained, those who were suspected of more serious offences were more likely to be left to 'sweat' in the cells. In addition, the denial of requests could be used to punish those who were non-compliant, demanding or were seen as being rude to staff (SNS11). An example of this was observed in GMPO7; during his detention reviews one of the inspectors fetched a suspect some water, which was unremarkable except that this suspect had been banging on his cell door for some time asking for water and the jailor had ignored his request. It transpired that this suspect had also ripped the jailor's shirt during a scuffle with him when he arrived in the custody area. Similarly, SND4 reported that part of the reason that the police staff did not feel the need to be 'nice' to her and deal with her requests for a phone call or for a drink of water was because she had been rude to them. It appeared, therefore, that staff worked on the principle that they treated suspects based on how the suspects treated them. However, in view of the powerless position of suspects this meant, in practice, that as long as suspects were deferent to the police and respected their authority their requests were worthy of a response.

There are three possible explanations of these petty displays of control in which staff wilfully ignored cell buzzers and/or suspects' requests. First, these responses to suspects could be due to the relatively short-term nature of relationships between the police and suspects. In relation to prison officers, Warr (2008) argues that managerialist changes in the prison environment which have taken power away from wing officers mean that displays of control offer an avenue for certain wing staff – particularly in prisons with high levels of prisoner turnover where staff did not have opportunities to build relationships with prisoners – to regain some sense of power and authority. Parallels can be drawn between the powerlessness of the disenfranchised prison wing officers and the privatized security staff in Sunnyside and the DDOs in Gormiston, who are arguably at the bottom of the police hierarchy and who work in an environment where there are few opportunities to build relationships with suspects, with the exception of the 'regulars'. Secondly, police and to a lesser extent police staff may believe it important to display authority and suppress challenges to it (e.g. through abuse of the buzzer system by suspects) if they believe that this is what is expected of them in the job. Choongh (1997: 83, 98) found that the police distinguished between the 'good as gold' and the 'obnoxious' based both on current as well as previous encounters. Indeed, this categorization of suspects is regarded as a part of the occupational culture of rank-and-file officers (Reiner, 2010: 123–5). Flashpoints over the buzzer system are also similar to the ones that Loftus (2010) identified in her study of police culture, which found the persistence of 'authority' as a key occupational characteristic. Thirdly, these displays of authority could be a form of self-legitimation, so that the young and experienced police and police staff who act as jailors, DDOs and custody assistants have confidence in their right to use their authority, which Tankebe (2007: 56–63) calls endogenous legitimacy.

Access to the facilities – exercise, showers and food

In Sunnyside, access to the exercise facilities (which prior to the smoking ban had doubled up as smoking facilities) depended on the discretion of staff, which in turn depended on the busyness of the custody area. By contrast, in Gormiston, there were no exercise (or smoking) facilities. An inspector (GMS8) explained that, as with many London police stations, space was at a premium and the only outdoor space was the car park at the back of the station which was in constant use. This meant the gates were regularly opening and closing and it was insecure for suspects to be out there.

According to GMD8, access to the showers depended on the availability of supervisory staff of the appropriate sex. It also depended on whether the facilities worked. The showers worked in Gormiston but not in Sunnyside; this was one of a number of problems with the building that Security Ltd had been slow to fix. Given that there were fewer staff in Gormiston and no exercise facilities and given that the showers did not work in Sunnyside, this meant that, in both sites, even if suspects had been in police custody for lengthy periods of time (e.g. Friday to Monday), this did not guarantee that they were allowed any time in the exercise yard (either to smoke or to take some fresh air) or that they could take a shower before they appeared in court. Suspects were understandably upset about not being able to shower. In spite of asking staff if she could shower, SND4 who was arrested for shoplifting and who was detained in total for 38.5 hours, was not given an opportunity to shower before going to court, which she felt was 'diabolical'.

However, smoking was the issue which caused suspects the most consternation. In Sunnyside, the research took place prior to the smoking ban. Sunnyside had a discretionary policy whereby suspects were allowed out to the exercise yard to smoke if a member of staff was going out there (SNS6). However, even this was not enough for some committed smokers, such as SND4 who complained that she had only four cigarettes over the 38.5 hours that she was in police custody.

The reason that smoking was important to suspects was because they believed it to calm their nerves and anxieties, and allowed them to cope with the stresses of being in police custody, including if they were 'clucking' or withdrawing from heroin (e.g. SND2, GMD4 and GMD8). Others reported feeling irritated, frustrated and aggressive, for example, kicking their cell door repeatedly when they were not allowed to smoke (e.g. GMD4 and GMD5), although, and unusually, one suspect said that he just coped with it (GMD6). Moreover, as one of the drug workers pointed out, nearly all of her clients smoked and so nicotine withdrawal added to the stress and tension of being in police custody (SNS13). Similarly, a solicitor, GMS1, noted the powerful effects of nicotine withdrawal, recounting how one client had threatened to attack the police in the absence of being allowed to smoke.

However, the discretionary nature of the smoking policy in Sunnyside meant that there were disparities between suspects in terms of their opportunities to smoke with some suspects, such as SND9, feeling that he had unfairly missed out. An independent custody visitor, GMS11, tried to dispel this sense of unfairness among suspects by finding out from staff, before she went on her tour of the cells, about the smoking policy. This was so that she could accurately inform people about whether they were entitled to smoke, as she believed that it was valuable for suspects to hear this from an independent person.

It was not just busyness or staffing issues that determined whether staff used their discretion to allow suspects to smoke. In both sites, smoking was also used as a bargaining tool by the police and police staff to encourage compliance. For example, in Gormiston a solicitor described cigarettes as a 'huge' bargaining tool. Similarly, a drug worker noted that:

> [O]fficers . . . don't want the job to be harder than it is, they will do everything they can to make the process go sweetly, if the client's

> cooperating and behaving, they will see if they can take them out for a cigarette . . . the police used to really like to be able to do that, it's a great bargaining chip . . . I'll tell you what we'll do, we'll do your prints, we'll go out for a cigarette . . . it was a way of placating things at the beginning. (GMS6)

Staff in Sunnyside also viewed the cigarette as a tool for 'keeping suspects quiet' (SNPO1). Hence, Security Ltd employee (SNS6) noted that probationary police officers were instructed not to promise arrestees a cigarette when they arrived at the custody area, as the staff in the custody area could not always deliver this promise, creating problems when the arresting officers left. Similarly, a different Security Ltd employee (SNS7) expressed annoyance at legal advisors for promising their clients cigarettes when there were no staff willing or able to take them outside. It was not just staff that recognized the cigarette as a bargaining tool. So too did suspects; one described how she refused to be interviewed unless she was allowed a cigarette, which she was after she was interviewed and before she was returned to her cell (SND4).

In Gormiston, the research took place shortly after the smoking ban had been introduced so it was difficult at this early stage to assess its impacts on the police custody process. One impact, however, was that it had meant that suspects had to seize opportunities to smoke prior to arriving at the custody area; for example, GMD4 reported that he had been allowed to smoke in the car on the way to the custody area, which he had appreciated. An inspector (GMS8) was pleased about the smoking ban as it had eased the pressure on the police to take people out for cigarettes: it was easier to decline suspects' requests by blaming the change in the law rather than having to say that staff did not have enough time.

In terms of food, PACE stipulates that suspects should be fed three times per day, although as SNS4 pointed out it says nothing about the quality of the food that is served. A Security Ltd staff member (SNS4) said that while they did not have to feed suspects outside of allotted meal-times, they normally would because it made suspects happier and more compliant. Suspects in Sunnyside were virtually unanimous in their views on the food served in the custody areas, whereas only some hated the food in Gormiston. In Sunnyside, the food came in boxes and was microwaved by the custody assistants shortly before serving. Suspects found the food to be inedible, even if they were in there for long periods of time. They described it as 'disgusting' (SND2), 'diabolical, absolutely foul, you wouldn't give it to your dog' (SND3), 'If you're dying of hunger you cannot eat that food' (SND4), 'definitely not healthy, and I mean, it goes straight through you' (SND5). The food was viewed with such disgust because it was microwaved, and it was sometimes badly microwaved resulting in it being warm on the outside and cold in the middle (SND2), or in Gormiston because it was simply cold by the time it was served to suspects (GMD12) or just 'tasted bad' (GMD5). In Gormiston, suspects were also vehemently opposed to eating the food because they did not trust the police, not even to make them a cup of tea (GMD2), and that they would 'rather starve' (GMD11).

In Gormiston, suspects were not uniformly opposed to the food. Some described it as 'inedible and disgusting' (GMD12); 'the food is terrible ... my dog wouldn't eat it' (GMD4); 'terrible' (GMD5). There were also some neutral views about the food, though. For example, this suspect described the food as 'edible, but then it's free food, and you're not ... at a holiday camp are you ... I wouldn't by any means say it was disgusting' (GMD13). Similarly three other suspects (GMD7, GMD8 and GMD9) said that the food was OK. However, two of them (GMD7 and GMD8) distinguished between the food served at the regular mealtimes which they believed to be (leftovers) from the staff canteen and the food that was served outside of mealtimes and was microwaved and which one of them described as 'atrocious, honestly they're horrid, they're not worth throwing at the wall' (GMD7). Another suspect (GMD6) who had been in the custody area at least six times even went so far as to say that he liked the food and that he looked forward to eating it.

Suspects' attitudes towards the food and drinks reveal mistrust of the police, especially in Gormiston. Moreover, if the food is inedible a lack of nourishment is likely to impair suspects' cognitive functioning at a time when they are likely to need it to make important decisions and answer police questions. Arguably food is of less importance than access to procedural rights such as legal advice, but access to food, showers and exercise all contribute to the overarching experience of stress, depression, isolation and boredom. These seemingly small matters do count towards suspects' overall experience of custody.

Conclusion

In this chapter I have described the nature of the police custody facilities. Sunnyside was a newer, cleaner and altogether more pleasant custody area while Gormiston was dirtier, more cramped and busier. In both, CCTV covered the custody area, as well as the majority if not all of the cells. Staff and suspects broadly supported its use, but the cameras were fallible in part because they were not monitored all of the time. Interestingly, the cameras were not only used for the purposes of caring for and controlling suspects, they were simultaneously used, in Sunnyside, to monitor the performance of individual members of Security Ltd.

Since Newburn and Hayman (2002) conducted their research, little seems to have changed in terms of the stressful nature of the custody environment and process. For staff, working in the cell-block could be stressful due to the busyness, constant noise, lack of natural light and shift work. Therefore, for staff, police custody was a bridge to something else; for junior police officers and police staff, it was a bridge to promotion and for police officers with lengthy service it was a route to retirement.

Suspect stress was due to uncertainties, for example, about how long they were likely to be there or what might happen to them. In addition, suspects reported being depressed, bored and isolated while they were in the cells. Suspects also reported that they experienced a loss of control, in part, because they were deprived of their liberty and because they were reliant on staff to provide them with things that they took for granted in the outside world. Their powerlessness was also reinforced by slow or non-existent responses to the cell buzzers or suspects' requests. Like the suspects in Choongh's (1997: 105) research, few objected to what happened to them, choosing, instead, the path of least resistance. Suspects tended to defer to the police knowing that it might enable access to things like cigarettes, showers or a breather outside.

The exertion of control over suspects was inadvertent as well as deliberate. While on occasions suspects were deliberately 'punished', mostly staff were too busy for this, particularly in Gormiston. Instead, the power and control that staff exercised over suspects stemmed from the routinized way that the custody process worked. Staff simply went through the motions of booking in a suspect, putting them in a cell, performing cell checks, responding to cell buzzers and so on. Bearing in mind the volume of suspects that staff processed, where in the busy periods they booked in over four times as many as their colleagues in the late 1980s according to Brown's (1989) research, it is unsurprising that police custody was so routine and monotonous that it was widely disliked as a job. This routinized approach also meant that staff, particularly those that worked regularly, if not permanently, in custody areas, could become desensitized to the needs of those in their care.

The findings I have outlined imply that police custody was both procedurally just, as well as unjust, in relation to five of the six constituent components outlined in Chapter 2:[5]

- *Representation.* The buzzer system gave suspects a voice, but this was taken away from suspects who challenged the authority of the police or who were too demanding.
- *Consistency.* The discretionary nature of access to things like showers and smoking meant that there were inconsistencies between suspects; as with representation, access to cigarettes and showers was granted to those that complied. At the same time, the PACE framework and the routinized nature of police custody meant that that there were also likely to be a preponderance of consistencies between suspects.
- *Impartiality and neutrality.* The police appeared to behave in a largely impartial way, except in relation to certain kinds of suspects, most

notably the non-compliant and the disreputable. While stereotyping occurred of drug users, women and suspected illegal immigrants this was not always manifest in police behaviour.

- *Correctability*. The buzzer system gave suspects some opportunities to complain about their treatment. Of course, it was not always the case that these complaints were acknowledged or acted on.
- *Ethicality*. Politeness and the respecting of suspects' rights was manifest in staff responses to suspect requests. These were mostly met, albeit slowly, except for the recalcitrant or those who made their requests impolitely. However, this dimension of procedural justice is best thought of in terms of suspects' access to their rights and entitlements which are examined in Chapter 5.

All of these factors might contribute to an overall sense of whether a suspect's treatment was procedurally just. While the present research did not test the impact of suspect experiences on police legitimacy, the bulk of the research evidence (reviewed, for example, in Tyler (2003)) suggests that suspects who felt there were treated in a procedurally unfair way in police custody would be less likely to cooperate with the police within the confines of the custody area and be less likely to comply with the law on leaving police custody.

Having described the roles of the key *dramatis personae* of police custody areas and the police custody environment, in Chapter 5 I explore suspect access to a range of rights and entitlements and the circumstances in which police practices diverged from the law. The aim in Chapter 5 is to provide an insight into how the custody environment and the working practices of staff in police custody areas can sometimes have negative consequences for suspects' experiences of justice.

Notes

1 For example, in Sunnyside, a Polish suspect's rights were not read to him when he repeatedly demanded a solicitor and interpreter to the annoyance of the detention supervisors and custody officer booking him in. In Gormiston, a suspect's rights were withheld when he began to throw his possessions at the custody officer who was booking him in (GMPO5). Another suspect's rights were delayed when she was dismissive, abusive and obstructive to the custody officer by giving false details (GMPO4).

2 A major delay to the booking-in process was caused by suspects who did not speak English as a first language and who required an interpreter. At the booking-in stage, this would be done via Language Line which is an interpreters' service provided over the telephone; this meant the telephone was passed backwards and forwards between the booking-in officer and the suspect.

3 These data are taken from my recent British Academy-funded comparative study of police custody, the findings from which will be forthcoming.
4 An inspector (GMS8) said that there were too few consultation rooms and that there was little that could be done about this short of knocking the building down, while also acknowledging that this caused delays.
5 Data about the sixth component, 'accuracy' – that is, the competence of decision-making and its founding on valid information – are examined in Chapter 5.

Chapter 5

Access to rights and entitlements at the police station

PACE sets out suspects' rights and entitlements, as well as providing a framework to regulate police practices. However, police practices can and do still diverge from the law; it is possible for those who work in custody areas to either inadvertently sidestep legal requirements or deliberately manoeuvre around them. For example, on arrival at the police station, as I have already described, the authorization of detention can be a routinized affair meaning that the necessity of police detention is automatically assumed by custody officers (e.g. Phillips and Brown, 1998: 49; McConville *et al.*, 1994: 55; Sanders and Young, 2006: 184).

The purpose of this chapter is to explore how certain practices within the police custody process, on occasions, diverge from the formal requirements set down in PACE and the circumstances in which these arise. Suspects' rights and entitlements are wide-ranging. Here, I focus on the reading of their rights; their right to have someone informed of their arrest and to phone calls; access to legal advice; and their experiences of legal requirements about interviews and detention reviews. These rights are covered roughly in the order in which they are given as the suspect moves through the custody process. The purpose of examining access to these rights and entitlements is also to further explore procedural justice as it is manifested in the police custody process. Of the six constituent parts of procedural justice outlined in Chapter 2, access to rights and entitlements can illuminate representation (when suspects may be given a voice by the police during detention reviews and interviews or through their legal advisor) and ethicality (when suspects' rights are respected). In short, access to rights and entitlements is being used as an indicator of the operation of procedural justice in police custody.

Moreover, as I discussed in Chapter 1, suspect access to rights and entitlements is a fundamental issue and one that has occupied researchers' attention for decades. In the interests of providing a comprehensive account of the police custody process, it is vital to include this chapter, even if it does lead us away, temporarily, from the main focus of the book on different philosophies of control employed by practitioners in multi-professional police custody areas. In examining access to rights and entitlements it is important to note that while police, police staff and legal advisors all contributed to the bestowing of rights examined in this chapter, the police had primary responsibility for this. As described in Chapter 3, the granting or denial of rights to suspects was largely done by custody officers (not police staff), in particular the so-called 'white-boarding' sergeants or the 'skippers' who were in overall charge of the custody area. Furthermore, in Chapter 7, I argue that, in spite of the involvement of a range of practitioners in custody areas, including legal advisors, police custody has remained 'police territory', suggesting again that the party that dominated the granting or denial of suspects' rights was the police. These two findings also reflect the custody officer's responsibilities under PACE to 'perform the functions in the PACE Codes of Practice' (PACE Code C, 2008: 1.1A). In the discussion that follows, where possible I distinguish between the contributions of police, police staff and legal advisors; otherwise, it can be assumed that the police were in charge of bestowing suspects' rights because it was their responsibility.

Informing suspects of their rights at the police station

On arrival at the police station, suspects should be informed verbally and in writing of three ongoing rights while in police custody, namely to receive free and independent legal advice, to have someone notified of their arrest and to consult the PACE Codes of Practice (PACE Code C, 2008: 3.1). These rights, when provided verbally, are separate from being informed of the (qualified) right to silence which was not something explored in the present research.[1] Previous research has shown that suspects are not always informed of these rights at the police station; Bridges and Sanders (1990) found that 2.9 per cent of suspects were not read their rights and Sanders *et al.* (1989: 46) found that 10 per cent of suspects had not signed to say they received their rights. How and whether suspects are read their rights may be a deliberate ploy to deny them their rights or it may simply be that officers neglect their duties, for example because of time pressures or out of boredom or laziness or because they view the process as an 'empty ritual' or that for certain suspects, such as the intoxicated, they view their rights as dispensable (Smith, 1997: 332; Sanders *et al.*, 1989: 46)

In the present research the custody records showed that for 23 out of 882 suspects (3 per cent) there was no record of the police having read them their rights,[2] and that there was no significant difference between the two police stations in the number of people who were not read their rights. Interestingly, however, twice as many suspects were not read their rights in week two in Sunnyside compared to week one, when the researchers were present (4 per cent compared to 2 per cent); the presence of the observers in week one may have contributed to this difference.

The small numbers of suspects that were not read their rights meant it was difficult to systematically examine the relationships between this variable and other independent variables. However, there were a few significant findings. Suspects who were identified as being at risk, which normally included vulnerable adults or juveniles ($\chi^2=6.5$, $p<0.01$), for whom a doctor was requested, primarily because they were intoxicated as a result of alcohol or illicit drugs ($\chi^2=3.5$, $p<0.05$), and those who were not interviewed, perhaps because they were suspected of a less serious offence not requiring an interview ($\chi^2=20.7$, $p<0.01$) were significantly less likely to have their rights read to them. For some suspects it may also have been that the police merely intended to delay the reading of their rights – for example, because they were *perceived* to be intoxicated on arrival at the police station, as was the case for SND5, or they were non-compliant, as was the case in SNPO7, or both, as was the case in GMPO4 and GMPO5 – and then the suspect was released before their rights were read to them.[3]

Delaying the reading of suspects' rights at the police station does not appear to be a breach of PACE, although Code C is vague on this point.[4] What is a breach of PACE Codes of Practice, though, is if suspects are not informed of their rights at all at the police station, even if the suspect is vulnerable (because they are a juvenile, mentally ill or intellectually impaired). For vulnerable suspects paragraphs 3.15–3.19 say that an appropriate adult should be sought for vulnerable suspects and then the suspect, with the help of an appropriate adult, should be informed of their rights at the police station. Similarly, citizens who are taken to the police station, as a place of safety under mental health legislation should be informed of their rights at the police station, including the right to legal advice (Cape, 2006: 432).[5] Yet on at least two occasions this did not happen, including one involving a 17-year-old female detained in Sunnyside police custody areas, as a place of safety under s. 136 of the Mental Health Act 1983. She was not read her rights in the presence of an appropriate adult yet demanded to consult with a named solicitor. However, the custody officer actively dissuaded this suspect from requesting a solicitor; he told her that a solicitor would merely be able to ascertain whether her detention was lawful. The custody records showed that despite her vociferous request, it was ignored and she never received legal advice. This suggests that for those detained under mental health legislation, the reading of their rights could be regarded as dispensable.

In the present research, police officers mostly viewed their role as informing suspects about whether and how to use their rights, such as to consult with a legal advisor. During participant observation, officers explicitly stated to suspects that they could provide them with information but could not advise them about what to do. Consequently, in the custody area at least, which is monitored by CCTV, staff were reluctant to engage in conversation with suspects about how long they might have to wait for a solicitor, whether the seriousness of the offence warranted it and how a solicitor would be able to help (e.g. with ensuring the interview was conducted fairly), although there were also variations between staff in terms of how much advice they offered, which depended, for example, on whether the suspect had mental health problems or on the suspect's prior experience of police custody. Moreover, because officers viewed their role as informing suspects of their rights, little was done to challenge suspects' decisions. In fact, as Brown *et al.* (1992) found, officers rarely even asked, as they should, why suspects had declined legal advice (PACE Code C, 2008: 6.5). In the present research, if this question was asked, the information was rarely recorded on any of the custody records that the researchers looked at. These findings contrast with Kemp and Balmer's (2008) survey of prisoners, where they found that 80 per cent of prisoners reported that they had been recommended to seek legal advice, and of these 82 per cent said that recommendations came from the police, largely by implication, rather than through a direct statement.

The present research found that there were also three kinds of inconsistencies in *how* suspects were read their rights,[6] which may have affected suspects' comprehension of them. First, officers varied in terms of how much information they provided. Sometimes they omitted important information, for example, about whether legal advice was 'free' through the duty solicitor scheme or about the fact that their rights were ongoing and could be exercised at any time during their detention. On the morning GMPO7, a suspect who had been intoxicated on the previous night was being read his rights, he was asked if he wished to consult with a solicitor. He said he did not 'coz they're too expensive', yet the custody officer did not inform him that legal consultations through the duty solicitor scheme are 'free'. Officers also varied in how many times they read suspects their rights; for example, some would keep reading them until suspects appeared to have understood rather than reading them just once.

Secondly, the police varied in terms of how quickly they read suspects their rights. In her field notes, one researcher described the differences between custody officers: 'Some explain very carefully, others are clear, but brief, whereas one gallops through them very quickly and doesn't really check that the suspect has understood what is being said to him.' The speed at which suspects were read their rights may also reflect the routinization identified by Brown *et al.* (1992). In GMPO1, one officer appeared to circumvent the routine of the booking-in process by making light of the reading of a suspect's rights. For example, he described the

PACE Codes of practice as being there to ensure that the police did not beat him up and when the suspect said he did not want legal advice he replied 'marvellous' in a slightly jovial but sarcastic tone. Indeed, it may have been 'marvellous' for the police that this suspect declined legal advice as it meant that there was less work to be done by them. Equally, this jovial attitude is understandable in view of the number of times this officer had probably booked in a suspect, yet making light of the situation may be disarming for suspects so that they do not fully appreciate the gravity of the situation. On balance, as Brown *et al.* (1992) argue, it is not deliberate obstruction by the police, rather overfamiliarity with and the routinization of the process that affects suspects' decisions about their rights.

Third, the police varied in terms of whether or not they gave suspects their rights verbally or on paper as well, which is required by the PACE Codes of Practice. Yet the use of paper copies of suspects' rights could be particularly helpful for suspects who did not speak English as a first language. In GMPO2, an independent custody visitor complained to the inspector that a Kurdish suspect had not been given a paper copy of his rights in Kurdish, which the inspector acknowledged should have been done. Without paper copies of rights in other languages, staff were entirely dependent on using a telephone interpretation service, which was another source of frustration because it was costly to the police and delayed the booking-in process. For suspects, if staff did not have the time or could not be bothered to seek out a translation of their rights, it is likely to have added to suspects' fear about being detained by officers with whom they could not communicate and being involved in an unfamiliar process.

The right not to be held incommunicado

Suspects have a right not to be held incommunicado. This means that they may request that someone with an interest in their welfare be informed via telephone of their whereabouts as soon as is practicable and at public expense (PACE Code C, 2008: 5.1). If that person cannot be contacted suspects can choose up to two alternatives and more, if staff use their discretion to allow it. This right can be delayed, for example, if it is believed that the suspect will interfere with or harm evidence or witnesses or that they will alert others suspected but not yet arrested for an indictable offence (PACE Code C, 2008: Annexe B). The decision to delay informing someone of a suspect's whereabouts has to be authorized by someone of the rank of inspector or above.

In the present research, the proportion of suspects requesting intimation was slightly higher than in previous research, perhaps because suspects were more aware of this right.[7] As Table 5.1 shows, overall, 30 per cent requested intimation and 22 per cent received intimation, albeit that some

Table 5.1 Access to intimation

Police station	*Sunnyside*	*Gormiston*	*All*
Requests for intimation, of all suspects (%)	33	27	30
Received intimation, of all suspects (%)	27	17	22
Request unmet, of suspects who requested intimation (%)	18	37	27

of those requests (N=22) were not recorded on the custody record, particularly in Gormiston, which was the busier of the two sites. However, the request rate could be inferred by counting those who received intimation but whose request did not appear on the custody record.

In previous research, delays with intimation occurred for relatively small numbers of suspects; for example, Brown (1989) found that in total approximately 1 per cent of suspects had their request either formally delayed or formally denied, meaning they were held incommunicado. In the present research, the average wait between the request and the phone call being made to the nominated person was on average 1 hour and 42 minutes (mean) or 24 minutes (median); the mean was skewed by some lengthy waiting times with eight suspects having to wait more that ten hours, although presumably this was because they were being held incommunicado, for example, while searches were conducted of their houses. Unfortunately, no data were collected on which suspects were held incommunicado which could have been used to clarify this. Being held incommunicado annoyed some suspects, although they also acknowledged that phone calls to friends and family could interfere with the police investigation.

In addition, it took the police in Gormiston significantly longer than their counterparts in Sunnyside to make the phone call to the nominated person ($t=3.278$, $p<0.05$). This may have been because the custody area in Gormiston was busier than in Sunnyside, so staff did not have the time to deal immediately with a suspect's request to notify someone of their arrest. Moreover, in Sunnyside there was a dedicated staff member, the custody administrator, whose responsibility it was to make these kinds of phone calls. Another possibility was that because of the busyness of the custody area there were delays recording the details of the phone call on the custody record, which were compounded by the use of paper records, perhaps because the paper record was in use when staff wanted to record the relevant information.

However, as Bottomley *et al.* (1991) found, these delays to intimation may have occurred for other reasons, both official (e.g. the police were concerned about evidence being destroyed or hidden) and unofficial. They also argued that the unofficial reasons could also be either intentional (e.g.

to allow officers time to search a premises) or unintentional (e.g. if a suspect was released before the person they had nominated had been contacted), particularly when the custody area was busy, and that this was enabled by the phrase 'as soon as practicable'. This shows that not all requests for intimation were acted on. Similarly, Brown (1989) found that only two-thirds of suspects requesting that someone be notified of their arrest had their request met, while Choongh (1997: 145) found evidence that the police could be lax and unwilling to make an effort to notify people of a suspect's arrest.

In the present research, of those who requested intimation, 27 per cent of requests went unmet. However, this figure was much higher for Gormiston than in Sunnyside. This means that in 27 per cent of cases the police failed to inform a family, friend or carer of the whereabouts of a suspect in police custody when that person wanted them to. Admittedly, for a small and unknown proportion of suspects, it may have been necessary to keep them incommunicado, but for the remainder this figure seems unacceptably high, even though the police, particularly in Gormiston, might have been too busy to make the telephone call.

It was difficult to discern the quality of the service that the police delivered when they made the phone call to a suspect's relative, friend or carer. However, one suspect's daughter who accompanied her to the interview complained about the police not providing enough information when they called her to inform her of her mother's arrest (SND4). Another suspect in Gormiston did not like the way that his girlfriend was informed of his arrest because he was worried that the police officer was scaring her:

> I didn't actually like the way they [the police] dealt with that [notifying his girlfriend of his arrest] . . . I said that I wanted to call my girlfriend. She was at home waiting for me, and the police officer actually called her and like said, yes, it's so and so from Gormiston police station, and I said, I wasn't rude about it, but I said to him, can't I talk to her please because you're going to scare her, and he was like, no, I was like, OK, alright then . . . I didn't want to argue with him. (GMD4)

In addition to the telephone call to the nominated person, suspects are also allowed to make use of a separate right to telephone one person for a reasonable amount of time (PACE Code C, 2008: 5.6), although the police are not obliged to inform suspects of this right. This right can be delayed or denied altogether for similar reasons to their right to have someone informed of their whereabouts (PACE Code C, 2008: Annexe B). It was difficult to ascertain how frequently suspects made use of this right as this information was not routinely recorded on the custody record and if so, it could be easily confused with information about their right to have someone informed of their arrest. The most recent figures suggest that the right to a phone call is exercised by 6 per cent of suspects (Brown, 1989), which is considerably less than those requesting that someone be notified of their arrest. In the present research, it seemed to be the more seasoned suspects who were aware of this right and demanded 'their phone call'. Similarly, Bottomley *et al.* (1991) found a small proportion of suspects requested a phone call because the custody officers rarely informed suspects of this right, prioritizing it below the right to legal advice and to have someone informed of their arrest. Choongh (1997: 145–6) also found that it could be difficult for suspects to exercise this right, for example staff kept suspects waiting for prolonged periods, if letting them exercise the right at all. Since access to a phone call depends on whether suspects know to ask for it, this raises questions about fairness and about whether it is a right at all. While the right is set out in the Codes of Practice, its availability depends on police discretion in informing suspects of the right. Like other rights (e.g. access to exercise and/or cigarettes), which depend on police discretion, it might be used as a bargaining tool to secure compliance and to assert control over the suspect.

The right to legal advice

The right to legal advice is an area that has generated a large amount of research. Consequently, I delve into this right more deeply than others. This section addresses two key issues, first the extent of access to legal advice and second, the factors affecting access to legal advice.

Extent of access to legal advice

Prior to PACE, the discretionary nature of the Judges' Rules meant that few suspects were informed of their right to legal advice and the police used this to either delay or prevent access to custodial advice, resulting in small numbers of suspects requesting and receiving legal advice (McConville and Hodgson, 1993). This situation was criticized by the Royal Commission on Criminal Procedure (1981) as disadvantaging suspects and it was recommended that suspects be informed of the right to legal advice, be given the opportunity to waive it and that provisions be made for legal advisors to provide advice when requested through the creation of a centrally run, publicly funded duty solicitor scheme. Subsequently, these rights became enshrined in PACE.

Since PACE, all suspects are statutorily entitled to ongoing access to free and independent legal advice as soon as is practicable after their request is made, and this is likely to have contributed to the increase in access to legal advice from 1978 to 2000 as shown in Table 5.2. It is also important to note that access to legal advice varies immensely between police

Table 5.2 Access to legal advice 1978–2000

Year of data collection	*Request rate, of all suspects (%)*	*Consultation rate, of all suspects (%)*	*Requests unmet, of suspects who requested legal advice (%)*	*Study*
1978	11	7	36	Softley *et al.* (1980)
1984	17	9	47	Bottomley *et al.* (1989), cited in Bottomley *et al.* (1991)
1985	17	27	59	Bridges (1985), cited in Maguire (1988)
	27	23	15	
1986 – when PACE took effect	20	15	25	Maguire (1988)
1987	26	22	15	Bottomley *et al.* (1989), cited in Bottomley *et al.* (1991)
	25	Unavailable	Uncalculable	Brown (1989)
1988	25	19	24	Sanders *et al.* (1989: 183)
1993–4	38	33	13	Phillips and Brown (1998: 58)
1995–6	40	34	15	Bucke and Brown (1997: viii)
1999–2000	45	Not collected	Uncalculable	Newburn and Hayman (2002: 47)
2007	60	48	20	Present study
2009	45	35	22	Pleasence *et al.* (2011)
Average 1978–2009	31	25	27	

stations, even those within a single police force (e.g. Pleasence *et al.*, 2011; Phillips and Brown, 1998: 60; Sanders *et al.*, 1989: 183; Brown, 1989; Bottomley *et al.*, 1991). Even so, there appears to have been an upward trend in accessing legal advice. Table 5.2 also shows that the request rate can vary from the consultation rate. This can be for a variety of reasons; for example, it might be that the suspect is released before the solicitor arrives or that the suspect changes their mind or that the police forget to act on their request and therefore the suspects do not receive the legal advice they requested.

As shown in Table 5.3, request and consultation rates were higher in the present research than in previous studies. In total, the custody records showed that 60 per cent of suspects requested legal advice and 48 per cent consulted with a legal advisor. This is higher than in the most recent previous research and these figures are also double or more the average request and consultation rates from 1978 to 2009. This high request rate suggests an increase in requests for legal advice, perhaps because of a growing awareness among suspects of their rights (Irving and Mackenzie, 1989: 117), or because the police offer more encouragement, particularly in more serious cases where they are concerned about the future admissibility of a confession obtained in the absence of a lawyer. In addition, these request and consultation rates were not just due to an 'observer effect'. Had there been an observer effect, for example causing staff to conscientiously observe the rules in the presence of the researchers, then request and consultation rates would have been higher in the week that the researchers were in the custody area. Chi-squared analysis showed that there were no such differences. However, caution is needed in interpreting the seeming increase in requests and consultations because the findings from the two police stations in the present research may not be generalisable to all police stations (see Pleasence *et al.*, 2011).

For consistency and comparability with previous research, Table 5.3 includes both request and consultation rates. The latter can be misleading as the consultation rate is the proportion of the entire suspect population that consulted with a legal advisor, yet not all suspects request a legal advisor. For this reason, I have calculated the proportion of requests for legal advice which went unmet for the previous studies, as well for the present research. In the present study, overall, 20 per cent of requests for legal advice went unmet, which is a lot more than in the most recent study by Phillips and Brown (1998: 58), but less than the average proportion of requests that went unmet between 1978 and 1993.

In the present research, request rates did vary between sites. Suspects in Sunnyside were significantly more likely than in Gormiston to request legal advice ($\chi^2 = 24.2$ $p < 0.01$). As I have argued elsewhere, this may have been because suspects were more willing to wait to receive legal advice, given that in Sunnyside the custody environment was better and there were more staff to respond to suspects' needs (Skinns, 2009b). This higher

Table 5.3 Requests and consultations with a legal advisor

Police station	*Sunnyside (privatized)*			*Gormiston (publicly run)*			*All*
Time of data collection:	*Time 1 (observers present)*	*Time 2*	*All*	*Time 1*	*Time 2 (observers present)*	*All*	
Request rate, of all suspects (%)	68	68	68	52	50	51	60
Consultation rate, of all suspects (%)	54	57	55	39	39	39	48
Requests unmet, of all suspects who requested legal advice (%)	21	16	19	25	22	23	20

proportion of requests for legal advice translated into a higher absolute number of consultations with solicitors, although neither site was significantly better than the other at meeting suspects' requests for legal advice. Therefore, it can be argued that, as with private prisons, newer custody areas offer suspects a better experience relative to the older custody areas by virtue of their being new. This highlights that the public sector does not routinely provide a better service and that privatization can have hidden and unexpected consequences. As I argue elsewhere, however, the question is whether advantages such as this outweigh the disadvantages, including the costly and burdensome nature of contract management (Skinns, 2009a). Moreover, it may be that in the longer-term, once the privatized custody area is no longer new and once the 'honeymoon period' is over and the custody area is expected to make a profit (e.g. by reducing staff costs), these advantages may disappear.[8]

Explanations of access to legal advice

Previous research has identified a number of factors impacting on access to custodial legal advice, which include those related to the suspect, police and legal advisors. Here, I briefly review and integrate the findings from previous research with the qualitative and quantitative findings from both sites in the present study. However, a more detailed examination of these findings can be found in Skinns (2009a) and Skinns (2011).

Socio-demographic characteristics of suspects

In terms of the suspect, demographic factors, have been found to be significant, with black suspects being more likely to request legal advice (Phillips and Brown, 1998: 62; Kemp, 2010: 22) and with juveniles being less likely to request legal advice (Pleasence *et al.*, 2011; Bottomley *et al.*, 1991), although for the latter this was because juveniles are suspected of less serious matters (Brown, 1989). As I have noted elsewhere, age and sex were not significantly related to whether suspects requested legal advice or whether that request was met (Skinns, 2009b). However, this was not true for ethnicity, as black suspects were significantly less likely than white suspects to have their request for legal advice met, though this may have been mediated by differences in the alleged offences committed by white and non-white suspects.

Furthermore, research has found that intoxicated suspects are more likely to request legal advice, than the non-intoxicated (Phillips and Brown, 1998: 62). This seems counter-intuitive given that suspects may not be in a fit state to request legal advice. While the findings were not significant, the results in the present study pointed in a similar direction: those identified as being at risk by custody staff were more likely to request legal advice but less likely to have that request met (Skinns, 2009b).

Let's get it over with

Suspects are also concerned that consulting with a legal advisor is likely to prolong detention (Sanders *et al.*, 1989: 59; Choongh, 1997: 149). This logic of not wanting to wait to see a solicitor held true even for suspects in both sites, even for GMD4, who had used this reasoning to decline legal advice in the past and then regretted it. It seemed that some suspects did not care about the longer-term consequences of declining legal advice and were prepared to take the risk of not having one because of their more immediate need to be released from police custody. This 'let's get it over with mentality' arose in part because suspects lacked information about why and for how long they would be waiting, but also because the police, sometimes rightly,[9] informed suspects that their detention would be prolonged by seeking legal advice.

Seriousness, complexity and likely penalty for the offence

The seriousness of the offence also affects access to legal advice, although the relationship between the two variables is complex (e.g. Maguire, 1988; Brown, 1989). Generally, in the present and previous research, those arrested for moderate and less serious offences are less likely to request and receive legal advice compared to those arrested for serious offences (Pleasence *et al.*, 2011; Choongh, 1997: 149; Phillips and Brown, 1998: 203; Bottomley *et al.*, 1991). Pleasence *et al.* (2011) also found that lower levels of offence severity were also associated with lower levels of requests. Furthermore, the present research showed that not requesting advice may also be mediated by suspects' perceptions of the strength of the evidence against them (see also Skinns, 2009a) and their perceptions of the likely penalty for the offence. For instance, GMD9 said that he did not request a solicitor for less serious offences, such as possession of cannabis for which you would be cautioned or receive only a fine in court. Moreover, suspects' calculation of the relative seriousness of the offence (and whether it warranted a legal advisor) may have been (informally) influenced by the police 'leading them to believe' that what they had been arrested for was 'not that serious' (GMD11).

'I'm innocent. What do I need a solicitor for?'

Suspects are also concerned about the police inferring guilt from requests for legal advice (Choongh, 1997: 149; Bottomley *et al.*, 1991). They have a 'don't need one. I've done nowt' mentality (Dixon *et al.*, 1990: 122) and they assume that a solicitor is unnecessary if they are innocent and have nothing to hide (Sanders *et al.*, 1989: 59). In the present research, suspects also appeared to decline legal advice either because they believed they were innocent or because they were guilty. A suspect in Sunnyside said: 'If you're pleading not guilty then you don't need a solicitor' (SND4) and, in GMPO3, two suspects said 'I don't need it coz I ain't done nothing wrong' and because 'I haven't done anything'.

There were two reasons why innocence or guilt was believed to negate the necessity of legal advice. First, rather than viewing a solicitor as being there to protect their rights, some suspects viewed a solicitor as redundant either because they were innocent and had nothing to hide or because they were guilty and would simply go to interview or court and tell the truth which, for the latter, suggested a degree of fatalism (Sanders *et al.*, 1989: 73). Second, because they believed themselves innocent, suspects were concerned that the police would infer guilt from their request for legal advice and therefore you only needed a solicitor if you were guilty of the suspected offence.

Prior experience of custody

Prior experience of custody can mean that suspects feel that they know enough to get by without a solicitor and consequently those with previous convictions are less likely to request advice. Phillips and Brown (1998: 203) found that those with previous convictions (and therefore prior experience of police custody) were 1.5 times more likely to request legal advice than those without. Unfortunately, data on previous convictions were not collected in the present study. However, the qualitative data illustrated that the impact of prior experience of police custody on access to legal advice was complex. On the one hand, inexperienced suspects requested legal advice because they were scared and/or declined legal advice as they did not understand the custody process or appreciate its importance. On the other hand, the more experienced suspects appeared to know when to use their right to legal advice, for example requesting legal advice for more serious offences or declining it because they believed that they knew enough to get by without the help of a solicitor.

Police practices: ploys and informal conversations

In the past, the police have been found, on occasion, to use informal conversations and ploys to dissuade suspects from seeking legal advice, the most common one being to read suspects their rights incompletely or incomprehensibly (Choongh, 1997: 150; Dixon *et al.*, 1990; Sanders *et al.*, 1989: 59), although there may be new ones too. However, there is little evidence that these ploys necessarily impact on suspects' decisions about legal advice (Sanders *et al.*, 1989: 58; Antoniou, 2008), particularly in the light of the growing proportion of suspects who request and receive legal advice in the police station. This may have been due to the surveillance of staff by CCTV cameras and by other criminal justice practitioners. At the same time, informal conversations between the police and suspects almost certainly took place and while the content of these conversations was unknown and unknowable, suspects (e.g. GMD14) and solicitors (e.g.

GMS12, SNS11) believed that they could influence whether suspects accessed legal advice.

The availability of legal advisors

The availability of legal advisors can impact on whether a suspect waits to have their request for legal advice met (Choongh, 1997: 154; Brown, 1989; Sanders *et al.*, 1989: 26; Maguire, 1988). At the time, in the present research, there was a chain of events that needed to occur in order for a suspect to consult with a legal advisor. The suspect had to request a legal advisor, the police had to act (promptly) on this request, and the police had to successfully contact either the legal advisor of the suspect's choosing or the duty solicitor. The legal advisor then had to agree to represent the suspect and agree a time, if at all, when they would arrive at the police station, and then arrive at the agreed time. The research showed that any of these stages could go wrong, thereby derailing the sequence of events. Moreover, the wait to see the solicitor was probably as much to do with solicitors (e.g. because there were not enough duty solicitors) as the police (e.g. while they completed their investigation) (see also Kemp and Balmer, 2008; Skinns, 2010). To an extent, though, who was to blame was irrelevant to the suspect, as the effect was the same: they had to wait longer before they were released and they were likely to be confused about why they were waiting as well as frightened and uncomfortable in a police cell.

Prior experience of legal advisors: experience, role and quality of advice

Prior experience of legal advisors can impact on whether someone requests legal advice in the first place; as Choongh (1997: 149) found, suspects in the present research were mistrusting of legal advisors, especially those they did not know and when the charge was a serious one (e.g. GMD3, GMD8 and GMD14). This suggests that suspect choice is important when it comes to legal advice, a matter which has been ignored with the introduction of telephone advice only for certain offences provided by Criminal Defence Service Direct. In addition, advice *can* be inadequate: solicitors can be slow to respond to requests; advice can be given over the telephone rather than in person; firms have been shown to make use of underqualified and poorly supervised staff; legal advisors may take a dim view of suspects and the kind of service that they deserve; and even when legal advisors are present they give poor advice, such as to 'tell the truth', and may fail to intervene in interrogations or fail to adopt an adversarial stance more generally (Pierpoint, 2006; Cape, 2004; Choongh, 1997: 157–61; Hodgson and Bridges, 1995; McConville *et al.*, 1994: 126; McConville and Hodgson, 1993; Bridges and Sanders, 1990; Irving and McKenzie, 1989: 164; Bottomley *et al.*, 1991; Baldwin 1992).

In the present research, while some suspects did not trust legal advisors, the rest expressed predominantly positive opinions about them, describing them as 'good', 'amazing', 'blinding', 'pretty good', and that they were 'reasonably happy' because their legal advisor stood up for their rights. It was also common for suspects to have multiple consultations and to spend, on average, over an hour in total in consultation with their legal advisor. However, suspect satisfaction with their legal advisor should not be overemphasized, particularly without knowing about the quality of the advice or about whether suspects were convicted: some suspects, like GMD13, were simply grateful to see a friendly face after being in police detention for some time. Moreover, some police officers and suspects were sceptical about the adequacy of the advice provided by hard-pressed duty solicitors who worked into the small hours providing advice to multiple clients in busy police stations like Gormiston.

Telephone legal advice and privacy

The quality of legal advice was also compromised when it took place over the telephone because of a lack of privacy. In Sunnyside, telephone conversations took place over a two-way intercom in the cells while in Gormiston they took place via a telephone on the custody desk. Either way conversations were audible to staff and conversations could also be recorded by the microphones associated with the CCTV system. As an alternative, suspects could be brought from their cells to use the telephone in the custody desk, but this was regarded as too resource-intensive by Security Ltd to be practical all of the time. Consequently, suspects and legal advisors were both concerned about the lack of privacy for telephone legal consultations, particularly when suspects were only eligible to receive advice over the telephone (i.e. for less serious offences dealt with by Criminal Defence Service Direct). Moreover, this lack of privacy is unlawful because it violates human rights legislation, guaranteeing suspects a right to a fair trial (Pattenden and Skinns, 2010).

Identifying the most important factors

Table 5.4 below shows data from regression analysis used to tease out which of the above factors are most important in predicting whether or not suspects requested legal advice (see Skinns, 2009b).[10] While this analysis was limited because not all of the variables identified above could be quantified and included, it is also helpful in that multivariate analysis of this kind enables researchers to simultaneously explore the relative value of a range of different independent variables. The factors significantly predicting requests for legal advice were: case disposal, with those charged rather than diverted being more likely to request legal advice; the police custody area, with suspects in Sunnyside being more likely to request legal advice; whether the suspect consulted with the doctor, with suspects consulting a doctor being more likely to request legal advice; the

Table 5.4 Variables predicting requests for legal advice

	B	*Sig.*	*Exp(B)*	*95.0% CI for EXP(B)*	
				Lower	*Upper*
Area	0.778	0.000	2.178	1.608	2.951
Day of Arrest	−0.366	0.017	0.694	0.514	0.937
Seriousness of arrest		0.002			
Medium	0.755	0.000	2.128	1.425	3.177
High	0.562	0.005	1.755	1.181	2.608
Breaches, warrants, recalls, mental health	0.637	0.011	1.891	1.161	3.079
Doctor consulted	0.619	0.000	1.857	1.361	2.535
Informal conversations	0.942	0.016	2.566	1.196	5.507
Case disposal	−0.971	0.000	0.379	0.254	0.564
Constant	−0.457	0.024	0.633		

Source: Skinns (2009b).

reason for arrest, with those arrested for serious offences being more likely to request legal advice rather than those arrested for less serious offences; conversations between suspects and the police, with suspects who informally spoke to the police being *more* not less likely to request legal advice, perhaps because those that talked to the police were more seasoned suspects familiar with the custody process; day of arrest, with those arrested on a weekday being more likely to request legal advice than those arrested at the weekend, which was related to suspects' concerns, described above, that legal advice would prolong detention.

Due to difficulties finding a model that fitted the data, regression analysis could not be used to explore the factors predicting whether or not suspects' requests for legal advice were met. Nonetheless bivariate analysis of the data shown in Table 5.5, indicated that suspect requests for legal advice were significantly more likely to be met if the suspect had *not* been arrested for a bail offence, on warrant, on recall to prison, for an immigration offence or under mental health legislation;[11] if they were white; and if they admitted to the offence (and were cautioned) (Skinns, 2009b).

Police interviews

One of the main reasons suspects are arrested and detained in police custody is to investigate the alleged offence and, in part, this takes place through the questioning of suspects.[12] In the present research, the interview was described to the suspect as 'an opportunity to give their

Table 5.5 Bivariate analysis showing factors associated with whether a suspect's request for legal advice was met

	Requests met		
Variable	*Odds ratio*	*Significance*	*N*
Area	0.985	0.941	868
Sex	0.742	0.311	868
Age	1.609	0.169	868
Ethnicity	0.689	0.092	867
Day of arrest	1.023	0.914	857
Time of arrest	1.185	0.458	868
Arrest seriousness		0.000*	883
Medium (property, fraud and drugs)	1.177	0.612	
High (violent and sexual)	1.288	0.445	
Other (breach, warrant, recall, immigration)	0.236	0.000*	
Identified risk	0.844	0.456	845
Rights read	0.406	0.217	868
Consulted FME	0.778	0.232	868
Consulted AA	1.59	0.18	868
Fitness of suspect	0.933	0.834	868
Informal conversations	0.937	0.886	868
Length of detention	1.074	0.737	868
Case disposal	2.513	0.007*	868

*$p<0.01$

side of events'. Yet as a solicitor, GMS12, explained, this is disingenuous; instead, he regarded the interview as being about discovering if an offence had been committed and if so by whom. This concurs with Sanders and Young (2006: 177), who note that officers no longer collect evidence before they arrest someone; rather they arrest someone in order to collect the evidence that they need. Therefore detaining someone to collect evidence by questioning is assumed to be necessary rather than optional. This partially explained why not everyone arrested was interviewed; overall, only 66 per cent of suspects were interviewed at least once, while the figures were 61 per cent in Gormiston and 70 per cent in Sunnyside. At the same time, there are other legitimate reasons why someone might be arrested but not interviewed, for example if they were arrested for their own safety under mental health legislation, or for breaching a court order or on warrant.

On average, suspects spent 33, 22 and 13 minutes, respectively, in their first, second and third interviews, although the majority had only one interview. This compares with 52 minutes in Brown (1989: 45) and 40 minutes in Irving and McKenzie's (1989) 1987 sample and 60 minutes in their pre-PACE sample. In the present research, whether or not suspects were interviewed was significantly affected by the type of offence that they were arrested for ($\chi^2 = 231.22$, $p < 0.01$). Those arrested for violent, sexual, property or drug offences or fraud were more likely to be interviewed compared to those arrested for breaches of court orders, warrants, prison productions and recalls to prison or under the mental health act. This makes sense given that decisions about breaches of court orders, warrants and recall to prison are made in court and decisions about mentally ill suspects are taken by approved social workers and psychiatrists, and neither requires investigation by the police. Suspects arrested for disorder and for driving offences were as likely to be interviewed as not.

There appear to be two main ways in which rules about the police interview may be deliberately or inadvertently broken. First, formal interviews may be used to put pressure on suspects to provide information, leading to either false confessions or the eliciting of inaccurate information, particularly in the absence of a legal advisor or appropriate adult (e.g. RCCP, 1981: para. 1.10). Inaccurate information can also be elicited if the interviews take place when suspects are vulnerable, for example, because the police have failed to recognize or acknowledge mental illness or intellectual impairment, or when they are unfit for interview because they are tired, intoxicated or withdrawing from drugs.

In the present research, the only scope for pressure being put on suspects in police interviews and inaccuracies in their evidence related to the use of night-time interviews. Of the suspects that were interviewed, 10 per cent were interviewed at night-time. This figure seemed high, given that this practice is discouraged by PACE because suspects are entitled to an eight-hour rest period overnight (see PACE Code C, 2008: 12.2). This experienced suspect provided one explanation for the use of night-time interviews:

> [T]he police, they're very tactical in their ways, they won't let you have a fag, they'll wait till they see you fall asleep, then bang half an hour later, come on, interview, to try and catch you out, because you're like that, eerr, half asleep, to just try and make you spill your guts . . . (SND9)

It was also the case that the police simply wanted suspects processed as quickly as possible. As this police officer explained, 'we don't just put people in a sleep period just because it's 2 o'clock in the morning, if we can do them quick, it's best to do them quick, and out of custody' (GMS10). Similarly, perhaps suspects agreed to a night-time interview in the belief that it would expedite their release from custody. When faced with the choice of being detained overnight or possibly being released after a night interview, they may have had the same 'let's get it over with' mentality as described above. Indeed, suspects were right to believe this.

As discussed in Skinns (2010), being interviewed at night was significantly associated with shorter periods of detention.

PACE Code C (2008) states that answers to questions and statements should not be obtained through the use of oppression (para. 11.5), which was defined by the Court of Appeal in *R* v. *Fulling* [1987] as 'the exercise of authority or power in a burdensome, harsh or wrongful manner; unjust or cruel treatment of subjects, inferiors, etc.; or the imposition of unreasonable or unjust burdens', as well as involving impropriety on the part of the police interviewer through the use of bullying, intimidating and discourteous practices, and lengthy interviews, and where there is a link between oppression and confession (cited in Cape, 2006: 486–7). According to this definition, night interviews could be seen as being on the cusp of being oppressive: they could be burdensome for the suspect in that they take place at a time when they are vulnerable. It would be more reasonable to conduct the interviews at a time when suspects are more alert. While night interviews may serve the crime control aims of the police, including their desire to process suspects as quickly as possible, they might also wrong-foot suspects, thereby jeopardizing their access to justice.

Second, previous research shows that informal conversations could be used to elicit information which could be later discussed in the formal interview and to put pressure on suspects to confess.[13] While they could not gauge the extent of the conversations, Sanders *et al.* (1989: 157) and McConville *et al.* (1991: 58–9) found evidence that informal conversations took place at various points after arrest such as when officers took suspects on the 'scenic route' to the police station, at the booking-in desk and in the cells. Moreover, they argue that these unofficial visits to the cells could be concealed on the custody record by saying that the suspect wished to speak to the officer who visited them or that the officer visited them on welfare grounds or they were simply not recorded at all. In the context of reductions in legal aid expenditure, it is rare that legal advisors are present in the police station throughout the course of a suspect's detention to protect them from such occurrences. Choongh (1997: 169), however, was able to gauge the extent to which informal interviews took place. He found that 15 of 79 suspects were spoken to off-the-record in police cars, search rooms, cells, fingerprint rooms, outside interview rooms, in the charge room and inside interview rooms before the tape-recorder was switched on. Importantly, Choongh (1997: 169) also says that these informal interviews place an unknown amount of pressure on suspects (e.g. if officers say to the suspect that it would make things easier for them if they admitted to the offence).

In the present research, as described above, informal conversations almost certainly took place. It was reported that in these conversations the police downplayed the seriousness of the offence or frightened suspects in order to make them admit to the offence. One suspect, SND9, remarked that informal conversations had been used to 'put the frighteners on' him;

for example, he was told that he would receive a number of years for the offence he was suspected of and that he could help himself by 'coughing' to it. By contrast, GMD11 described an occasion when he was arrested for possession of cocaine, whereupon he had a conversation with police officers in the back of the police car on the way to the station about his concerns about jeopardizing his career and university course, whereupon the police officers told him not to worry. Platitudes such as this could be regarded as reassuring, but also potentially misleading. Similarly, GMD3 – a less experienced suspect, who was arrested for common assault following a domestic incident at his home involving his stepfather and mother – had a lengthy conversation in the back of the police car about the events preceding his arrest, as he explained:

> [T]he policewoman who arrested me was very nice, and very understanding of the situation . . . she told me, not in so many words, that she knew I was innocent, but because of the state of my stepdad, they had to arrest me while they investigated, and she said that I would more than likely be released without charge . . . She was quite informative, and caring . . . I just basically told her exactly what happened. (GMD2)

No further action was taken against this suspect. On this occasion, while this police officer broke the rules, she had meant well. In sum, informal interviews were reportedly used to reassure suspects, but could also frighten them, inadvertently mislead them or be deliberately used to find out evidence relevant to the case (or to dissuade the suspect from seeking legal advice, as described above).

Detention reviews – 'you're not going anywhere until it's done'

Under the PACE Codes of Practice, the review of detention is performed by an inspector. If the suspect is asleep at the time of the review they are informed of it when they awake. The reviews take place 6 hours after detention is authorized and then no later than 9 hours after the first and subsequent reviews. That is, the review is conducted before 6 and 15 hours of detention by an inspector and before 24 hours of detention by a superintendent. After that, a suspect can be held for no more than 36 and 96 hours, but this has to be decided by a magistrate. Reviews of detention are concerned with 'periodically determining if a person's detention, before or after charge, continues to be necessary' (PACE Code C, 2008: 15.1). Therefore the reviewing officer has to consider the details of the case and allow representations from relevant parties such as legal advisors and appropriate adults. During the review, the suspect should also be reminded of their ongoing right to free and independent legal advice and the reviewing officer is to make a note of any comments made by the suspect.

However, in the past, detention reviews have been found sometimes to be tokenistic and routinized. For example, Dixon *et al.* (1990) observed that detention reviews sometimes amounted to nothing more than the inspector asking the suspect through the wicket 'are you alright mate?' and that early reviews at 6 and 15 hours, especially if they were over the telephone, involved custody officers simply adding a standard entry on the custody record, such as that detention was required for questioning. Dixon *et al.* went on to say:

> The review system is conducted in a way which produces records apparently complying with the letter of PACE, but that its spirit is largely dissipated in the routinization of procedure . . . the quasi-judicial, independent role of the review officer which PACE seems to demand has been implemented as merely administrative routine. (1990: 131–2)

Other than this, there has been little research on detention reviews, although they were recently discussed in the review of PACE with plans to allow, for example, reviews to be done remotely (i.e. over the telephone), which is likely to reinforce the routinization that Dixon *et al.* (1990) note as well as the scope for (inadvertent) rule-bending.

In the present research, the data collected about detention reviews showed a pattern whereby an interview was followed by a review of the

Table 5.6 Reasons for continued detention at the first three reviews*

Reason for continued detention		*Detention review 1*	*Detention review 2*	*Detention review 3*
Interview	%	51%	52%	6%
	count	229	96	3
Unfit	%	16%	1%	0
	count	74	1	0
Further evidence, review and charge	%	17%	14%	10%
	count	77	26	5
Attending court	%	9%	24%	61%
	count	39	44	31
Other including mental health assessments	%	7%	9%	24%
	count	31	17	12
Total count		450	184	51

*There was no significant association between the area and the reason for continued detention, so the data included in this table refer to both sites. The first three reviews of detention only were included because there were too little data for subsequent reviews.

evidence and charge, with the process being delayed if the suspect was unfit. Table 5.6 shows the reasons most commonly given for continuing detention at the first three reviews. In both sites, at the first and second reviews, the most common reason given for continuing a suspect's detention was to interview them, although at the third and subsequent reviews the most common reason was because the suspect was waiting to attend the next available court.

In the present research, detention reviews were done in a routinized way, as the reviewing officer went through the motions, merely rubber-stamping the decision to prolong detention. An inspector in SNPO7 spent no more than a couple of minutes per review. The inspector reminded the suspect of their right to legal advice and then informed them about what was happening with the case, for example that they were going to be interviewed. None of the suspects complained about their continued detention. This inspector said that he was supposed to remind suspects about why they were being detained, for example to secure and preserve evidence, but that this information was lost on most so he did not bother. He also said that he felt as if he was 'going through the motions' when performing the reviews and that he only reviewed the details of the case and contacted the officer in the case when a suspect complained. If the officer in the case had done little to move the case forward, he would even consider bailing the suspect to punish the officer. Similarly, a solicitor in Gormiston (GMS1) regarded detention reviews as a routinized matter; he noted that the information on the custody record was repeated verbatim for all suspects. This was also observed to be the case when the researchers collected data from the custody records.

In addition, it appeared that further detention was regarded as a given by suspects and staff during the detention reviews. When reviewing detention, an inspector, GMS8, described himself as 'the bearer of bad news' that further detention was necessary, saying to suspects that 'you're not going now' and 'I'm authorizing your detention', rather than admitting the 'truth that the investigation isn't complete'. Suspects, such as SND4, also regarded the detention review as a routine process with little possibility of challenging the decision. Like GMS8, she accepted further detention as a given and simply asked for things (such as cigarettes, a blanket and food from a local supermarket) that would make her continued detention more bearable. This straightforward acceptance of further detention among experienced suspects was also remarked upon by an inspector who said that reviews of detention were better received by those who had been arrested before because they knew they were 'not going anywhere until it [the investigation] was done', whereas explaining this to first-timers only compounded their distress (GMS8).

This routinization of the process, as well as busyness in Gormiston, may explain why officers sometimes forgot to inform suspects of the review of their detention, for example if they had been asleep at the time of the review (e.g. GMS11). The implication is that detention reviews were not accorded the priority that they deserved. This was also confirmed in GMPO1; an independent custody visitor raised the issue of suspects not being informed of reviews undertaken while they were asleep with the inspector, who replied that it was only best practice to do so rather than it being a legal requirement.

Without adequate detention reviews, suspects are unlikely to be fully informed of the progress with their case. This explains why an independent custody visitor (GMS11) felt that suspects were not given enough information about what was happening to them and the reasons for delays. Yet if they were kept informed, the wait might not have seemed as unfair. This was illustrated by a suspect, GMD11, who had been arrested for cannabis possession; he said that he was happy with how he was treated on this occasion by the police because he was dealt with within an hour as he was told he would be.

The inadequacies of detention reviews also show the limitations of PACE as a tool for regulating police custody practices; police officers' discretion allows them to accord priority to other matters. Research on police legitimacy suggests that detention reviews may have wider implications for how the suspect regards the fairness of the custody process as well as having consequences for their attitudes towards the police in the future (e.g. Tyler, 2003). Given that little appeared to have changed in relation to how detention reviews were conducted since the 1990s when Dixon *et al.* (1990) conducted their research, it suggests that once a practice such as detention reviews becomes routinized it is likely to remain that way.

Conclusion

An important conclusion that can be drawn from the preceding discussion is that the police and other relevant practitioners such as legal advisors mostly enabled suspects' access to their rights and entitlements. That is, most suspects were informed of their rights, most suspects who requested that someone be notified of their arrest had that request met, most suspects who requested legal advice consulted with a legal advisor, most suspects were not informally interviewed nor were they interviewed at night, and most suspects had their detention reviewed. In addition, the evidence implies that there may have been improvement on access to things like legal advice since the research studies conducted in the mid-to-late 1990s. However, as has been shown, there were some occasions when police practices diverged from the law.

In examining the reasons for these divergences from the PACE Codes of Practice, it is important to think beyond the immediacy of the situation to some of the cultural and structural factors affecting access to rights and entitlements. Part of the conditions of policing that enable these divergences from the law is the inevitable but necessary existence of police discretion (Waddington, 1999: 38–9), that is mandated authority to choose between particular courses of action (Gelsthorpe and Padfield, 2003: 3). The application of discretion is also partially shaped by officers' agency, as well as the cultural knowledge and the wider structural context of policing (Chan, 1997: 73–5). One of the consequences of police discretion is that, within certain parameters influenced by cultural and structural factors, it allows the police to pursue organizational objectives which may or may not be in keeping with the law. Two organizational objectives seem to be of particular importance to the police custody process, namely, crime control and informal punishment of suspects.

First, the structural position of the police within the criminal justice process means that, arguably, one of their organizational objectives is to contribute to prosecution, for example by efficiently processing suspects, irrespective of their rights and entitlements being safeguarded. This expresses the tension at the heart of the crime control and due process models, where due process values such as the presumption of innocence and the right to legal advice are supposed to act as a break on the efficient processing of suspects. The emphasis on crime control can lead the police to deny suspects their rights. In the present study, as well as others, this helps to explain why some suspects were denied appropriate adults when they needed one or were interviewed when they were sleepy or why the police dissuaded them from seeking legal advice or dissuaded them of the seriousness of the offence or held suspects for long periods without being fully informed about what was happening to their case.

Second, divergences from the law in relation to police custody are not just driven by a need for crime control. Choongh (1997: 227) argues its so-called primary purpose is social discipline (e.g. to remind suspects that they are under constant surveillance or to punish or humiliate them, as well as to convey contempt or control). This is so as to coerce suspects into understanding and accepting the normative dimensions of the police–suspect relationship. He also argues that this coercion is disproportionately directed at those suspects who are known to the police and regarded as 'undeserving' during stops, arrests and in police detention, thereby locking them into a regular and long-term relationship with the police. Data from Chapter 3 and from this chapter suggest that, in the present study, the disreputable and undeserving were the non-compliant, problematic drugs users, the mentally ill (particularly, those brought to the police station as a place of safety under mental health legislation) and suspected illegal immigrants. This stereotyping of suspects can also be regarded as part of the cultural knowledge of the police, more specifically what Chan (1997: 76–80) calls 'dictionary knowledge', which is the devising of categories based on who the police come into contact with.

These categories act as summaries, which are of use in complex and ambiguous situations where the police have to take action quickly.

While denial of access to rights and entitlements was sometimes part of a deliberate strategy, this was and could not be the case all of the time. The flaw with Choongh's (1997: 227) argument is to state that social discipline is the *primary* purpose of police custody. In reality, it is probably one of a number of purposes. For it to be a primary purpose, it implies a degree of foresight and malice on the part of the police to always consciously arrange the custody process in a way that suits their ends. In practice, the custody process, as has been seen in Chapter 3, is too busy for this, with discontinuity from one shift to another. Moreover, in a busy custody suite like Gormiston which was in London, not all suspects were part of a group of 'regulars' with whom they were locked into a punitive relationship based, for example, on avenging past wrongs.

In practice, the police acted as much inadvertently as deliberately, albeit that the effect is the same in that suspects can be denied their rights and entitlements. Police practices were also shaped by the monotony of the custody process. There appeared to be an unthinking compulsion on the part of the police which meant that they simply did things in the ways that they had always done them before; indeed, this was the path of least resistance. The idea that denial of rights was inadvertent offers a better explanation of the routinized way in which suspects were informed of their rights and entitlements or the way in which detention reviews were conducted. Staff paid lip service to the idea of fulfilling their PACE obligations, but in reality these rights were a hollow shell, albeit that this was still better than there being no framework at all.

In addition, divergences arose because, structurally speaking, the criminal justice process does not function as an effective deterrent to police malpractice. Suspects may complain about the way that they are treated to their legal advisor, the police or the IPCC, or they can take civil action against the police, but the onus is on them to make these complaints stick and such complaints are notoriously difficult to substantiate (Gleeson and Grace, 2009: 11), since it is the suspect's word against that of the police. Even if the events surrounding a complaint are recorded on CCTV, recordings can go missing, as has been the case in a recent investigation into the death of Sean Riggs who died in the holding area known as 'the cage' at the back of Brixton police station (*Guardian*, 2009). Breaches of PACE might also be identified when the case is at court, yet the judiciary have been reluctant to act in punitive ways towards the police when ruling about the admissibility of evidence and whether it was fairly obtained (Cape, 2002; Dixon, 1997: 70–1; Choongh, 1997: 221). Therefore the police are largely left to regulate themselves when it comes to PACE provisions (Sanders, 2008). Without effective legal deterrents, it encourages the *perception* that the police have absolute control over the custody environment and that it is entirely up to them whether they act in accordance with the rules or not. As argued in Chapters 6 and 7, it is likely that the presence of other criminal justice practitioners in the police custody areas has also done little to alter this perception or deter the police from malpractice because these other practitioners lack power in what is regarded as 'police territory'.

The second aim of the chapter was to explore the implications of access to these rights and entitlements for procedural justice and the legitimacy of the police custody process. Divergence from the law, on occasions, shows, as argued in Chapter 4, that while police custody was mostly procedurally fair, there were aspects of it that were not. This was in two key ways. First, in terms of representing suspects' views, which is one dimension of procedural justice identified by Paternoster *et al.* (1997), there were occasions when this was not as effective as it might have been. This failure to represent suspects' views was evidenced by the ineffectiveness of detention reviews and the requests for legal advice that went unmet. This meant that suspects may not have spoken a great deal either to the police officer conducting the detention review or to their legal advisor. Second, in terms of ethicality, that is when suspects' rights are respected (Paternoster *et al.*, 1997), while the picture was broadly positive across all rights and entitlements, procedural *in*justice remained, such as when the police read suspects' rights in incomprehensible ways. Having not formally tested the relationship between these aspects of procedural justice and police legitimacy, cooperation and compliance, it is only possible to hypothesize that denial of rights and entitlements might have escalated unpleasant situations in the custody area and lessened suspects' compliance with the law on their departure from it.

While police custody was mostly procedurally fair but in some areas and on occasions procedurally unfair, these practices coexisted alongside practices that were instrumental in character in which suspects were not persuaded to cooperate with the police but were forced to do so. This and the previous chapter have shown that, on occasions, the police and police staff acted in ways that were deliberately coercive and punitive, whether that was by switching off cell buzzers or denying suspects access to material goods or dissuading them of the need to speak to a legal advisor. This suggests that any attempt to measure the quality of the police custody process needs to explore the existence of coercive as well as procedurally just/unjust practices. Moreover, it implies that police officers (and possibly other criminal justice practitioners) had different philosophies of control which were used to establish order in the custody area. Some used coercion and punishment suggesting an instrumental approach to the exercise of power while others treated suspects fairly suggesting a procedurally just approach to the use of their authority. In Chapter 6, the aim is to examine whether these philosophies of control varied between police and police staff and, in Chapter 7, between the police and other criminal justice practitioners in how they established social order in the custody areas.

Notes

1 The right to silence was not explored as no data were collected at the point of arrest, which is when suspects are supposed to be 'cautioned' by the police; this is when suspects are informed that 'you have a right to remain silent, but it may harm your defence if you do not mention when questioned something which you later rely on in court'.
2 There may have been mistakes on the custody records; for example, there were two rape suspects who were supposedly not read their rights. The gravity of the offence suggests that this was implausible.
3 Sanders *et al.* (1989: 47) found that such secondary reading of suspects' rights, for example once they were sober, only took place in 20 per cent of cases.
4 There is general advice in para. 1.7 about allowing suspects access to their rights as soon as is practicable, that any delays should be justifiable and that steps should be taken to prevent unnecessary delay and, more specifically, in para. 3.6 it says that any reasons for delaying information on rights at the police station should be recorded.
5 Cape (2006: 432) says that the only part of the PACE Code of Practice C that does not apply to suspects taken to a police station as a place of safety under mental health legislation is para. 15 which relates to reviews and extension of detention: these kinds of detainees can be held for up to 72 hours to allow examination by a doctor and an approved social worker to arrange a transfer to a psychiatric institution, if it is required.
6 Indeed, these inconsistencies in the way suspects are read their rights are inevitable, unless the police were to play an audio-visual recording for suspects to watch.
7 Bottomley *et al.* (1991) found that those requesting intimation had increased from 14 per cent in 1981 to 26 per cent in 1986 and to 23 per cent in 1987. Similarly, Brown (1989) found that 18 per cent of suspects requested that someone be notified of their arrest. However, in both studies the request rate varied depending on the seriousness of the offence and the police station, as well as whether the suspect was a juvenile.
8 In relation to private prisons, Genders and Player (2007) argue that an initial period of financial leniency can be followed by companies pressuring managers to make a profit.
9 Sometimes detention did take longer if a suspect requested a legal advisor, although this could be as much to do with legal advisors as the police (Skinns, 2010).
10 In total, data from 855 cases were included in the step-wise binary logistic regression used to analyse predictors of requests for legal advice. The Hosmer Lemeshow test showed that the model was a good fit on the basis of the five police-related factors alone ($\chi^2=9.093$, $p=0.334$); this indicated that the model does not differ significantly from the observed data. The estimates of R^2 ranged from 0.111 to 0.150, which is the proportion of the variance explained by the variables in the model.
11 For example, the researchers observed a 17-year-old female being denied access to legal advice when she had been taken to the police station as a place of safety under mental health legislation. This incident was described in the section above on 'informing suspects of their rights at the police station'.

12 That arrest is used as a start rather than an end-point to the police investigation is controversial because, for example, arrest can be used to quash lawful public protest (e.g. Gearty, 2007: 102).

13 In theory, the recording of interviews since 1991 reduces the likelihood that informal conversations take place. However, in practice, informal interviews may simply take place immediately before the recording commences; indeed this happened in 10–31 per cent of cases (Brown *et al.*, 1992; Moston and Stephenson, 1993, cited in Royal Commission on Criminal Justice, 1993; McConville and Hodgson, 1993). Hence the Royal Commission on Criminal Justice (1993) recommended that revisions should be made to the PACE Codes of Practice to discourage these practices and to allow suspects to comment on the nature of any such discussions at the start of the tape-recorded interview.

Chapter 6

Plural policing and the police custody process

Having mostly focused thus far on suspects' experiences of the custody block and their access to their rights and entitlements, the book now begins to explore the experiences of those who work in police custody areas. In this chapter, the emphasis is on the experiences of police and police staff and their impact on suspects, while in Chapter 7 the focus is on the other practitioners who work in the custody area who were described in Chapter 1, that is legal advisors, doctors, appropriate adults and drug workers.

The purpose of this chapter is to outline the findings from the present study about plural policing and police custody while also comparing and contrasting them to some of the existing research on workforce modernization and the police. In so doing, the aim is to explore whether the strategies of control used to maintain social order in the custody area varied between police and police staff. First, I conceptualize the meaning of plural policing, situating it within a discussion of why workforce modernization has arisen. Second, I examine again the roles and responsibilities of police officers relative to police staff, as well as assessing their power to use force and its implications. Third, I explore staffing and line management arrangements, pointing to difficulties with training and conditions of service. Fourth, I explore police–police staff relationships, examining whether they acted and felt as if they were part of a team. Fifth, I examine suspect experiences of police staff compared to the police. Finally, I consider the implications of plural policing in police custody areas for police accountability.

Plural policing in England and Wales

Prior to 1829, much police work was done by private individuals and organizations, although the state played a role too. Dixon (1997: 50–1) notes that the village constable in the early Middle Ages partly reflected the context of self-governing, responsible local communities. However, they were also concerned with mediating between the norms of village communities and the central state's attempts to impose new standards of moral and social discipline. From the eighteenth century, they performed both administrative duties (e.g. conducting driving tests and licensing butchers) as well as crime prevention duties and order maintenance.

The modern police, however, are largely regarded as having been born in 1829 with the Metropolitan Police, whose influence slowly spread throughout the regions, culminating in the County and Borough Police Act 1856. However, the distinction between the old and the new police was not clear-cut and indeed there was some continuity between policing arrangements prior to 1829 and developments afterwards. Rather than the Metropolitan Police Service being a completely new development, they professionalized and standardized existing developments in policing. For example, the formalization of patrols and the use of paid officers occurred over the course of the eighteenth century in London (Elmsley, 1991: 19–22). Similarly, village constables were being paid before 1829 (Dixon 1997: 53–4). The practice of the police charging individuals, companies and public bodies for services rendered is not new either. Before and after 1829, 'additional constables' were appointed to police private spaces such as theatres and casinos, as well as large industrial companies during industrial disputes, and they were requested and paid for by these private bodies (Williams, 2008). Indeed, this practice of the police charging for their services continued until the 1950s and it was only, temporarily, from the 1950s to the 1970s that scepticism arose and less use was made of 'additional constables'. This scepticism only lasted until the Court of Appeal ruling in 1987 in the *Harris* v. *Sheffield United* case, which enabled the police to charge Sheffield United for the policing of football games (cited in Williams, 2008).

While there has been continuity and discontinuity in terms of the role of the police in policing, it is possible to argue that with the 'birth' of the Metropolitan Police, policing became accepted by the public as being more firmly located within the state and non-state or private forms of policing were perceived to occupy a less significant role. However, in the late twentieth century, there were attempts to reverse this tendency, with the state taking a less prominent role next to other providers in a complex, fragmented and differentiated patchwork of policing (Crawford, 2008). Indeed, this is what is meant by terms such as the mixed economy of policing, plural policing, the extended police family, security partnerships and policing networks. As Jones and Newburn note, 'policing is now authorized and delivered by diverse networks of commercial bodies, voluntary and community groups, individual citizens, national and local governmental regulatory agencies, as well as the public police' (Jones and Newburn, 2006a: 1).

On the one hand, policing is delivered by Home Office-sponsored policing agencies. There are 43 police services in England and Wales, as well as one centralized service provider, the Serious and Organized Crime Agency. On the other hand there is growing civilianization of administrative tasks and police core functions, as well as privatization of police functions at the margins.

Administrative tasks not requiring the training and legal powers of police officers were 'hived off' to civilians during the 1980s and 1990s (Jones and Newburn, 2006b). In particular, there was a significant drive during the 1980s in the civilianization of functions such as financial management, legal services, personnel, research and analysis and forensic services, with some civilians being employed at senior levels equivalent to chief constables (Jones *et al.*, 1994, cited in Jones and Newburn, 2002). More recently, 'core police functions' such as patrol work have also been civilianized through the creation of non-warranted police community support officers (who do not have powers of arrest). By September 2009, there were a total of 144,833 full-time equivalent police officers, as well as 80,322 civilian staff (performing administrative roles), 16,814 PCSOs and 3,064 designated civilian staff (dealing with investigation, detention and escorting suspects) (Sigurdsson and Mulchandani, 2010). Since September 2008, increases in the overall police workforce have been greatest for police staff, PCSOs and designated officers, with these civilians now making up 41 per cent of the workforce and police officers making up the other 59 per cent. This recent civilianization has been partly enabled by the Police Reform Act 2002, which introduced PCSOs and enabled civilians employed by the police (known as police staff) to be given 'designated powers', e.g. to use force. These powers are decided by chief officers in each police service.

In addition to civilianization, there is also a degree of privatization of policing through the contracting out of police functions. As yet, there has been no firm establishment of purchaser–provider splits or any significant threat of exposing the police to competition from the private sector, although this is beginning to happen at the margins of police functions (Hough, 2007). For instance, there has been a return to some marketization of police services with the police being allowed to charge for special services such as the policing of football matches. The Police and Magistrates' Court Act 1994 also allowed the police to charge more generally for goods and services, and the contracting out of police officer time. Together, the growth of civilianization and the contracting out of police functions are referred to as workforce modernization.

Policing is also carried out by the commercial sector.[1] It is estimated by Jones and Newburn (2006b) that, in 2004, there were 146,000 private security personnel in the UK, making the commercial sector similar in size to other European countries but smaller than in the USA, Canada, Australia and South Africa. Commercial security has three main functions: staffed services (e.g. security guards, door staff on pubs/clubs); the installation and monitoring of security equipment; and private investigation services (Crawford, 2008). In addition to the policing conducted by the police/police staff and by the commercial sector, there are other forms of policing performed by other policing bodies, which Crawford (2008) classifies as: specialist policing bodies (e.g. intelligence services such as MI5 and MI6); regulatory authorities (e.g. the Waterways Agency); municipal policing carried out by local government (e.g. neighbourhood wardens and housing officers).

In relation to police custody, as with other areas of policing, civilianization has given way to privatization. Since the 1980s, there has been a growing number of civilians employed to work within custody areas, who are known as 'police staff'. Police staff are non-warranted civilians employed by the police and who work in police roles. In police custody areas, civilians are employed by the police as custody assistants and investigators (who help collect evidence for police investigations). HMIC (2004) found that in the police services employing civilian custody assistants and investigators, approximately half had been given designated powers appropriate to their role. HMIC were not able to quantify the composition of police staff acting as custody assistants and investigators, but they estimated that a significant proportion of investigators were retired police officers contracted on an hourly or daily basis, whereas there was greater involvement of the private sector in providing detention officers.

An important dimension of the privatization of the police custody process is the growing use of public finance initiatives (PFIs) which are partnerships between the public and private sector. Indeed, one of the sites in the research, Sunnyside, was a PFI site. PFIs involve a competitive tendering process in which the successful bidder is given a contract in which the private sector designs, builds, finances and often operates a facility throughout the life of the contract (usually for 25 years or more), while the state pays an annual fee for using it. The nature of PFI complicates the sale category, as the public sector does not simply own the PFI asset, rather they pay to use it and once the contract has expired ownership reverts to whoever is said to own it in the contract and this is not necessarily the public sector (Bochum, 2002: 2, cited in Johnston *et al.*, 2008). Hence Johnston *et al.* (2008) describe it as an 'elegant piece of hire purchase' (p. 227).

PFIs have been used most in the area of public transport at a cost of £22 billion (Johnston *et al.*, 2008). As of March 2006, however, the Home Office were committed to 42 projects costing £1.2 billion, and of these 23 were police-related, most being directed at ancillary functions such as the provision of new buildings and facilities management services rather than core services. In particular, three of these 23 projects related to police custody facilities (Buttons *et al.*, 2007). In the past, the police would have had to finance such projects through the Capital Building Projects fund provided by the Home Office, through which they were required to save up and ring-fence funds for projects. Under PFI they can now fund such projects in less time with the help of the private sector (Button *et al.*, 2007). Nonetheless, Johnston *et al.* (2008) show that PFIs place private security companies in a powerful position. For example, they found that the costly nature of the bidding process means that only a limited number of companies can effectively make a bid, which means in turn that competition between bidders is illusory. Public bodies are also inexperienced in the bidding process, resulting in them depending on the company for guidance about how to proceed (with a lack of guidance from government). However, PFIs may be relegated to being a thing of the past given that they have met with such structural, cultural and ideological barriers, but more importantly, in April 2004, the code of practice used for regulating borrowing by public authorities was amended, meaning that they can now borrow what they can afford for capital projects (e.g. new buildings), rather than having to save up and ring-fence the money (Button *et al.*, 2007). This means that public bodies will still be borrowing large sums of money, albeit from a different source.

Workforce modernization begs the question why? The answer to this question is complex. Jones and Newburn (2006a) offer two relevant explanations. First, constraints on public expenditure, in the face of growing demand, have meant that gaps have had to be filled by other policing providers and that there has been a deliberate transfer of functions from the public to the private sector.[2] In relation to police custody, workforce modernization has been partly connected to money. As argued in Chapter 1, police staff are viewed as a more cost-effective option because they supposedly free up the time of experienced staff to be redeployed on front-line duties and because police staff, in theory, cost less. However, it remains to be seen whether privatization will reap the anticipated benefits, particularly as the privatization of prisons has not. While it is difficult to compare public and private prisons (e.g. because they differ in their function, age, design and security), it is unlikely that privatization alleviates financial burdens on the state, for example because of the hidden costs of monitoring contracts with private companies (e.g. Padfield, 2006), and if it does, those savings are likely to be in the short term rather than the long term (e.g. Harding, 2001). Moreover, perhaps politicians are privately ambivalent about whether workforce modernization saves money. Johnston *et al.* (2008) argue, in relation to PFIs, that the point is not that financial gains are made in the short term, rather that the long-term cost of modernization is kept off the balance sheet until after the politicians implementing the changes have departed, for example when the police have to buy back a facility from the company contracted to run or manage it on their behalf.

Second, Jones and Newburn (2006a) argue that workforce modernization is explained by the shift to late modern society with its emphasis on neo-liberal politics, which makes privatization seem like an attractive option because it limits public expenditure. 'Ontological insecurity' and an emphasis on risk also mean that the public both demands more visible signs of being secure, yet is also frightened by these symbols in a self-perpetuating process.

As argued in Chapter 1, the civilianization and privatization of staff in custody areas are connected to this wider socio-political context. Concerns have long been expressed about the cost-effectiveness of the police, but Jones and Newburn (2002) argue that they are currently subject to a new variant of managerialism concerned with purchaser–provider, quasi-contractual arrangements, which are in turn connected to the rise of 'advanced liberalism' (Rose, 2000) and in particular the importance attached to free-market principles. In this context there are also ideological gains to be made from workforce modernization, which include short-term gains for government in appearing prudent in how public services are delivered and in appearing to hold underperforming areas of the public sector to account by introducing competitive tendering processes (Johnston *et al.*, 2008).

The power to use force and other roles and responsibilities

Figures 6.1 and 6.2 summarize the working relationships between police and police staff in the custody areas. As explained in Chapter 1, in Gormiston, jailors were police constables who were employed to look after the welfare of suspects in the cells, perform cell checks and accompany suspects to/from the cells. Designated Detention Officers (DDOs) were employed to collect biometric data, which included photographing, fingerprinting, drug-testing and the taking of DNA. Custody officers were police sergeants. They authorized detention, read rights and booked in suspects, and made decisions about whether to contact the doctor and/or appropriate adults. Custody officers line-managed the jailors and DDOs, and the custody officers were line-managed by the inspector. The latter also dealt with matters such as detention reviews but otherwise was not physically present in the custody area.

As Figure 6.2 shows, role and responsibilities and line management were more complex in Sunnyside. Custody administrators answered the phone and dealt with administrative matters. They were employed by Security Ltd. They supported the custody assistants who looked after the

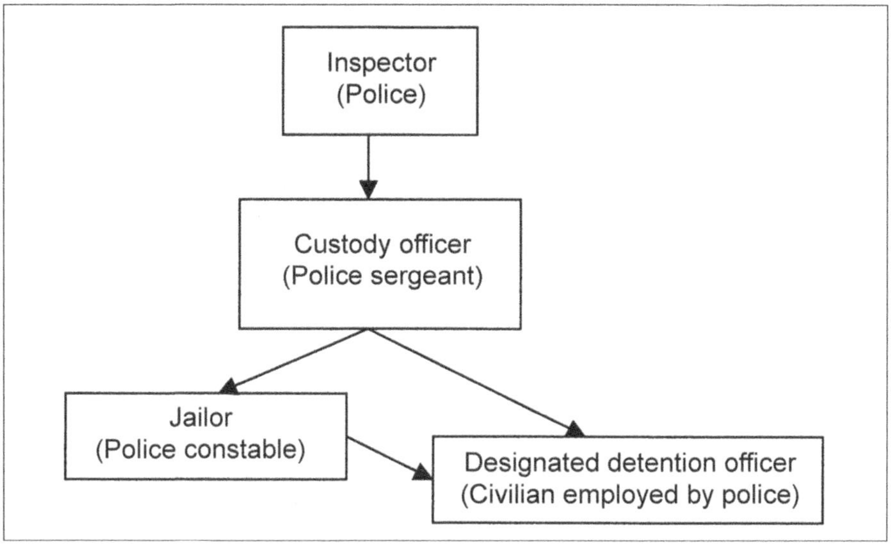

Figure 6.1 Roles in Gormiston

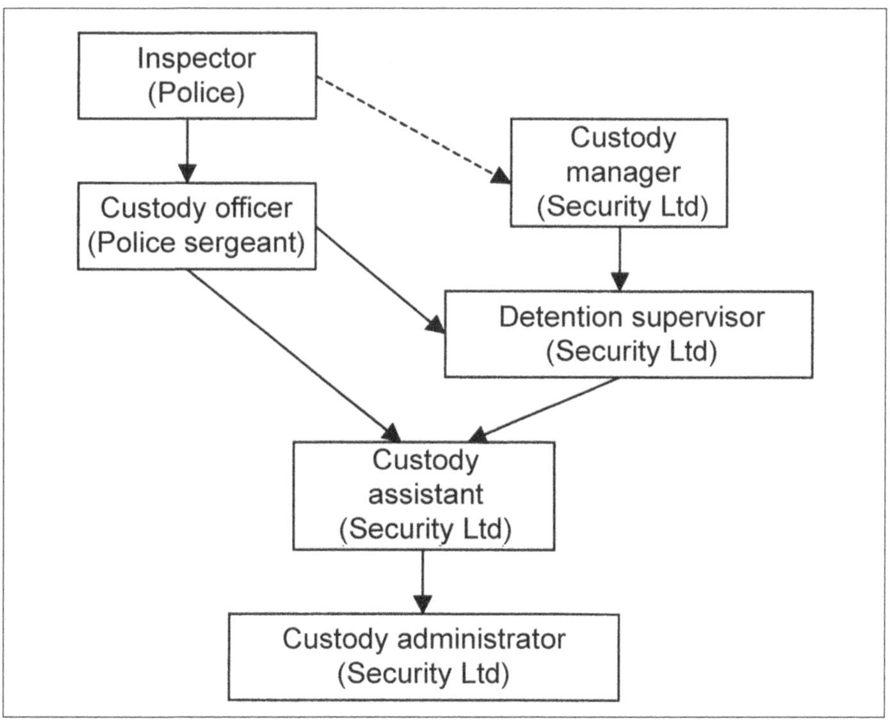

Figure 6.2 Roles in Sunnyside

welfare of the suspects, performed cell checks and accompanied them to/from cells as well as taking biometric data. They were employed by Security Ltd. The detention supervisor was a new role created to provide career progression for custody assistants. They booked in suspects but could not authorize the detention of suspects or read them their rights. This had to be done by a custody officer. As described in Chapter 1, this authorization process was sometimes cursory, involving only a nod from the sergeant without them thoroughly checking, as they should, whether someone's detention was legitimate, or sometimes it was not done at all. Custody officers were police sergeants. They authorized detention, read rights and booked in suspects, and they made decisions about whether to contact the doctor and/or appropriate adults. Inspectors line-managed the sergeants, while the Security Ltd custody manager line-managed the private police staff. None of the private police staff had designated powers, although they could carry out most duties, but had to seek the consent of the suspect first; however, in some circumstances consent may not have been sought, particularly when it was difficult to do so, for example for mentally ill suspects. If the private police staff used force, it had to be while assisting a police officer.

Roles and responsibilities were more clearly delineated in Sunnyside than in Gormiston, but there was also evidence of the blurring of roles and responsibilities in both sites, as discussed in Chapter 2. In Gormiston there was an overlap between the jailors and DDOs and, in Sunnyside, there was an overlap between the detention supervisors and the custody officers, leading to the conclusion that 'mission creep', (where staff take on additional roles) and 'power creep' (where staff take on additional powers) had occurred after the civilianization and privatization of the police custody process. This blurring may lead to confusion among the suspects about what to legitimately expect from staff in the custody area. Some suspects noticed the police staff (e.g. SND2, 3, 4 and 9 or GMD 3, 6, 7, 8, 9, 11, 13), but some did not (e.g. SND7 and GMD4) and some seemed unsure (e.g. GMD2 and GMD4). This was not helped by the fact that police staff in Sunnyside, in particular, wore a similar uniform to the police.[3]

It seems that power creep and mission creep arise when there are uncertainties about roles and responsibilities. This creates a vacuum allowing staff to take on new tasks and once such behaviour takes root it is not challenged. For example, Button and John (2002) found that the police engaged in a form of mission creep in the policing of public protests when under-sheriffs (who were normally solicitors working in private practices and appointed by the high sheriff), who had legal and operational responsibility for the removal of protestors from private land, did not have relevant experience or training. Consequently, they turned to the police for advice particularly during the planning stages, and sometimes the police had to take the initiative during the removal of protestors and when it came to dealing with the media.

In the present research, there was creep in the way police staff used force. In neither site were police staff designated with the power to use force. Indeed, some did not want the additional responsibilities that came with being given a baton or pepper spray, preferring to talk their way out of difficult situations (e.g. SNS7). Similarly, PCSOs have been regarded as reliant on policing by consent, drawing on personal skills in the absence of having formal coercive powers, albeit that they would use these coercive powers if they had them (Crawford *et al.*, 2005: 42–3). In the present research police staff did use force, though they were allowed to use it either in self-defence or when assisting police colleagues. In addition, however, police staff reportedly felt pressured to use force when they were not supposed to, for example if a suspect was trying to escape from a cell, meaning that some had in fact used force when they were not permitted to do so. It is possible to see how these practices become a regular occurrence: the habit of using force in unpermitted circumstances sets a precedent, making its use, eventually, an official part of staff powers and responsibilities. Indeed, one police officer in Sunnyside hoped that a change of chief constable would enable him to seek designated powers for police staff to use force.

Another explanation for the creep in the use of force by police staff is that it reflects a shift in the way that the police and others view this power. Johnston and Shearing (2003: 54) argue that coercion, such as capital punishment, used to provide a visible and symbolic deterrent and righting of wrongs, but now has taken on a neutral and instrumental character simply being used to terminate a life. They argue that this routinized and efficient administration of coercion reflects a new mentality and one that has affected the way that the police and prison staff use coercion. Similarly, Reiner (2010: 101–3) argues that the police no longer use a strategy of minimal force – evidenced by the militarization of policing and growth in the excessive use of force – and that there is a pragmatic acceptance of tougher policing tactics in the belief that the risk of mistakes and malpractice are necessitated by the problems the police face. This view of force as a 'necessary evil' helps explain the automatic, unquestioning and pragmatic acceptance of the transference in the use of force, at least in practice, from the police to police staff.

There are three potentially negative consequences of police staff taking on the power to use force for which they were not authorized and were not trained. First, it places staff and suspects at risk, as there are recognized unarmed defence practices which can help to protect both suspects and the police. For example, Button (2003) found that private security staff with limited training on how to deal with disorder experienced verbal abuse, threats of violence and physical attacks, ranging from punches, kicks and even an attempted hit and run. Forty per cent had been assaulted in the year before the research as a result of their job. Similarly, Johnston (2007) found that while the police, more than PCSOs, believed that PCSOs had been adequately supported when they were introduced, they also pointed to shortcomings in safety training and equipment which may have resulted in injuries to PCSOs. In police custody, suspects are more vulnerable, but also more likely to be in need of restraint than the general population, given the high levels of drug and alcohol problems and mental illness, making it all the more crucial to know when it is necessary to restrain them and how to restrain them appropriately, if it is necessary at all.

Second, without training, there is scope for staff to abuse these unofficial powers. Indeed, staff may not have been selected with a view to them being able to use force, other than in a supporting capacity. Button and John (2002) found some unscrupulous practices used by private security staff appointed to assist under-sheriffs involved in the policing and eviction of protestors on private property. Even though these private security officers were authorized to use force, they had little training on how to restrain people, and some appeared to actively want to engage in a fight. Indeed, managers were found to encourage staff to hit protestors in such a way that they could not be caught.

Third, police staff are likely to lack accountability for their actions, a matter discussed later in the chapter.

This tension between rhetoric and practice has another implication which is connected to the role of the police in policing. By officially denying police staff the power to use force, the police maintained an illusion that the power to use force rested solely with them. On this rhetorical level, therefore, Bittner's (1970: 122) view that only the police have a monopoly over the use of force remains true. This may have ideological benefits in a situation in which police monopoly over policing is slipping through their fingers as a result of the mixed economy of policing.

However, based on what happened in practice – that is, the finding that police staff used force in situations when they did not have the power to do so – challenges Bittner's understanding of police coercion. In an interview with Jean-Paul Brodeur, Bittner argues that in situations where both the public and private sector are involved in policing, as was the case in Sunnyside, the police can simply deputize matters to the private police. He says, '[p]rivate police forces to the extent to which they are empowered to use force are told the terms under which they operate' (Brodeur, 2007: 118–19). This may be true, but as with any kind of rule it does not mean that it is followed in practice. The present research showed that, in theory, police staff were deputized by the police in relation to the use of force, thus the police symbolically retained their monopoly over the use of force, but in practice police staff acted in ways which made them nearly an equal to the police. For example, a custody assistant commented that when using force, rank was forgotten and that police officers and police staff became equally respected (SNPO3).

Finally, it is worth noting only briefly here that in spite of the confusion about roles played by the police and police staff, indicated by power creep and mission creep, when interviewees were asked about where, ultimately, the responsibility lay for the care and fair treatment of suspects, most regarded responsibility as resting with the custody officer. This was true for most types of research participant including the police staff. In both sites, police staff said that while everyone, themselves included, played a part in caring for and fairly treating suspects, the ultimate responsibility rested with the custody officers. This resonates with Button *et al.*'s (2007) assessment of PFIs in which they argue that the balance of financial risk remains with the police not the private company and that, even if a private company were obliged to pay a fine for breaching their contract with the police, the suspect would sue the police authority or the police not the private company for any failures or mistreatment. This is a matter that I return to in Chapter 7. It also reflects the role of the custody officer in PACE.

Plural policing and staffing arrangements

It may have also been that custody officers were regarded as being ultimately responsible for suspects, in part because police staff, particularly private police staff, had less training, which was reportedly of a poorer quality than that of the police. In relation to PCSOs, Johnston (2007) found that they undertook only three weeks of formal training, which was not assessed, before being given further training on the job. A team of independent consultants that assessed this training found that it was inadequate because it was too short, because the competence of attendees was not assessed at the end of it and because parts of the training (e.g. on human rights and diversity) was too theoretical rather than practical. Moreover, he argues that the shortness of the training meant that it had failed to inculcate in police community officers values that were appropriate to a disciplined organization and consequently they routinely turned up late, failed to call in sick and failed to wear appropriate uniforms. However, Merritt (2009) argues that more recently PCSO recruits have six weeks of classroom training followed by a year-long probationary period. While this is an improvement, it is still relatively little compared to the training for police constables who have a two-year probationary period underpinned by ongoing classroom training.

In the present research private police staff, in particular, also identified shortcomings in their training. The private police staff had two weeks of training compared to the seven weeks given to public police staff. Consequently private police staff expressed dissatisfaction with their training (e.g. their medical training and training on how to use force) with operational staff reporting that they initially felt ill-prepared to do their jobs effectively, as this custody assistant explained:

> Yes, use of force, I had two days, and then if you're going on shift the next day for the first time . . . there are tried and tested methods that are accepted that mean you can restrain a detainee without getting into trouble. However, having two days of it, not enough really . . . their [Security Ltd] training methods are crap. When you do your fingerprints, I was shown on their machine once, and then I went live, and you learn live, you're dealing with live prints, that if you cock up could, like, damage the outcome of a case. (SNS4)

He said that he learned the most while 'on the job' and from colleagues familiar with the procedures in the custody block in which he worked and that he had felt thrown in at the deep end. This sentiment was also echoed by another custody assistant, SNS7, and a detention supervisor, SNS1, who had been trained some time ago. Security Ltd managers, however, felt that the training given to operational staff was sufficient to do the job.

In addition to more training, the public police staff in Gormiston were paid significantly more for doing very similar work to their counterparts in Sunnyside although less than police officers. The private police staff in Sunnyside would have been paid approximately £7.41 per hour for a 35-hour week, based on information available on Security Ltd's website (as of June 2008), which amounts to £12,449 per annum based on 20 days' leave. However, according to inspector GMS5, DDOs in Gormiston were paid around £21,000 per annum, which was slightly less than a PCSO.[4] Even allowing for a London weighting, this meant that public police staff in Gormiston were paid more than private police staff in Sunnyside. Public police staff also had better conditions of service than the private police staff, for example they were entitled to paid sick leave.

By contrast there were fewer opportunities for career progression in Gormiston than in Sunnyside. In Sunnyside, on the one hand, staff could move from being a custody assistant to being a detention supervisor. The latter was responsible for the custody assistants when the custody manager had gone home for the day, as he only worked during office hours. A Security Ltd manager said that the role of 'detention supervisor was introduced just over two years ago, so we have a natural progression now from custody assistant to detention supervisor' (SNS5). On the other hand, staff could also move to other departments, albeit this might be more a sideways than an upwards move. For example, during participant observation one of the private police staff moved to a new post in the 'identity unit' where civilians worked conducting identity parades. Even so, this was not enough for some Security Ltd employees who felt frustrated that they could not move up to management level. During SNPO4, one detention supervisor who used to be a custody assistant said that he was bored and frustrated with his job because he wanted more management responsibility which was not available. Consequently, he was actively looking for alternative employment.

In Gormiston, once someone was a DDO, there were few other civilian options available to them. A doctor, GMS2, described the role as a 'dead-end' and stressful job with poor pay and conditions, and wondered whether it would be better for police staff to have the option of rotating between being a DDO, PCSO and working as a civilian investigator so that there was more variety. This is in marked contrast to the stated aims of workforce modernization outlined by HMIC (2004) which were to support each of the branches in the extended police family with training and opportunities for career progression.

Not surprisingly, police staff were sometimes viewed as 'frustrated police officers', who were using their role in the custody area as a 'stepping stone' into the police, an approach which had worked for some (SNS6). Similarly, GMS4, a DDO, said that he was in a 'predicament' in terms of progressing with his career and that he was considering his options, which included joining the police or working as a civilian intelligence analyst. This view was further supported by inspector GMS5, who said that there were two sorts of DDOs. There were those who were happy with their role and would remain in it and there were those who saw it as a means of joining the police. He said that, in the past, potential new recruits who were not regarded as ready to be a police officer became special constables, but now they opted to be a DDO or a PCSO. In his survey of PCSOs in London, Johnston (2007) similarly found that the majority of them had taken the role in order to join the police.

In both sites, police staff were permanently based in the custody area, which could be a difficult working environment as described in Chapters 3 and 4. They spent their entire shift in pressured roles with poor pay and conditions, dealing with suspects with multiple and potentially life-threatening problems, doing shift work in custody areas that were either poorly ventilated and ill-lit, as was the case in Gormiston, or where essential building repairs were reportedly not carried out, as in Sunnyside. They had few options for career progression in either site. In Sunnyside, staff could move from being a custody assistant to being a detention supervisor and a few from both areas at least had the possibility of becoming appointed as police officers.

Together, these conditions reportedly contributed to staff turnover among public and private police staff, particularly in Gormiston, although no other data could be used to verify these views. Part of the pressure experienced by staff was attributable to understaffing. One Security Ltd employee regarded the understaffing as worse than when the police were running the police custody area because, unlike the police, Security Ltd were unwilling to draft in staff to cover things like maternity leave due to the cost involved (SNS7). This hinted that many of the issues above, including inadequate training, poor pay and conditions, staff shortages and higher staff turnover among Security Ltd employees, were connected to the need for the company to make a profit. Nonetheless, they still had a higher staff per suspect ratio than in Gormiston.

Police–police staff relationships

Research has found advantages and disadvantages in relationships between the police and other policing providers. On the one hand, there is evidence of growing cooperation between a range of policing providers in terms of the exchange of information and intelligence, the sharing of equipment or facilities and the undertaking of joint operations. Jones and Newburn found that '[c]ooperative relationships took a range of forms, including the following: swapping of general advice or information, specific intelligence sharing, sharing of equipment or facilities, passing over cases, joint operations, social contacts/"old boys' networks", and police response to calls from private security' (1998: 170). For example, the police and private security undertook joint operations whereby private security would carry out early investigations and collect enough evidence to build a case against a suspect and then call the police. Crawford *et al.* (2005: 17) also found, in a national survey of private security firms, that 61 per cent indicated that the level of cooperation with local police was good, but there was variation between forces and relationships were improved by private security managers having previously worked for the police.

At the same time, previous research shows that the police may resent police staff and police staff and private security staff may resent the police thereby hampering cooperative working relationships. For example, in 'Pleasure Southquay', Button (2003) found that private security guards did not welcome police involvement in incidents to the extent that one operational manager actively stood in the way of the police and was nearly arrested. Johnston (2007) found a decline in the proportion of police and PCSOs agreeing that PCSOs were accepted as part of the police team in his survey of police officers and PCSOs (conducted in December 2002 and September 2003), shortly after PCSOs were introduced into the Metropolitan Police in April 2002. He also found a decline in the percentage of those agreeing that PCSOs received support from police officer colleagues. This suggests that perhaps some respondents, particularly PCSOs, whose affirmative responses were initially high, had unrealistic expectations and that while there was some evidence of success, given the quick absorption of PCSOs into the workforce, there was still some way to go to fully integrate them into the police.

Worse still there may be competition between the police and other policing providers. For instance, Jones and Newburn (1998: 179) found little opposition to the privatization of prisoner escort, perhaps because it was a peripheral function, but this was not the case for proposals by the local authority to expand the work of the Parks Police patrol work, which were seen to encroach on the role of the police. Noaks (2000) also found competition between the police and private security firms providing residential patrols. On the part of the police, she found a reluctance to acknowledge the role of and contributions made by private police. This was partly due to a lack of regulation of private security, which meant that the police were wary of being seen to associate themselves with them. She also found that there was minimal communication and mutual suspicion.

Therefore, together, the police appear to have a complex set of 'cooperative' 'competitive' and 'coexisting' relationships with other policing providers (Jones and Newburn, 2006b: 51). Similarly, in the present research, there was a mixture of views about police–police staff integration and team work.

In Gormiston, staff suggested that there was growing integration between police and police staff, but that 'there's still a them and us thing with the police and the civilian staff, and the civilian staff aren't allowed into the Police Federation, as a union, and I know that that raises a few hackles' (GMS1). In Sunnyside, Security Ltd managers emphasized that integration between the police and police staff had occurred and was evidenced by staff socializing and going on training together, so that things were 'all kept as one' (SNS6). However, some of the operational police staff and police officers pointed to the fact that the police and police staff worked for different companies and had different goals, albeit probably compatible goals (SNS1).

In terms of teamwork, in Gormiston, the DDOs and the police did not always describe the police and police staff as a team. A DDO, GMS3, saw himself as part of the team with whom he worked; for example, he went out for drinks with them after work. However, he also felt separate from them as he did not go out with the team on patrol. The limited amount of integration of police and police staff into a team was also outlined by a custody officer, GMS10, who did not think that DDOs were 'integrated at all' into the police teams because the DDOs only worked in custody and were not involved in the social life of the team(s) or were fully cognizant of the police officers with whom they worked.

Yet, during observation, it was apparent that the DDOs made a significant contribution to the workload, going beyond the role that they were appointed to do (which was to perform drug tests) and outperforming the police constable jailors who were newer to and less knowledgeable about the job. Their willingness to 'muck in' suggests a kind of team spirit which was perhaps not fully recognized by the police.

Interviewees in Sunnyside, however, were more divided about whether the police and police staff were a team and it did not seem to matter whether the interviewees were police or police staff. On the one hand, there were those who thought that Security Ltd and the police worked as part of a team. In SNPO5, a custody assistant said that they worked as part of a team and that this was shown by custody officers 'having a word' with suspects who behaved badly towards the police staff. One of these custody officers, SNS3, later said in interview that he would fill in for Security Ltd staff if they were too busy by taking suspects to the cells. He argued that this was quicker than waiting for Security Ltd to do it and he would do it even though he was not technically supposed to and even though Security Ltd might be fined for not performing their allotted duties. Similarly, while SNS1 and SNS4, who were Security Ltd employees, seemed ambivalent about whether they worked as a team with the police, they erred on the side of saying that there was a team spirit in that the police and police staff 'covered each others backs' when it came to using force.

On the other hand, an inspector, SNS13, said that the police and Security Ltd staff were separate as a result of their differing roles and powers, and custody officers, such as SNS3, said that the differences between him and the police became apparent at social events when there would be separate groups of Security Ltd and police employees. There were others who also thought that the police and Security Ltd formed two separate teams. An appropriate adult, SNS15, said that there was a clear division between the two and that this was counterproductive for suspects, implying that they may find it confusing. A legal advisor (SNS11) and a custody assistant (SNS7) also felt that there had been more of a team spirit in the old and more intimate custody area, in which the sergeants used to routinely 'help out' the police staff. This was compared with the new custody area where the custody officers were regarded as more likely 'to shout a bit more', implying that the police were deputizing the Security Ltd staff rather than the custody area being given over to Security Ltd.

Taken together, it seemed that in Gormiston staff acted as a team but did not describe themselves as such, whereas in Sunnyside staff described themselves as a team but did not behave as such. This may have been a consequence of the nature of the custody areas: Gormiston was a smaller custody area with only one or two police staff per shift meaning that they had to integrate with the police rather than vice versa.

Plural policing also raises some interesting questions about police culture. While there has been little research on how *civilian police staff* engage with police cultures, that is, whether they assimilated into them, adapted to them or resisted them, Johnston (2007) argues that PCSOs failed to understand, through their training, how a disciplined organization like the police works. Although Johnston (2007) does not discuss this possibility, this seems to suggest that police staff did not fit readily into the police occupational cultures. By resisting police cultures, police staff may contribute to police reform, albeit that this may be of greatest significance for lower-ranking police officers with whom police staff regularly engage.

Nevertheless, the opportunities for reforming the police may be hampered by hierarchy. As one inspector, SNS8, explained, the police only accepted civilianization because police staff were employed to do menial jobs:

> [P]olice officers don't like a member of the public coming in and just putting on a similar uniform and doing a job perceived to be almost the same. That's a cultural thing. But I think it depends which job, and if you say to somebody, we can get you out of the cell block by employing civilians to feed the prisoners, and water them, DNA, fingerprint, photograph and other stuff, how do you feel about that, I think most of them would say, yes. (SNS8)

Police officers also questioned the authority of the police staff, talking down to them or 'pulling rank' on them. One of the detention supervisors in SNPO1 said that he occasionally had problems with officers talking down to him or being overly forceful, but that this was not a frequent occurrence and tended to be from police officers he did not know and from 'the old-school' officers who had a number of years' service in the police. By contrast, SNS7, a custody assistant, said that it was the new recruits that tended to think they were better than him because they had a 'uniform with numbers on it'.

In Gormiston, GMS13, a custody officer, also noted that it was the newly recruited police constables that tried to pull rank on the DDOs. He said '[t]here has been some problems with PCs who think, because you're a DDO you can't tell me my job, but that's usually easily fixed'. Similarly, a DDO noted that some people have an 'aura of power' and that sometimes the jailors tried to pull rank, but generally in the custody area he knew more about the process than the jailors and that consequently the PCs were normally asking him for things, rather than it being the other way round (GMS3). Furthermore, in GMSPO2 one of the researchers observed some banter between the custody officer and the DDO in which the custody officer said that the DDO was their tea-maker to which the DDO responded that 'they wouldn't talk to me like that if I were a white shirt', referring to the fact that the police wore white shirts while the DDO wore blue.

While those working in the custody areas downplayed this aspect of the police–police staff relationship and/or made light of it, it had serious consequences, not least because of the growing responsibilities of police staff in the custody area. An appropriate adult, SNS15, wondered whether some of the mistakes that were made about contacting appropriate adults were due to the police staff not being old enough or 'robust enough to ask questions of the police'. He said:

> I really want to say that I think the civilian custody staff do a great job as far as I can, but I just think they're hampered by that hierarchy

> . . . they just can't make some decisions that perhaps need to be made quickly, they can't challenge some of the things which are being asked of them.

While this was done in a jocular manner, at times the consequences could be serious in that it hampered the ability of police staff to do their job effectively and also meant that they did not or could not challenge unacceptable police practices. This suggests that the custody block remained police territory in which police staff are the deputies, not the equals of the police.

Plural policing and suspects

In the interviews, suspects said that they liked police staff more than the police and this was for a variety of reasons. Suspects reasoned that they were able to establish a better rapport with police staff and communicate better with people that were more compassionate and polite to them. The permanence of police staff (unlike police officers) in the custody area also meant that suspects who were regularly detained recognized some of the police staff and knew them by name. By contrast, suspects were not so charitable in their assessment of the police. One suspect said that the police should not look after suspects in the cells because they lacked compassion and because having a caring attitude did not fit with their objective of catching and locking up criminals. Others complained about the attitude of the police, who were described as being 'cocky', 'arrogant' or 'having big heads'. They also complained about being spoken to impolitely by the police. Similarly, while cell buzzers were reportedly switched off and suspects' requests were not met as described in Chapter 3, suspects generally felt that police staff were more responsive to their needs than the police.

This suspect explained why he preferred the DDOs:

> [I]f I ask them [the police staff] for a cup of tea, I get it there and then, if I ask a police officer, I'm not saying all of them are like that, but the majority of them it's, oh we're too busy . . . and you're waiting, you're on the bell again, again, again, but right them two fellas [the police staff], they bring me my tea all the time because they know me quite well in there . . . Yes, and I'm always pleasant, I don't kick police cell doors, and abuse them, and all that, I don't do that stuff, you know, but really, yes, they're a lot better I would say, definitely. (GMD4)

Similarly for SND2, aside from the rapport he had with the Security Ltd staff, he also liked them because 'they bring you your food, and if you ring the intercom they'll bring you a hot chocolate, or something, you know, if you ask a police officer that and he'll probably tell you to jog on . . . they're there to help you'.

Suspects also liked the fact that the police staff were 'more like them', which suggests that the power relationship between them was less one-sided. This lessening of the power differential is something that a colleague and I have noted in relation to research on snitching. We argue that while some young people looked down on PCSOs because they lacked the powers and authority of the police, they also felt that they could communicate more effectively with them because they had a regular relationship with them and saw them as being more like them (Clayman and Skinns, 2011). Similarly, in the present research, this suspect reported that he liked the police staff in the custody area because they were more like him, as he explained:

> I feel they do a better job than the police without a doubt . . . they're sort of like us . . . they're just wearing a uniform, whereas the police . . . they do it for the government, they're working for the government, they're higher than us. But them, they're sort of like us. (SND2)

Similarly, two other suspects said that the Security Ltd staff were easier to talk to and did not look down on them and 'treated them like an equal', did not judge them, as well as viewing them as innocent and 'normal'. However, an alternative interpretation of this relationship is that the police staff lacked the authority of the police. Certainly, Liebling (2006) has reached similar conclusions in her research on public/private prisons. She found that prison officers in privately run establishments lacked the authority of their public counterparts (e.g. to carry out searches of their cells), meaning that prisoners feel more fairly treated but less safe. Similarly, Zander (2005) expresses concern that civilian custody officers would be unlikely to command the same respect and authority as police officers.

A number of research participants agreed that police staff were like a neutral buffer who were less threatening than the police because of their more limited powers. Furthermore, it was also the case that the police staff deliberately cast themselves in a different role to the police in order to act as a neutral buffer and because they believed that this role could be useful in diffusing difficult situations. That is, police staff mediated in the sometimes antagonistic relationship between the police and suspect, as this Security Ltd employee explained:

> [B]ecause they know it's Security Ltd staff that are looking after them, it's civilian staff that are looking after them in the cell, it's not a police officer, because police officers, if they're fighting with a detainee, they've got the red mist and the best thing is to get those officers out of the cell, because they're the ones that are scrapping and fighting

> with them, and probably sprayed them, and whatever, out on the street, so they're adrenalin pumping like mad, and really you want them out of the situation to try and calm the situation down, and the Security Ltd staff are probably the ones doing that . . . they will be shouting and swearing at us, and we say, hang on, we're not police officers, and then they'll see, oh no, you're the ones that feed and water us, and very rarely do our staff get assaulted. (SNS6)

Alternatively, this might be seen as the police staff acting in a disingenuous manner to secure compliance or as them passing the buck (e.g. for delays) to the police. Moreover, police officers did not appreciate the police staff passing the blame to them. For instance, one custody officer was sceptical about what he called Security Ltd's 'distancing tactics' and about the fact that Security Ltd blamed the police for delays. He said 'I listen to them all the time on the intercom saying, it's up to the police when you're dealt with, so they are distancing themselves, and saying, I'm the custody assistant' (SNS3).

Accountability

In theory, the police are held to account through democratic, organizational and legal forms of governance (see Jones, 2008 for a review). In practice, police officers in the research pointed to the importance of PACE, for example describing it as their 'bible', while also acknowledging its limitations, such as when they were unfamiliar with amendments to it. In spite of the growing micro-management of the police (Hough, 2007; Smith, 2007b), there was little organizational accountability for police custody through performance targets, with the exception of targets for successful drug tests and biometric data collection.

However, with the introduction of police staff in the custody areas – particularly police staff employed by Security Ltd – who were found to take on new powers and new responsibilities, accountability becomes a more complex matter, making it more difficult to deduce how they might be held to account. For example, if police staff were authorized to use force then it would be reasonable to expect that line managers routinely checked on whether their performance conformed to policies as well as ensuring that their training was regularly updated. Without these powers to use force being officially authorized, then there would be no reason even to write a policy about their use of force, other than to say that they are not supposed to do it. Moreover, for private police staff and depending on the nature of the contract between the security company and the police, this could leave the police open to criticism for neglecting their duty of care towards suspects. Judging by Johnston *et al.*'s (2008) findings about PFI contracts and also by the findings discussed in the section below, it is likely that contracts between security companies and the police are likely to be stacked in favour of the private security company not the police.

Line management was potentially one accountability mechanism and a form of organizational governance, but its complexity in Sunnyside raised questions about its effectiveness. As described above, in Sunnyside, Security Ltd staff were managed by Security Ltd managers and police officers were managed by the police. Police managers and Security Ltd managers did regularly converse with each other over staffing issues, but this was not as simple as in Gormiston where police officers and police staff were simply line-managed by the police. This complexity in line management in Sunnyside was also translated into the police complaints system; there was confusion in Sunnyside about who and how staff could be disciplined for poor working practices. In Sunnyside, minor matters were dealt with by Security Ltd and more serious matters were dealt with by the police, whereas in Gormiston all matters were dealt with by the police. Moreover, it may be difficult for suspects to ascertain about whom they should complain, the police or police staff. This may be because roles and responsibilities were unclear for suspects, but also be because, in Sunnyside, the private police staff wore similar uniforms to police officers. In theory, these may be matters that are resolved in the contract between the police and the private security company.

In theory, police staff in both sites could also be held to account through the police complaints process. Regulation 30 of the Police (Complaints and Misconduct) Regulations 2004, which are statutory, suggests that police staff can be the subject of disciplinary actions. Furthermore, the Police Reform Act 2002 extended the range of people who could be subject to a complaint to include police staff employed either by the police or by another company through contracting-out arrangements (Gleeson and Grace, 2009: 10). Gleeson and Grace (2009: 11) found that in 2008/9, 91 per cent of complaints were made against the police, compared to 5 per cent against police staff, 2 per cent against PCSOs and less than 1 per cent against contracted-out staff. These data imply that complainants complain less about police staff and contracted-out staff relative to police officers. However, Gleeson and Grace (2009) do not provide the figures for police staff and contracted-out staff as a rate per thousand workers, which makes it difficult to substantiate this claim. Nor do they differentiate between police staff or contracted-out staff in police custody areas compared to other police settings so it is difficult to tell the relationship between the complaints and their location. Therefore the impact of civilianization and privatization of police custody areas on suspect complaints remains unclear.

Private police staff in police custody areas are also likely to be held to account through specifications in their contract. Harding (2001), a supporter of privatization, argues that in private prisons the state is placed in an advantageous position to hold private contractors to account by being able to carefully specify processes and targets to be met by the contractors. For example, in private prisons, contracts can detail minimum standards in relation to living conditions, facilities and regimes. Moreover, financial incentives can also be written into contracts to ensure compliance. In private prisons, the full fee is only paid when targets are met, and specific penalties are incurred for failures, particularly in sensitive areas such as if prisoners abscond.[5] In the worse case scenario, contracts can be cancelled. Furthermore, public accountability is enhanced in private prisons in the US by making contracts publicly available, including to prisoners. Moreover, as Genders (2002) notes, contractors can be shielded from the vagaries of the criminal justice process, in which overcrowding, for example, can result in incursions into the prison regime (e.g. the research budget). Under contract, budgets can be ring-fenced and therefore protected. In theory, these advantages described in relation to private prisons have a bearing on contractual arrangements in police custody areas.

Clearly, the success of contractual accountability mechanisms in part depends on strategies for monitoring compliance. In hybrid custody areas (with police and private police staff), the police can directly monitor compliance with the contract or use CCTV cameras to monitor activities after the event. Moreover, with the rolling-out of NSPIS – the electronic system used to log information that used to be recorded manually on paper records – there may be new means available to police to monitor the performance of private police staff.

However, private security companies in police custody areas, like those that run private prisons, may succumb to the financial pressures. Indeed, financial pressures may override public interest when there is conflict 'between shareholders' interests and what is in the public interest' (Genders, 2002: 299). Paradoxically, this may have unintended consequences. The necessity to make a profit may be so great that it may be an incentive for private companies to conceal malpractice or evidence that they are not meeting contractual targets. This would seriously undermine accountability. This seems likely in police custody areas, since Rose (1996) describes the number culture in the police as 'an engine of malpractice, a direct incentive to manufacture the vital cough' (cited in Genders, 2002: 300).

In addition the pressure to meet key performance indicators written into contracts through larger numbers of lower-cost police staff suggests an emphasis on the quantity rather than quality of staff. Consequently, while suspects may be processed more quickly, this does not mean they will necessarily be processed fairly and with due care. They may simply be processed in a routinized and bureaucratic fashion and this can militate against upholding due process and justice (e.g. McConville *et al*., 1994: 20). On the other hand, perhaps the police custody process is already bureaucratic and routinized. As such, as Liebling notes in relation to prisons, privatization can be an opportunity for public sector bureaucracies to improve their 'game' by learning from 'successful and disastrous experiments with privatization' (2004: 480).

Ultimately, the success of contractual accountability mechanisms in police custody areas depends on how the contract is written and whether it is tailored to an individual police service or police station. In essence, the content of the contract revolves around what constitutes a 'good' police custody area, which is likely to be contentious and difficult to define. In this respect, the tendency may be for the contract to identify aspects of the police custody process that are easy to measure (e.g. how many suspects are being processed and how quickly), rather than other factors (e.g. the number of suspects that request and receive custodial legal advice). Button *et al.* (2007) argue that in relation to PFIs it is difficult for the public sector to commit to a 25–30 year contract as it is difficult to predict future requirements. In addition, they found that contracts were restrictive and difficult to change. For example, requests for fridges, which were not originally included in one contract, were estimated to cost £13,000, reflecting the price of hiring this item for 30 years. More fundamentally, as Reiner (1993, cited in Jones, 2008) argues, market-based reforms such as the privatization of police custody facilities might 'circumvent or even undermine the traditional "political" models of accountability' which have hitherto focused on democratic, organizational and legislative mechanisms.

In the present research, in theory, contractual arrangements between the police and Security Ltd were an additional accountability mechanism in Sunnyside. The contract reportedly specified two different types of performance targets, although the contract was never seen by the researchers, perhaps because of concerns about commercial sensitivity. First, Security Ltd had targets for how long it took staff to book in suspects. Staff, such as SNS6, were proud that they had reportedly halved the booking-in time in the first month of moving to the new custody area from 35 to 18 minutes and more recently it took them, on average, five minutes.

Second, Security Ltd were paid a fixed amount of £120 per 'prisoner' rather than providing a certain number of staff in the custody area. In addition, in the contract there were reportedly fines for critical tasks such as punctuality with cell checks or with fingerprints. This was monitored through the logging of information on the computer. In SNPO1 one custody assistant kept a constant eye on the computer screen, explaining that the screen went pink when the time was approaching for the performance of a check on a suspect in the cells. Ideally, Security Ltd were meant to inspect the suspect before it turned pink but this was reportedly not always possible. Once the check was complete, the custody assistant filled in the screen to say so. If the check was not entered as having been completed before the screen went red, then Security Ltd could be fined.

In practice, however, Security Ltd were left to monitor punctuality themselves through random 'dip checks' into custody records, and there was evidence that late cell checks for instance were easily excused (e.g. if staff were busy elsewhere) and Security Ltd were not fined. Again one of the researchers observed in SNPO6 how this was possible, albeit in legitimate circumstances on this occasion:

> When I came back from visiting the cells with the custody assistant, one of the boxes had gone red on her screen and she rushed over to type in that the person had been checked. The custody assistant explained that the way round this was to type in CHS (Custody Handling System) which meant that it was a problem with the computer system that resulted in it going red, rather than that the check was late ... She also told me that they used to have regular reviews with managers about the number of times they had boxes go red in which they had to explain what had happened in each case, but this had not happened for months and she said that managers 'must be getting a bit slack'.

Similarly, in SNPO7, a custody assistant said that she was once visited by a manager at her desk and asked to explain why all her suspects had gone red on the computer. She said that they were black and then she had pressed F8 which refreshed the page. During the time that the boxes had gone red, she had been preparing breakfast for one of the suspects. The manager was satisfied with her explanation and also pleased because it saved Security Ltd a fine. She pointed out that if serious questions were raised about her explanation, it could always be checked against the CCTV recordings of her visits to the cells.

This side-stepping of the rules suggests that there were opportunities for Security Ltd to conceal malpractice. In addition, Security Ltd were not fined for poor performance for fear of upsetting the balance of their working relationship and, even if they were, Security Ltd were somewhat accepting that fines were an inevitable part of the contractual arrangements which had therefore presumably been taken into account when the contract fee was agreed. This raises questions about how effective such fines are for delivering an effective police custody process. Interestingly, Security Ltd were not so lenient when it came to fining the company contracted to deliver medical services in the custody area.

Conclusion

In summary, as shown in Table 6.1, the findings were mixed about the advantages and disadvantages of the two different types of custody area. There was not much to choose between the two custody areas as both did

Table 6.1 Key findings on plural policing and the police custody process

Theme	*Sunnyside (private)*	*Gormiston (public)*
Roles and responsibilities	Greater separation	Greater blurring
Pay and conditions of service	Less pay, no sick leave	More pay, sick leave
Working conditions	Less busy and new custody area	Busier and old custody area
Career progression for police staff	Some	None
Team	Less cooperative behaviour	More cooperative behaviour
Hierarchy	Police staff deputized	Police staff deputized
Suspects' experiences	Police staff more liked than the police	Police staff more liked than the police
Accountability	Unclear line management and uncertainty about complaints but contractual obligations and fines	Clearer line management and disciplinary process but unclear roles

some things well and other things less well. The publicly run custody area, Gormiston, had staff who were better trained and paid, with more cooperative behaviour between police and police staff and clearer accountability. However having fewer staff, whose roles and responsibilities were also blurred, contributed to a busier custody area, which was also housed in an older building. The privatized custody area, Sunnyside, had more staff, a newer and less busy custody environment and clearer roles and responsibilities, but also less well paid and trained staff and uncertainties about accountability. In both, suspects preferred police staff to the police and police staff were deputized by the police.

The research shows a growing role for public and private police staff within police custody areas. There was also a blurring of the roles leading to 'power creep' and 'mission creep', including in the use of force. Private police staff, in particular, lacked the skills, training and necessary remuneration to ensure that they could perform these roles. When coupled in Sunnyside with uncertainty about accountability mechanisms, this may provide scope for errors, some of which may be of little significance while others might compromise justice or harm suspects. Therefore the empirical evidence suggests that civilianization is preferable to privatization, if civilians are to be involved at all in the police custody process.

At the same time, police staff in both sites were regarded more highly than the police by suspects, for example because they felt more fairly and respectfully treated by them, but also perhaps because they did not have the same powers as police officers. In relation to the use of force, this meant that some staff felt compelled to use words not force, as well as preferring not to have the additional responsibilities of a baton or pepper spray. In combination with the empirical evidence discussed in Chapters 4 and 5 about suspects' experiences of coercive police practices in the cells (e.g. through the buzzer system) and the coercive ways in which they could be denied access to their rights, this suggests a need for a differentiated understanding of police and police staff, allowing for the possibility that they employed different strategies of control. Police staff employed a more procedurally just style of policing, leading suspects to feel more fairly treated by them, while the police were more likely to use coercion, giving suspects little or no choice in how they behaved, thus employing a coercive style of policing. These two categories are similar to those identified in May *et al.* (2010: 39). They found in the policing of young people that members of neighbourhood policing teams varied between 'adversarial/street control' in which officers focused on crime control and assertion of their authority and 'rule of law/procedural justice' in which a more consensual approach to policing was taken to secure commitment to the rule of law.

In the present study, the fact that police and police staff had different ways of using their authority begs the question why? Police officers perhaps struggled to be caring and compassionate in the way that police staff were because these qualities are not regarded as part of the police role. Certainly, caring and compassion are not part of the core characteristics that Loftus (2010) argues have remained a stubborn feature of the occupational culture of the rank and file. Indeed, they are inimical to some of these characteristics such as a crime-fighting mission, cynicism, suspicion, pragmatism, authority and machismo. Alternatively, perhaps the police had to use coercive strategies as police staff were not designated with the power to use force. In addition, May *et al.* (2010: 58) found that contextual exigencies shaped the style of policing – for example, in high crime areas and in areas where there was a history of citizens mistrusting the police there was a tendency towards 'adversarial/street control'. Similarly, one might expect the wider social and historical context of police–citizen relationships in the two areas in the research to influence these interactions between individual suspects and the police/police staff in the custody areas.

The more positive experiences that suspects had with police staff also suggest that police staff, but to a lesser extent the police, enhanced suspects' experiences of procedural justice. If Tyler (2003) is correct about the relationship between procedural justice and legitimacy, then police staff may have a role to play in securing compliance with the law both in the shorter term while they are in police custody, but also in the longer term once they leave and in spite of the outcome of their case. In fact, that is precisely how police staff behaved, as they were called on to diffuse aggressive and difficult situations. At the same time, suspects' encounters with the police and police staff in police custody may be one of a number of encounters which contribute to what Bottoms and Tankebe (2010) call a 'dialogic relationship within an institutional normative order' in which power-holders and their audience engage in a claim and response dialogue, which cultivates power-holders sense of their own legitimacy. This 'dialogic relationship' suggests that legitimacy is negotiated on an ongoing basis and can also help to understand strain and change in organisations like the police.

The danger of this conclusion is that workforce modernization (either civilianization or privatization) might concentrate attention on procedural justice, but this might mean less of a focus on fair outcomes for suspects. Indeed, this is one of the critiques of Tom Tyler's work. This may amount to persuading suspects (indirectly, through the use of police staff) into accepting outcomes which are unfair to them. Of course, there may be other pay-offs, though, such as fairer outcomes for potential victims who might be protected by the increased likelihood that suspects cooperate with the police and comply with the law. At the same time, police custody needs to be fair for the sake of being fair not because it secures compliance. Moreover, attention needs to be given to both procedural justice and substantive justice in police custody and the relationship between them. For instance, what impact does lack of access to legal advice have on the outcome of a case and on a defendant's perception of the fairness of this outcome?

The research also found that the police staff were deputized by the police and that police custody remained police territory. This was evident in relationships between the police and police staff, for example, with the former trying to pull rank on the latter. In addition, the police retained symbolic control over their use of force because police staff were not officially authorized to use force, even if they did do in practice. In part, this suggests that Johnston (2007) is correct to argue, in relation to PCSOs, for a greater focus on the intra- not inter-organizational dimensions of civilianization. However, contrary to Johnston's (2007) expectations about the possibilities of police reform, the present research suggests that the dominant position of the police in the hierarchy means that the culture of the police officers in the custody areas has not had to change. The police have been 'absolved' from changing because characteristics which have not been traditionally regarded as part of the job (e.g. being caring and compassionate) have simply been taken on by the police staff. This picture of a largely unchanging police culture is further supported by Loftus (2009), who found, for example, that the diversity agenda had only altered behaviour not attitudes.

This deputizing of police staff by the police implies that, in both police custody areas, police–police staff relationships were not 'nodal networks' in which the state is only one of a number of equal players involved in the delivery of security, as Johnston and Shearing (2003: 25–6) have argued. While it is possible to see how in a community context having nodal networks as a model of relationships between the state and other policing providers may be beneficial, for instance in terms of enabling communities to build sufficient capacity to deal with some of their own problems, this makes little sense in police custody. This chapter shows that much importance was attached to the role of the police in their relationship with the police staff (and in their relationship with other criminal justice practitioners, as argued in Chapter 7), and perhaps this is how it ought to be. In dealing with complex and contentious matters such as suspects' rights and welfare the police do and should have 'the final say' rather than police staff, although the police should not have the 'only say', particularly as suspect welfare was largely the responsibility of police staff. This illustrates what Loader and Walker (2006, 2007: 192–4) call 'anchored pluralism', in which the state not other policing providers is in a position to act as an arbiter in decisions about security, thereby retaining it as a public good.

In the following chapter, I extend the discussion of the relationship between police and police staff to an exploration of working relationships between the police staff and other practitioners in the custody area, including legal advisors, doctors, appropriate adults and drug workers. I argue that practitioners in the custody areas were not engaged in a partnership of equals with police and police staff, thereby limiting the capacity of criminal justice practitioners to use their authority. This further contributes to the idea that strategies of control used to maintain order in the custody area varied between police, police staff and other criminal justice practitioners.

Notes

1 Indeed a lot of research on the changing role of the police in policing has focused on the private security industry. See, for example, Wakefield (2003, 2008), Williams (2008), Noaks (2000, 2004, 2008), Button (2002, 2003, 2007), Shicor and Gilbert (2001), Sklansky (1999), Forst and Manning (1999), Jones and Newburn (1998), Johnston (1992), Ocqueteau (1990).

2 By contrast, research on police departments in Illinois in the United States found that civilianization increased the most in agencies that declined in size and were in rural areas, as well as where there were substantial increases in their budgets and decreases in the crime rate (Crank, 1989).

3 The practice of civilian staff (street wardens or *stadswachten*), wearing uniforms the same as or different to the police has also been noted in the Netherlands

(Hauber *et al.*, 1996). Where the uniforms were the same, the public found it difficult to distinguish between the street wardens and the police (Hofstra and Shapland, 1997).

4 Merritt (2009) confirms this. He found that PCSOs' level of pay depended on the police service, with some being paid around £19,000, which was the same as a newly-recruited police constable.

5 For example, between 1 March and 31 December 1999, Securicor incurred penalties of £199,950 for breaches of contract in relation to Parc prison, mainly for incidents of prisoner self-harm, prisoners failing to see a medical officer on arrival, failures to respond to prisoner complaints and failures to provide sentence plans (Genders, 2002).

Chapter 7

Multi-professionalism and the police custody process

This chapter is concerned with the interplay of working relationships in police custody areas and the likely impact on suspects. It builds on the descriptions of roles and responsibilities of the police, police staff, legal advisors, doctors, appropriate adults (AAs) and drug workers described in Chapter 3 and I examine the relationships between them, police staff and the police. Before introducing the concept of multi-professionalism, it is necessary to draw a distinction between the 'hard' and 'soft' ways that the term professional is used. In sociological terms 'a profession includes some central regulatory body to ensure the standard of performance of individual members; a code of conduct; careful management of knowledge in relation to the expertise which constitutes the basis of the profession's activities; and, lastly, control of numbers, selection, and training of new entrants' (Scott and Marshall, 2009: 'professions'). This professional status also limits the supply of possible practitioners, increases their market value and ensures that they have a monopoly over their area of work and expertise. Typically, only a small number of occupations, such as doctors, lawyers and teachers, have gained acceptance as professionals. By contrast, police officers cannot be included in this group: they lack a body of knowledge, unlike lawyers or medical doctors, and undergo relatively little training, for example they undertake only two years' training compared to the eight or so years it takes to become a medical doctor or the five years it takes to become a solicitor.

Nevertheless, the police may still assert that they are professionals, as some of them did in the present research, as did other practitioners, such as police staff, drug workers and some appropriate adults. This was probably because they were using a different and 'softer' understanding of the meaning of the term to refer to working in a reasonably detached manner and paying attention to the requirements of the job. Based on the definition of a professional given above, only doctors, nurses, solicitors and social workers (who acted as appropriate adults) can be regarded as professionals in the custody area. As for police, police staff, drug workers and appropriate adults, they may have acted in a professional manner, but this is not the same as saying that they are professionals. This is pertinent to the research as professional status may have entitled some practitioners to claim greater autonomy than others.

Because of these differences between the 'hard' and 'soft' use of the term professional, it has been avoided thus far, with reference being made, instead, to practitioners or staff, except if I am quoting or paraphrasing an interviewee who described themselves or others in the custody area as a 'professional'. The only other exception to this is within the concept of multi-professionalism, in which the term professional merely denotes occupations found within police custody areas. This was partly because it was linguistically convenient, but also to avoid the concept of inter-organizational or intra-organizational relationships. Multi-professionalism conveys that two practitioners, such as public police staff and doctors, can be employed or paid by the same organization but have different professions, roles, responsibilities and powers. This meaning is not captured in the concept of inter-organizational relationships, which implies that practitioners belong to different organizations. To an extent it is possible to conceive of these relationships in terms of intra-organizational relationships, as Johnston (2007) urges, but this overstates the extent to which practitioners such as doctors or public police staff belong to and are integrated into the police organization. As argued in Chapter 6, there were limits on the extent to which police staff acted as and were viewed as being part of the team of police officers working in the custody area.

It is important to examine these multi-professional relationships because, while they have been the subject of research, for example on crime prevention partnerships, there has been little attempt to systematically examine them in relation to the police custody process, although Newburn and Hayman (2002: 136–40) touch on this subject. Yet, as hinted at in Chapter 5, multi-professional relationships can have a bearing on suspects' access to their rights and entitlements, such as to legal advice – the tendency was for the police and legal advisors to blame each other for delays with legal advice and difficulties coordinating service provision. As I shall argue in this chapter the same was true for other practitioners such as appropriate adults and doctors.

This chapter first examines the wider context of partnership working and how this relates to the police custody process. Second, I empirically examine how staff viewed multi-professional relationships in the custody area. Third, I critically assess the promises and pitfalls of various aspects of multi-professionalism in the custody area, including: the sharing of objectives and whether police custody areas remain police territory;

delays and difficulties with coordination, communication, resources and information sharing; where the ultimate responsibility for the care and fair treatment of suspects lies; and the difficulties of bureaucracy, joining up service provision and how this is to be reconciled with practitioners' independence. Finally, I explore the implications of multi-professionalism for accountability and for governance.

Partnership working and police custody

The notion of partnership working has come to be seen as an important way of tackling crime and disorder. Indeed, the principle which grew out of the community policing movement, as well as Home Office documents such as Circular 8/1984 and the Morgan Report in 1991, has come to be enshrined in legislation like the Crime and Disorder Act 1998, so that the concept of partnership working is advocated at all levels, from local practitioners to national politicians. There has also been a proliferation of sometimes overlapping multi-agency partnerships, settings and practices including:

- Crime and Disorder Reduction Partnerships (CDRPs) to improve community safety;
- Youth Offending Services (formerly known as youth offending teams) to tackle youth offending;
- Local Strategic Partnerships, which work alongside the CDRPs;
- Drug Action Teams to commission drug services;
- Criminal Justice Integrated Teams to broker services for drug-using offenders including treatment, housing and benefit payments from a range of service-providers;
- Multi-Agency Public Protection Arrangements (MAPPA), which are the multi-agency arrangements used to supervise sex-offenders in the community;
- Circles of Support and Accountability used to supervise sex-offenders once formal arrangements with MAPPA and the probation services have ceased.

While there is agreement about the importance of partnership working, the concept itself is interpreted and implemented in locally varied ways, but also with limited evidence of effectiveness (Skinns, 2005: 186, 248–50).

The popularity of partnership working stems from the advantages that partnerships are believed to offer practitioners, citizens and government alike. Multi-agency criminal justice partnerships between the police and other agencies are considered to contribute to efficient and effective crime control by 'doing more with less'. This is partly because by drawing a number of partner agencies together, they are believed to be more effective at tackling the causes of crime. Since the 1980s, there has been a growing recognition that the causes of crime are wide-ranging and beyond the direct control of the police alone (Home Office, 1984, cited in Crawford, 1997: 67; Home Office, 1991). In essence, it is believed that many agencies are better than one at tackling crime and disorder. Partnerships are also believed to contribute to efficient crime control by minimizing duplication and reducing the chance that social problems fall between the gaps of different agencies. Therefore social problems, such as noisy neighbours, can be responded to as they are experienced by citizens, rather than as they are defined by these agencies. In this sense, partnerships also offer the opportunity to enhance the legitimacy of the criminal justice process.

In theory, partnerships also create new opportunities for practitioners to break down barriers, build trust between agencies, share information and maximize their skills, capacity and knowledge. Moreover, inter-agency differences in police partnerships provide an opportunity for a different kind of accountability. As Thacher (2001) notes, partner organizations can act as checks and balances on each other. For example, in the Crime and Disorder Reduction Partnerships (CDRPs), the voluntary sector may have a role in challenging the status quo of statutory organizations (Skinns, 2005: 303). Citizen involvement in multi-agency criminal justice partnerships also enables both participation, and possibly even ownership of the issues and enhanced accountability, which could compensate for the low level of participation in democratic processes. Finally, criminal justice partnerships have the potential to free up capacity allowing organizations to specialize and focus on their 'core business', that is on the things that the agency regards as their essential duties as defined in policies and in law. For example, the civilianization of roles such as jailors and investigators allows police constables who would normally do this kind of work to be redeployed on front-line duties (e.g. as part of the neighbourhood policing teams) and police staff to develop specialist skills (e.g. IT skills) which may not have been readily available among the police ranks.

In practice, the extent to which these ambitions have been realized is a contentious matter with some areas, partnerships and multi-agency settings doing better than others. For example, partnerships such as the CDRPs have struggled, as evidenced by the report by the Audit Commission in 2002 which found that the CDRPs had not made a measurable impact on crime and disorder, and the Review of the Crime and Disorder Act in 2005 which cited difficulties with basic matters such as getting the right people present at meetings. This led to the Police and Justice Act 2006, the promulgation of national standards in 2007 and, more recently, the creation of comprehensive area assessments which for the first time simultaneously examine the performance of both the police and local authorities. The Criminal Justice Integrated Teams (CJITs) have also struggled but to a lesser extent than the CDRPs; after all, research began to show that the teams contributed to a decrease in self-reported offending behaviour, even though this did not result in the projected savings to the public purse (Turnbull and Skinns, 2010). Part of this difference in impact is explained by the relatively poor focus of the CDRPs; in the twenty or so years since the notion of community safety arose, there has been little attempt to clarify exactly what it means. This kind of uncertainty breeds failure. From this perspective, police custody areas, as multi-agency settings, have the advantage of having a clearer and more tangible focus on suspects who may have a variety of social problems requiring assistance from a more limited range of agencies and within a limited time frame, although this is not to say that police custody areas always run smoothly, as there are other challenges that have to be managed.

Some of the organizations in multi-agency criminal justice partnerships do not have a history of working cooperatively alongside each other. For example, in the adversarial system, the police (i.e. the prosecution) and the defence build competing cases to either support the innocence or guilt of the defendant (Hodgson, 2004). More recently, agencies involved in the police custody process have also been affected by a managerialist culture, which can undermine inter-agency cooperation. As has been seen with the CDRPs managerialism can contribute to competition rather than cooperation between agencies, for example in meeting conflicting key performance indicators (Crawford, 2001; Skinns, 2005: 238). Furthermore, inter-agency relationships can be fraught with difficulties associated with different levels of commitment and involvement, with the police tending to dominate partnerships such as the CDRPs, as well as conflicting organizational priorities, occupational cultures and ideologies.[1] These inter-agency differences impact on how partner agencies view the problem and its solution and can limit the amount of common ground between them. For example, drug users in the criminal justice process might be seen by the police as problematic because of their involvement in acquisitive crime, while drug workers and health workers may see such offenders primarily in terms of the harmful nature of their drug use. While this example oversimplifies the issues, it serves to show how inter-agency differences can affect not only offenders, but also the agencies that deal with them. Similarly, in an evaluation of a newly established court-based psychiatric diversion scheme, Turnbull and Beese (2000) note the differences in language used by police and mental health practitioners; one of their interviewees, a mental health worker, says 'talking to the police you would talk in terms of serious mental illness diagnosis or medication, and they talk in terms of lunatics and gooks . . .' (p. 294).

Police custody areas are also sites of multi-professional practice, but previous research shows that one occupational group – the police –

dominates the scene. As Newburn and Hayman (2002: 136–40) found, practitioners such as legal advisors, AAs, independent custody visitors (formerly known as lay visitors) and doctors are dependent on assistance and cooperation from the police. Similarly, Choongh (1997: 85) says that, simply because a wider array of practitioners is allowed in police custody areas, it does not follow that they are no longer in police territory; the police tell these practitioners 'when to wait, where to wait, where to stand, when to sit down'. Like other kinds of partnerships, relationships between practitioners in police custody can also break down due to different occupational cultures, working practices, organizational priorities and levels of power and status. For example, Newburn and Hayman (2002: 136–40) found that these relationships could sometimes be fraught due to mutual suspicions (e.g. the police thought solicitors were obstructive, while AAs disliked solicitors for keeping them waiting), mistrust (e.g. solicitors did not trust the police not to record consultations that took place in cells where there was CCTV) and a lack of familiarity with each other's roles (e.g. the police did not understand the role of the lay visitor). Moreover, if other practitioners begin to take on police conceptions of normality and reasonableness (Choongh, 1997: 86), then there is a chance that these practitioners will lose their independence which may be fundamental to their role.

Perceptions of multi-professional relationships

Research participants suggested that relationships between some practitioners were better than others. More specifically, GMS12, a legal advisor, said his relationship with the police would always be compromised by his adversarial role, although other practitioners such as drug workers were a better example of partnership working in the custody area. Relationships between the police, police staff and legal advisors differed in terms of how much contact they had with each other. In Gormiston it was recognized that the changing role of the custody officer – whereby custody officers were no longer primarily responsible for decisions about charging suspects – meant that designated detention officers and jailors, not custody officers, dealt with legal advisors. Similarly, in Sunnyside, the custody administrators and custody assistants, not the custody officers, dealt with legal advisors.

Relationships between police, police staff and legal advisors also differed in the extent to which they were viewed as cooperative. Interviewees in Sunnyside felt that there was a reasonable degree of cooperation between police, Security Ltd and legal advisors founded on familiarity and the long-standing nature of their working relationships. One Security Ltd employee noted that 'when you've worked in an area for seven years you know all of them [solicitors] on first name terms and so I'd say we have good relationships with the solicitors' (SNS1). Furthermore, there was recognition of their different roles and responsibilities, which enabled the police and Security Ltd to treat solicitors with respect as they recognized that each has a job to do. One police officer remarked that it may be true that some solicitors and police officers cannot 'stick each other', but 'I think we all appreciate we've got a job to do and we get on and do it as best we can' (SNS8). Moreover, it was also noted that police/Security Ltd and solicitors had a shared goal of justice and that unnecessary delays caused by either party could hinder the pursuit of this goal.

In Gormiston there was some recognition of the shared aims and objectives of the police and legal advisors which are noted below. However, this is where the similarity with Sunnyside ended as some police officers, especially custody officers in Gormiston, expressed outright dislike and animosity towards solicitors rather than expressing a desire to cooperate with them. GMS10 said that 'we don't really work together with solicitors' and they caused problems by demanding 'too much'. When asked why, he said some of them just seemed to get out of the wrong side of bed. Another PC who passed through the custody area in GMPO4 felt that solicitors deliberately infuriated the police by interrupting in interviews and by advising their clients not to comment just as they were about to answer a question or break under the pressure of the interview.

The comments from GMS12 at the start of this section suggests that, at the time of the research, relationships between police/police staff and legal advisors were poor but that the relationships between drug workers and the police and police staff were reasonably cooperative. However, this has not always been the case. For example, in the early days of the arrest referral scheme, there were difficulties with the referral process and with drug workers and the police having different priorities. Drug workers depended on the police to inform them of potential clients and to facilitate access to them. Hunter *et al.* (2005) found that this had two main consequences. First, the drug workers lost prospective clients as the police appeared to filter out some suspects (such as 'old people', white-collar offenders, anyone who required an interpreter or those who would take umbrage at being asked if they had a drug problem). Second, dependence on the police also meant that police priorities could take precedence when it came to notifying drug workers of potential clients. Therefore, Hunter *et al.* question whether the relationship between the police and drug workers was 'a partnership of equals' (2005: 17).

By contrast, drug workers in the present research had a great deal of freedom in the custody area in Sunnyside; for example, a custody officer (SNS3) explained that drug workers were allowed unsupervized access to the custody area because it was believed that the presence of a uniformed officer would inhibit effective working practices and take up too much of police/police staff time, although these views were not supported by the 'old-school' police officers. Drug workers SNS13 and SNS14 also said that they had a good relationship with the police and police staff partly because the drug workers helped to train the police staff and because they fitted around the police staff by only asking them to help when they had a free moment, but also because their relationship with the police had become inescapable as a result of it being formalized through the Criminal Justice Integrated Teams.

This was not the case in Gormiston, however, where the police staff, rather than the police officers, had good working relationships with the drug workers. A custody officer in Gormiston said that he 'did not have a relationship with the drug workers'; rather, they just worked in the same environment and the jailors dealt with the drug workers (GMS13). Similarly, an inspector, GMS5, said that the police were not involved with what drug workers did. Unsurprisingly, therefore, drug workers GMS6 and GMS7 said that their primary relationship was with police staff with whom they regularly chatted during the drug-testing process, enabling them to build a rapport with them.

While relationships between drug workers and the police/police staff were reasonable, drug workers had only a limited relationship with legal advisors and doctors. Drug workers (SNS13, SNS14, GMS6 and GMS7) said that they did not have a relationship with legal advisors, except perhaps at court when they provided information about whether a client was engaged in drug treatment which could be useful in decisions about restrictions on their bail conditions. Similarly, a legal advisor (GMS1) said that he had 'very little' contact with drug workers: 'What they do is confidential, and they really keep it that way, they don't talk to us about what the client said, they don't talk to the police about it, as far as I'm aware'. Similarly, drug workers had few dealings with doctors except when sharing information about a suspect's drug use.

Like drug workers, it seemed that the medical staff had good working relationships with the police and police staff in Sunnyside. A doctor said that there was a good team atmosphere between the forensic medical staff, Security Ltd and the police, suggesting that they shared similar goals in the custody process. Similarly, an inspector (SNS8) said that relationships with medical staff were very good and that 'failings' only occurred when 'people are too busy and forget to do things', as opposed to there being 'an unwillingness to be a part of the process'.

By contrast, in Gormiston, the doctors mainly had a relationship with the police officers and not the police staff. One legal advisor (GMS12) said that it was natural for doctors and police officers to strike up a relationship since they were both regularly present for long periods of time in the custody area. Police officers were aware that the police needed the medical staff in order for the custody area to function. One custody officer said that the police 'couldn't survive without them [the medical staff]. At the end of the day, it's one of those invaluable services and we've got to have them ... to make sure the codes of practice are complied with' (GMS10). In addition, doctors such as GMS9 and in GMPO4 and in GMPO6 described relationships with the police as based on mutual trust and respect.

The same was not said of AAs. While some research participants, such as GMS5, recognized the importance of the work of AAs, this did not guarantee that they commanded respect from the police, police staff or others working in the custody area. For example, an AA, GMS14, complained that the police and legal advisors did not respect her until she reminded them of her qualifications as a social worker. An inspector's views summed up the lack of respect for AAs. He described a recent incident in which an AA had insisted that her client stay in a secure waiting room rather than being returned to the cells. She had also become 'stroppy' when the police did not agree to her request. Tellingly, this inspector said, 'well, it wasn't her client because she was *only* an appropriate adult. She has no influence as such, they're there just to look after the interest in a sort of an appropriate adult way, not a legal thing' (SNS8). An AA, SNS15, said the police viewed AAs as a bunch of 'do-gooders', forgetting that they were vital to ensure that convictions were sound.

Table 7.1 summarizes multi-professional relationships based on the data presented here and in Chapters 3 and 6. The shaded area refers to relationships between practitioners in Sunnyside, while the other half of the table refers to relationships between staff in Gormiston. In the latter, doctors were mainly dealt with by the police and drug workers were mainly dealt with by the police staff, which perhaps conveys that doctors were more highly regarded than the drug workers perhaps because of the necessity of their role. Legal advisors had a fairly limited and/or poor relationship with the police and police staff. In Sunnyside, drug workers and doctors seemed on more of an equal footing with the police and police staff, being given unrestricted access to the custody area and the electronic police custody records and being dealt with by both the police officers and the police staff. Legal advisors also had moderately good relations with both the police and police staff, in part through familiarity and in part through their occupation of a room in the custody area. In both sites, AAs were not accorded the same level of respect as doctors, drug workers or legal advisors, perhaps because their professional reputation, as adding little to the process (as was explored in Chapter 3), preceded them.

Assessing multi-professionalism: the promises and pitfalls

Trust and familiarity

Building cooperation and good working relationships was partly related to familiarity. This theme applied mainly to legal advisors and drug

Table 7.1 Perceptions of multi-professional relationships*

	Police	*Police staff*	*Legal advisors*	*Doctors*	*Appropriate adults*	*Drug workers*
Police	–	Described themselves as a team, but did not act like one	Limited but poor	Good	Poor	Good
Police staff	Acted like a team, but did not describe themselves as one	–	Poor	Good	Poor	Good
Legal advisors	Limited but moderately cooperative	Moderately cooperative	–	No data	Poor	No relationship
Doctors	Good	No relationship	No relationship	–	No data	No relationship
Appropriate adults	Poor	No data	Poor	No data	–	No data
Drug workers	No relationship	Good	No relationship	No relationship	No data	–

*The shaded area refers to relationships between practitioners in Sunnyside, while the other half of the table refers to relationships between practitioners in Gormiston.

workers. A solicitor, GMS12, explained that the size of Gormiston meant that there was little familiarity with the police in the custody area and that, anyway, he did not want to 'pally up to the police' as over-familiarity might undermine his independence and his clients' confidence in him. This conveys what a difficult balancing act it could be to manage multi-professional relationships based on mutual interdependence. Similarly, designated detention officers such as GMS3 and custody officers such as GMS10 and GMS13 made similar points that they were familiar with certain firms but were unfamiliar with specific legal advisors, except for some duty solicitors, and that they preferred it that way so as to maintain some independence from each other, saying that legal advisors 'don't have a professional relationship with me, and I don't have a professional relationship with them'. One opposing view to this was expressed by legal advisor GMS1 who said that familiarity helped with relationships with the police and that police officers recognized him, but he did not recognize them.

By contrast, in Sunnyside, there was greater familiarity between police and Security Ltd employees and legal advisors. Familiarity was facilitated by there being fewer solicitors that frequented the custody area and a dedicated custody team of police/Security Ltd employees permanently based in the custody area, and because, unusually, solicitors had their own office in the custody area, meaning that they did not have to wait outside in reception. There were few opportunities for this kind of relationship-building in Gormiston. Consequently, it was unsurprising that officers, such as GMS10 said that they did not trust solicitors 'as far as they could throw them because they are trying to get as much information out of us as possible, and to try and find the loopholes to get their client off'. In the light of this lack of trust and familiarity between the police and legal advisors in Gormiston, relationships with legal advisors in Sunnyside appeared to be more cooperative, as described above.

As for drug workers, in Sunnyside, one of them, SNS13, who had worked there for some time, was described as having done a lot of the 'leg-work' to develop a cooperative relationship with the police, but that it took time for the police to change their attitude to drug users and to the service offered by the drug workers. Similarly one of the AAs said that having a personal relationship with the custody assistants could prevent his time being wasted, as he explained: 'It does work where you've got those personal relationships with people. They will phone and let us know if the situation's changed, and that sort of thing, and originally we just sent a volunteer on the way and we got a phone call back saying, oh actually the detained person is quite upset and has been kicking off, so the interview's not going to happen for a while now' (SNS15).

By contrast, the lack of familiarity between drug workers and police officers (as opposed to police staff) created difficulties in Gormiston. One of the drug workers (GMS6) interviewed said that he had been mistaken for being a suspect. In addition, a different drug worker, GMS7, said that the lack of familiarity and the suspiciousness that he encountered from the police 'got his back up': police officers did not even say hello to him and, instead, looked him up and down and demanded to know who he was. This drug worker also thought it paradoxical that for an organization, which was renowned for being observant, officers did not recognize him, even though he had worked on the same shift as them on a number of occasions. However, as with other practitioners, these drug workers did not want to appear overly familiar with the police for the sake of their working relationship with suspects. Together this suggests that a sense of familiarity coupled with professional independence contributed to good working relationships between the police/police staff and others working in the custody area.

Being involved in training police/police staff provided another opportunity for those working in the custody area to develop a better understanding of each other's roles and responsibilities. For instance, the drug workers in Sunnyside provided the private police staff with training on substance misuse. One of the drug workers (SNS13) said that 'the training we offer, it's entitled Substance Misuse training, but to my mind it's how I can advise the custody assistant to be the most help to me, so that's my agenda for going up there and offering that substance misuse training, and explaining how they can be of use to me, but selling it as substance misuse training'. Similarly a different drug worker (SNS14) described the training as 'laying the groundwork for that joint working', although later this drug worker also said that she saw her role as educating custody staff about drug users and about her role in the custody area.

While these structural and organizational issues may be of importance to building cooperative relationships between professionals in custody areas, so too were individuals. As one of the drug workers (SNS13) noted, on an organizational level relationships with the police were good, but there were certain individuals who were 'different' and 'difficult to deal with'. Similarly, other research participants said that cooperation depended on 'personalities' and on the 'good-will' of staff (e.g. in GMPO1 and SNS1). This independent custody visitor summed up these views when she said that cooperation between practitioners depended both on individual personalities and occupational cultures, for example of the solicitor and the police officer, and that 'I don't think there is a sort of combined effort, because everyone's coming at it from a different angle' (GMS11). This conveys that practitioners of all kinds had agency.

Stereotyping and adversarialism

In interpreting the behaviour of solicitors, the police and police staff in both sites appeared to employ negative stereotypes about solicitors as 'demanding', 'pushy', 'arrogant', 'unnecessarily obstructive', 'awkward', 'disruptive' and 'money grabbing' (e.g. SNS4 and GMS10). This Security Ltd employee explained:

> There are guidelines about what each block [custody area] will do for a solicitor, they do try and push those guidelines, they expect us to be a waiter. They'll order a coffee or ask us to go and get a DP [detained person] . . . a lot of us take umbrage to that sort of thing, because we're not their servants . . . but overall most of the solicitors seem to be okay, they've got a job to do as much as us, it's just sometimes they need reminding that actually we can escort you off the premises or you can be by the police, if you're rude and arrogant, and expect too much. (SNS4)

This quotation also gives the impression that police staff as well as the police could be territorial in terms of how they viewed the custody area.

Police officers such as GMS3, GMS10 and GMS13 also believed that legal advisors behaved unprofessionally by either acting for a client when they knew they were guilty or by helping their clients to concoct stories to get them off. For example, GMS13 said that solicitors helped clients to concoct stories that got the client off and helped the legal advisor secure future work from the client. He argued that this strategy was unlikely to backfire on legal advisors because there was no way of proving these kinds of allegations, as consultation rooms were private, and even if the police did overhear a solicitor helping a client to concoct a story it would be inadmissible in court. And furthermore, even if there was enough evidence of a solicitor's involvement in concocting an alibi to go to court a judge was more likely to believe a solicitor over a client. However, as a solicitor, GMS1, argued, this would be against their professional codes of conduct and also not in their interests.

However, there may be occasions when legal advisors are obstructive, pushy and unprofessional; for example, an inspector in Gormiston, who dealt with police complaints, including complaints about solicitors, described a situation he had recently dealt with in which a solicitor had been obstructive to the progress of the interview. He was not present in the interview, but watched the videotape of it. He said that the legal representative was:

> [A]rgumentative, personally insulting towards the officers, and if you excuse the language, one quote on the tape was . . . shall we stop buggering about with the mind-fucks and get on with the interview please officer, which any normal person can see is not particularly professional or constructive to either officers or to the suspect. (GMS5)

The point is that some police officers generalized from the behaviour of a few legal advisors and used this to understand and interpret the behaviour of all, perhaps because it suited their interests to do so. This negative stereotyping of legal advisors was also noted by Irving and Mackenzie (1989), who found that the only threat to productive inter-professional relationships was police officers' prejudices about solicitors stemming from the unprofessional conduct of a small number.

The police may also have misinterpreted some aspects of the behaviour of legal advisors; for example, awkwardness might in fact have been assertiveness. And assertiveness in the custody area is part and parcel of their adversarial role which is 'to protect and advance the legal rights of clients' (PACE Codes of Practice, 2006: 6D para. 7.51; Cape, 2006). Their assertiveness was also warranted given that solicitors were 'invited' into police/Security Ltd territory where they inevitably did not hold as much sway. At the same time, their assertive behaviour, if misconstrued by custody staff, could impact on suspects' access to custodial legal advice; for example, as one Security Ltd interviewee remarked, it made him reluctant to help certain solicitors and thereby implicitly suspects.

In sum, it is likely that a minority of solicitors can be obstructive and unprofessional, but the problem is that the behaviour of a few leads to a generalized and stereotyped view of solicitors, especially among custody officers who are deeply embedded within the custody process and the stresses and strains that this engenders. In addition the behaviour of solicitors, which was stereotyped by the police as pushy and demanding, was regarded by legal advisors as them taking an adversarial stance while on police territory.

These two interpretations of the same behaviour illustrate the influence of adversarialism on police–solicitor relationships. Adversarialism was also referred to indirectly in other contexts, such as disclosure, when the police described police–solicitor relationships as a 'cat and mouse game' or a 'chess game'. For example, one custody officer described how he disclosed as little as possible to solicitors knowing full well that this would affect the ability of a solicitor to properly advise their client. On one occasion, a solicitor had been furious with him because he had deliberately kept quiet about whether the Crown Prosecution Service were likely to charge or caution the client, knowing full well the Crown Prosecution Service were going to charge the detainee. The solicitor guessed incorrectly that the likely disposal was a caution and consequently his client admitted to the offence, at which point he was charged rather than cautioned. This example shows that adversarialism can cause the police to focus on the 'game' and thus lose sight of the bigger picture of just outcomes.

Delays and coordination: 'if it's not one, it's the other'

There could also be difficulties in coordinating the involvement of a number of practitioners who were needed either simultaneously or in a certain order, as was also found by Newburn and Hayman (2002: 136–40). In the present research, difficulties in coordinating practitioners partly arose because of delays reportedly caused by the police, but also by doctors (particularly in Gormiston), legal advisors, AAs and the Crown Prosecution Service, which were described in Chapters 3 and 5. However, who caused the delays depended on who you asked, as this legal advisor explained:

> The police always blame the solicitors, and the solicitors always blame the police . . . Or sometimes we both blame the interpreters, or God help us, the appropriate adult, especially if they come from social services, and it becomes a bit of a stand-off because say if I have a young person in custody and they need social services to send an appropriate adult, they seem to have a rule now that they won't attend until the solicitor arrives, which makes my hackles rise, and . . . presumably because their experience is that they attend and then wait for a solicitor and they don't like waiting, whereas our experience is we attend and wait for the appropriate adult, so you have to have a sort of element of trust, you know, that if we all agree an interview time of X that everyone will be abide by that. (GMS12)

As GMS12 and another legal advisor (GMS1) noted, the delays could lead to what were described as 'stand-offs' in which legal advisors would not attend until the AA was there or vice versa. He was not the only interviewee to note such stand-offs. So too did AAs (SNS15 and GMS14), particularly in the light of the introduction of fixed fees for legal advisors, which have added to their reluctance to wait at the police station as they are no longer paid a separate fee for this. Similarly, a custody assistant (GMS3) said that there could be delays while waiting for interpreters, AAs and legal advisors to arrive, especially late at night, and that this could result in 'clashes' and people becoming 'impatient'. A jailor in GMPO6 said of the difficulties coordinating doctors, legal advisors and AAs in the custody area, 'if it's not one it's the other'.

The difficult task of coordinating practitioners was left to police officers, although this probably also meant that they were better able to fit the arrival of practitioners around their own timescales. At the same time, police officers felt powerless to influence whether and when practitioners turned up, including other police officers. For example, this inspector said that 'once the officer in the case walks out the door, you can't tie them to a chair and say, right sit there and deal with your prisoner and don't leave till it's done, because that's not how it works' (SNS8). Similarly, in GMPO1, an Inspector said that it could be difficult coordinating the arrival of interpreters, solicitors and AAs, as each told the officer to call them when the other practitioner arrived and so his tactic was to lie to all of them to get them there at the same time.

Such practices left AAs, legal advisors and drug workers feeling disgruntled about being misinformed. An AA in Gormiston acknowledged that the police had a difficult job to do in coordinating practitioners, but that she would have liked more honesty from them about whether other practitioners had been contacted and when they were likely to arrive (GMS14). SNS15, an AA, also said that the police either deliberately or inadvertently misinformed either them or the custody administrator about whether the legal advisor was present and therefore when they should arrive, but used the custody administrator to relay the information to the AA in what felt like a game of 'Chinese whispers'. Similarly, a legal advisor in Gormiston said that his main complaint about the custody process was about being misinformed about when to arrive, not being able to contact anyone on arrival at the police station because none of the staff answered the telephone and then having to wait in reception without being given information about what was happening with the case, meaning that he did not know whether to go back to the office or to remain at the police station (GMS12). He said the same was also true for AAs, who he saw sitting in the waiting room having been told to attend the police station immediately.

Therefore, like suspects, practitioners were subject to ploys by the police about when to attend the police station. These were used to cajole and persuade practitioners, in part because of the difficulties of trying to coordinate their arrivals, but also so that these practitioners fitted around police objectives connected with the smooth running of the custody area. The introduction of the Defence Solicitor Call Centre (DSCC) will probably add a further layer of bureaucracy to this already complicated coordination process, as the DSCC, not the police, are now responsible for contacting legal advisors. While this may free up officers' time for doing other things, it may also add to it; for instance, if the legal advisor does not contact the custody area then the police officer will have to call the DSCC again and again and wait once more until the legal advisor contacts the custody area. Given that practitioners reportedly struggled to get through to the custody area in Gormiston, it may be that legal advisors and appropriate adults will also struggle to find out when they should arrive and about when other practitioners are arriving, thereby adding to the time that they spend on the case if they have to make a number of attempts to contact the custody area.

In order to further understand the challenges of coordinating practitioners and who was to blame for delays, elsewhere I have explored the issue using the quantitative data collected from the custody records (see Skinns, 2010). Using logistic regression, I examined the multi-professional factors predicting the length of detention from arrival at the police station to case disposal, that is when someone is charge, cautioned, bailed or released without charge. Of the factors that significantly predicted the length of detention, police-related factors such as the time taken to contact a legal advisor and the time taken from arrival at the police station until first interview (taken as a measure of police investigation time) were better predictors of the length of the detention than multi-professional factors, such as the time taken for the doctor to consult with a patient once they had been contacted, and suspect-related factors such as the reason for arrest or case disposal. Given that the police were largely responsible for coordinating practitioners and given that police-related factors predicted a larger portion of the variance in the regression model than the other multi-professional and suspect-related factors, this suggests that the police may be the main reason for delays to the custody process.

The issue underlying these delays, and difficulties with coordination and communication would appear to be the scarcity of resources, meaning that none of the practitioners could afford to have their time wasted or perhaps even their dignity undermined by the humiliation of waiting for hours in the waiting room. An inspector (GMS8) said 'everyone was trying to do the best they can with limited resources', including the police who he felt were inhibited by limited numbers of consultation rooms. Similarly, a custody officer (SNS12) said that all the practitioners in the custody area had broadly similar objectives, but that the problem was a lack of resources. He also said that that the situation had worsened for legal advisors and social services as their work had increased but their resources had not and that this affected multi-professional relationships.

This was an unfortunate state of affairs, particularly when it was not just practitioners who had to potentially wait in the custody areas – so too did suspects. As discussed in Chapter 5, concerns about waiting for the services of practitioners such as legal advisors meant that they would sometimes rather not request them or cancel their request than prolong their detention. The lack of resources and associated problems were therefore unfair to many parties: to suspects because it prolonged their detention; to practitioners (other than police or police staff) because they had their time wasted; and to the police staff, and to a lesser extent the police, as delays made the custody area impossibly busy.

Shared objectives or police objectives and police territory?

The practitioners in the custody area had some overlapping organizational objectives. First, the police concern with the safety and welfare of suspects was shared by other practitioners. One doctor (GMS9) said that the police and doctors had a shared appreciation of the need for a safe endpoint for suspects, although he sometimes came under pressure to do otherwise. Similarly, a different doctor (GMS2) said that the police and doctors shared the objective of wanting to prevent a death in custody, as well as ensuring that the suspect was treated fairly, even if this meant certifying them unfit for interview, which many suspects did not like because it prolonged their detention. However, later he said that a doctor's concern with the welfare of the suspect could clash with police investigative goals; for instance, the police had wanted him to conduct an intimate search for concealed drugs, which he refused to do in the custody area in part because of concerns about his own or the patient's safety and in part because of a lack of X-ray equipment which could have been used to find out where the drugs were allegedly hidden. He said that he was put under pressure because 'sometimes the police just want to achieve the objective, irrespective of how they get it'.

Second, police/police staff shared a concern with legal advisors to process suspects expeditiously, albeit for different reasons. One custody officer said of police and police staff: 'Let's face it, we've got one objective, which is to get as many people through the justice system that walk through those doors, as we can . . . sometimes things fall off the end . . . but I think we are all pulling in the same direction to get the job done' (SNS3). For Security Ltd quicker processing meant the use of fewer resources and therefore more profit (SNS1). As for a legal advisor, GMS1, his main aim was to get clients out of custody as quickly as possible, if that was what the suspect wanted. Later he said that this aim was compatible with the police, provided clients had not been involved with the police before.

Third, drug workers and the police also shared a concern with crime reduction, although not necessarily the means by which it was achieved. A custody officer (GMS10) observed that by engaging drug users in treatment, drug workers helped to prevent suspects being arrested and brought to the custody area in the first place. However, one of the drug workers was unhappy with the concessions drug workers had to make through their involvement in coerced treatment and their role in the police station. He said: 'I think we've taken on the sort of enforcement, the police side of things, so I don't feel we can have shared objectives. I'd imagine that they, the police, are happy when we get somebody into treatment, because it takes them away from crime'. That is, drug workers had become co-opted into helping the police meet their objectives rather than sharing those objectives.

While the police/police staff may have shared goals with some of the other practitioners in the custody area, it seemed that there was a tendency for police objectives to take precedence. One research participant (SNS11) said that police objectives to investigate and prosecute crimes caused them to forget their 'humanity'. For example, the view expressed above by one inspector (SNS8) that someone was *only* an AA conveyed the power imbalance that existed between some staff and the police. This meant that it was easy for the police to focus on their investigation and their timescales at the expense of the needs of AAs and suspects. Similarly, in both sites, the police and police staff tended to view the police station as their territory into which solicitors were invited or from which they were ejected if they 'misbehaved'. For example, this Security Ltd employee noted that solicitors are 'here at the invite realistically of the police, they've got rooms outside, that's where they are supposed to be, they're only here to deal with the client, and sometimes they forget to show a lot of respect for what we do' (SNS4).

However, it was not just legal advisors and AAs that felt pressured by the police and the detention clock, so too did doctors, as one explained:

> Now urgent can mean two things in the police, it can mean medically urgent . . . or PACE clock urgent, because they're running out of time. So we encourage them to make it clear what they mean. Asap is different from urgent or in your own time doc . . . if I get two, PACE clock problems or a Road Traffic Act blood option, on the other hand I've six cases somewhere else. Then rather than me be stressed I'd talk to the custody officers to say, sort yourself out and tell me where you want me to go, I'm your servant. That way they can't blame me, and they usually come to a very quick agreement, and then it all works quite smoothly. Not doing that sometimes gets the doctors into difficulties because they get over-stressed, you know, it's quite stressful when you've got 18 people backed up, and everybody's screaming for you, and the pager's going off left, right and centre, and you do have to concentrate. (GMS9)

This illustrates, however, that doctors were sometimes able to stand up to the police so that they could concentrate and do their job properly. It is possible to see how some AAs, particularly inexperienced volunteers, may not be robust enough to do this. This is hardly surprising given the status of the medical profession relative to AAs, as I outlined at the start of the chapter.

Drug workers in Gormiston, but not in Sunnyside, also noted a sense of power imbalance between them and the police when it came to using the custody block. One drug worker (GMS6) said that he preferred to speak to police staff and avoided speaking to sergeants because they made him feel uncomfortable and as if they were too busy to talk to him. There were also certain parts of the police custody area that were out of bounds; for example, he felt that the area behind the booking-in desk, where the custody records were stored, was out of bounds even though occasionally he needed to write things on the custody records. However, it was not just the police with whom they felt powerless; this was also true of their relationship with doctors. Indeed, drug workers in Gormiston had been encouraged by their managers to go along with doctors' professional judgements. A drug worker (GMS6) said that he had recently been e-mailed by his manager to say that even if the drug workers disagreed with a doctor's assessment about fitness to interview they had to go along with it.[2] This was in spite of the fact that sometimes suspects assessed to be fit by doctors were not fit enough for him to assess them, for example, because they were so intoxicated that they kept falling asleep.

Therefore the present research indicates that custody areas were police territory, for both suspects and a range of practitioners. The findings from Chapters 4 and 5 show how the police exerted control over suspects from the moment they arrived at the police station, albeit that this was also tempered by access to their procedural rights and entitlements. Chapter 6 showed how police staff were deputized by the police and, in this chapter, the findings show that legal advisors, AAs and drug workers, but also to an extent doctors, felt a power imbalance between them and the police. In spite of growing multi-professionalism, police custody areas remain police territory. As one sergeant in Gormiston (in GMPO1) said, the custody area was 'his kingdom' and that he liked to offer a professional, fair but firm service. This fits in with previous research which has reached similar conclusions, such as Britton (2000), Choongh (1997: 86) and McConville *et al.* (1991: 38), and suggests that, disappointingly, multi-professionalism has brought few changes in terms of how the custody area is viewed by practitioners and suspects.

Independence from the police

Police dominance of the custody area created a constant tension with other occupational groups who tried to assert their independence. This was also noted by Choongh (1997: 86). Legal advisors, perhaps because of their adversarial role, were particularly clear about this; they felt that they should be polite and friendly, but not familiar with the police as this compromised the trust invested in them by their clients to defend them. Doctors also expressed similar views about their independence. So, for example, SNS2 said that the medical staff did not share organisational goals with Security Ltd or the police and that so long as the medical staff provided the agreed service the police and Security Ltd did not have an input into the medical service. Perhaps these two groups were more able to assert their independence from the police because they were professionals in the 'harder' sense of the term, that is they belonged to external professional bodies and worked in a profession which commanded status and high levels of pay, even if they did not always maintain such independence.

It was not just legal advisors and doctors that wished to remain independent from the police, so too did drug workers. One drug worker (SNS13) said that he made it abundantly clear to clients that 'I'm not a copper, I'm not a solicitor, I'm a member of the public, I work with a charity, and I try and get that across, because then that puts them more at ease, and they're more inclined to want to engage with me'. A drug worker in GMPO7 said that he retained a degree of physical separation from the police by having a separate office which was a reasonable distance from the booking-in desk. He also said that his first response to working in the custody area was that he did not like all of what he saw there (e.g. the macho police culture and the derogatory language used to talk about suspects). However, he also said that, no matter how hard it was, it was important to retain these early impressions of the custody block because otherwise there was a risk that you could become desensitized to it and become co-opted into the culture of the custody area.

In practice, those who were regularly based in the custody area (e.g. legal advisors, doctors, drug workers and AAs), had to manage the risk that they would become co-opted into the culture of the custody block. For instance an inspector (SNS9) said that there was a danger with the police working too closely with legal advisors or AAs or any other practitioners because it meant there was scope for them becoming part of the team in the custody block and of them losing their independence. However, it was doctors more than other practitioners in the custody area that were least effective at managing this risk, even though they were professionals in the 'harder' sense of the word. For instance, in SNPO4, one of the researchers observed a situation in which the doctor overtly helped the police with their investigation rather than remaining independent, although this seemed to be because the officer in the case was new and in need of guidance. On this occasion, the on-call doctor was asked to conduct an assessment on someone suspected of driving under the influence of alcohol and drugs after he was stopped in his car and found to have cannabis on him. The arresting officer had not dealt with a case like this before. The doctor said to the officer in the case, 'the first thing you have to have absolutely clear is your reasons for stopping him'. The officer gave an account of the suspect driving and the doctor interrupted saying, 'you mean he was driving erratically?' 'Yes' said the officer. Later, while filling in the paperwork for the assessment, the doctor who was filling in the in form said to the officer 'I believe your words were that he was driving erratically?' No drug or alcohol impairment was detected.

Another legal advisor, in Gormiston, described the doctor as the 'police doctor' and said that the doctor provided a service to the police and not to the suspect. He seemed to suggest that the doctors did not just cooperate with the police, rather that they colluded with them in meeting police goals when it came to fitness for interview decisions, as he explained:

> I rarely find an FME [forensic medical examiner] who will find a client unfit for interview . . . in fact, on this case where the client had chopped the man's head off that I was telling you of, the FME went down, spent 10 minutes with them, and said they were fit for interview, whereas I had spent a couple of hours with the person, and it was absolutely as clear as day that he was absolutely unfit, barking mad in fact, as was later proved when he was found guilty on the grounds of diminished responsibility. (GMS12)

He also said that this lack of independence further impacted on suspects because of a lack of client confidentiality. Information given to the doctor, for example, about drug use was placed on their custody record and could be later used by the police as a reason to object to bail. Doctors were supposed to inform suspects that what they told them was not confidential, but suspects may not have appreciated the significance of this and, if they did, it may have inhibited the frankness of their conversation with the doctor. This poses a threat to the well-being of suspects, for instance if they failed to mention something of life-threatening significance to the doctor because of fears about the lack of confidentiality. This confirms the discussion in Chapter 3 and in Newburn and Hayman (2002: 135–6) that doctors, more than other practitioners, have a conflicting role in the custody area, since they have a duty of care towards and a need for confidentiality in their relationship with clients, but are paid by the police.

The ultimate responsibility for suspects: 'the buck stops with the sergeants'

In Chapters 4 and 5 I identified the ways in which the police exerted coercive control over suspects, whether that was through cell buzzers or access to rights and entitlements. In this chapter, so far, I have argued that the police also exercised control over the custody area in part because they were responsible for the time taken to investigate an offence, for coordinating practitioners required by suspects and for prolonging detention, but also because their objectives tended to dominate what happened in the custody process, making the custody area police territory, albeit that this was tempered by practitioners clinging on to their independence from the police. Furthermore, when participants were explicitly asked about who was responsible for the care and fair treatment of suspects most, regardless of site or occupation, argued that the buck stopped with the custody officers. This also reflects the central role given to custody officers under PACE (Code of Practice C: para. 1.1A).

Police staff (SNS4, SNS7 and GMS3) in both sites said that while everyone, themselves included, played a part in caring for suspects and ensuring that they were fairly treated, the ultimate responsibility rested with the custody officers. The remainder of the research participants in Gormiston were emphatic that custody officers were viewed as ultimately responsible. This was true for doctors (GMS2, GMS9), legal advisors (GMS1 and GMS12) and custody officers (GMS10 and GMS13). Research participants such as police staff (GMS3), doctors (GMS9) and custody officers (GMS10 and GMS13) said that this was because there was a clear chain of command in which the custody officer oversaw the different practitioners therein. Furthermore, an inspector (GMS5) said that inspectors were only there for administrative purposes, such as staffing and resourcing, but that only a superintendent could revoke a custody officer's decision, not an inspector. This meant that the custody officer had ultimate responsibility for the decisions unless challenged by a superintendent.

In Sunnyside, research participants other than the police staff were also emphatic that custody officers were ultimately responsible. Two medical professionals (SNS2 and SNS10) said that overall responsibility for suspects rested with the custody officer as they were the person authorizing detention and who had a duty of care towards the suspect. A legal advisor (SNS12) and this custody officer both agreed that the custody officer was ultimately responsible, even when private police staff were employed within the custody area:

> The custody officer ... anything Security Ltd fall down on is ultimately our responsibility, an example of that would be, somebody made a complaint ... a nominated person hadn't been called, and when I looked at the record, I was on duty, the bloke had asked for it, but the custody assistant hadn't seen it, or had seen it and then forgotten to do it, and that was my fault, I should have seen that, and checked it, and told him to get it done. (SNS12)

Similarly, a Security Ltd Manager (SNS5) and an inspector (SNS8) said that the ultimate responsibility was a legal responsibility because of PACE.

There were two examples in Gormiston of when the buck stopped with the custody officer; one was less serious than the other. In GMPO6, a French-speaking Algerian suspect was booked in, having been accused of 'pickpocketing' a mobile phone, which he had picked up from the floor of a nightclub. There was confusion about whether he intended to hand in the phone to the manager of the club with the suspect at one point saying that he was planning to keep the phone and at another point saying that he was not. The custody officer was concerned that the matter may have become confused because the suspect did not speak English as a first language. The suspect said he did not need an interpreter, but the custody officer overrode his wishes and requested one anyway, saying 'I don't care whether he agrees. He's having an interpreter and that's my decision'. Perhaps this custody officer's decision was motivated by a concern that he would be held responsible if charges could not be laid because the language barrier had not been addressed.

The second example of this was when a suspect had an epileptic fit in her cell and had not been found for some time. In GMPO5, at 20:46, a female suspect was found by the designated detention officer barely conscious in her cell, having had an epileptic fit. A jailor came to the desk to inform one of the custody officers that this was the case, although he did so quietly so as not to alert the researcher. Two of the custody officers immediately went down to the cell. At 21:18 the suspect was escorted by two PCs to hospital in an ambulance. One of the other custody officers said of the 'skipper' for the night that they thought he would be going 'fuckety-fuck'. This highlights that the 'skipper' was regarded as ultimately responsible for events that night.

The remainder of research participants in both sites either expressed confusion about who was ultimately responsible or said that the buck stopped with the inspectors. Two inspectors (SNS9 and GMS7) provided somewhat contradictory responses. For example, when asked where the ultimate responsibility lay for the care and fair treatment of suspects SNS9 initially stated that it rested with the sergeants. However, later he said:

> If Security Ltd don't carry out a task, or if staff members don't carry out a task, or are rude or offensive, or commit a crime, then there's a responsibility that's not the sergeant's fault necessarily. If they miss a check, that's not the sergeant's fault, although there is a liability to ensure, because of course, in theory, they should be checking as such, so they can't be responsible for their lack of training, or their poor action.

He could not seem to make up his mind. This was perhaps because the legal responsibility of the custody officer was at odds with the contractual responsibilities of Security Ltd and this inspector was struggling to distinguish between the two. This highlights a crucial difficulty with involvement of the private sector in police custody areas.

The drug workers (GMS6 and GMS7) were also uncertain about how to answer the question, for example saying 'I suppose it's the police and the designated detention officers'. In Sunnyside, however, the drug workers (SNS13 and SNS14) and the AA (SNS15) thought that the inspectors were ultimately responsible, not the custody officers. For example, SNS13 and SNS14 said that the ultimate responsibility rested with the inspectors, not the sergeants, saying the 'the buck would stop with the inspector' and that 'if shit happens on the inspector's shift, then it's down to him to work out exactly how that happened, and what went wrong there'. Similarly, an independent custody visitor (GMS11) said that she used to think it was the custody sergeant, but now that they had created a custody manager role for inspectors that it had become the inspector's responsibility 'because they can have such an effect because they can say, no I don't want this, yes I want this to happen, and, let's talk about how things might be improved'. This tension between operational command and legal responsibility highlighted another area of uncertainty about responsibilities in the custody areas.

Accountability and governance

As explored in Chapter 6, police officers and police staff largely thought about their accountability in terms of PACE, line management and, for the private police staff only, through contractual arrangements. The other practitioners in the custody area were accountable for their actions through their own organizations. The drug workers were line-managed within the structures of the drug intervention programme, except for one of them who was a sessional worker and who said that he was infrequently line-managed, if at all. The situation was similar for AAs. In Sunnyside, an AA (SNS15) said that there were national guidelines for the AA service and that they would be held to account through the Department for Children, Schools and Families in the local authority for the service that they delivered, including the use of volunteers.

Medical staff in Sunnyside were employed by a subcontractor of Security Ltd and were line-managed by managers from this subcontractor. One of the nurses (SNS10) said that he had to report daily to the most senior doctor, informing her of who he had seen, of any concerns he had and any action he had taken. He also conferred with her about decisions when he was uncertain about an appropriate course of action. This hierarchical line-management structure had been put in place because of the use of forensic nurse practitioners rather than just doctors. The doctor who line-managed him was also the manager of the subcontractor who was, therefore, held to account through their contract with Security Ltd. However, in Gormiston one of the doctors (GMS9) said that because he was an independent medical practitioner he was held to account by the General Medical Council.

The multi-professional nature of police custody areas raises another possibility of practitioners regulating each other by acting as checks and balances on one another. In other criminal justice contexts, such as restorative justice, this has been referred to as a kind of 'deliberative accountability' (Roche, 2003: 5), in which accountability is built into the decision-making process rather than occurring after a decision has been reached. It is premised on ideas from political science and theories of deliberative democracy that citizens should be involved in decisions that affect them not through the aggregation of votes but rather through deliberation, discussion and debate. Importantly, in relation to restorative justice, this kind of decision-making enables both the offender and the state to be held to account by the victim. The involvement of a variety of practitioners in the police custody process means that a suspect's case might be discussed by multiple players, thereby enabling each to act as a check and balance on one another, as well as deterring any untoward behaviour. In addition, if a suspect were to make a complaint about their treatment, there are likely to have been witnesses, other than the police, who could substantiate the complaint, which is important given the small proportion of complaints against the police that are substantiated (Gleeson and Grace, 2009: 9).

In the present research, a doctor, GMS2, said that he was constantly vigilant in the custody areas to ensure that staff were doing things properly, as well as being on first-name terms with staff and making himself approachable so that the police staff could ask questions of him. At the same time, there were limits to this, particularly in view of the evidence presented above about the dominance of the police in the custody area. A drug worker (GMS6) said that he was limited in his capacity to suggest to the police that they were not doing things properly perhaps because he lacked authority relative to the police. As Skolnick (2005) argues, the police officers' roles contain two important variables, danger and authority. Danger elicits self-defensive behaviour and suspiciousness, while authority becomes a resource for diminishing perceived threats, including those perhaps from other practitioners who question them.

This drug worker, GMS6, described a situation in which, when he arrived at work to relieve his colleague, his colleague was upset by how the police had treated a suspect who was drunk and had 'communication difficulties', and who had also vomited in the police station. His colleague felt that the police had been 'abusive', had failed to find an AA for the suspect and had not met the suspect's needs. On this occasion, the drug worker and his colleague said nothing as the change of shift meant that the suspect was treated differently by the incoming shift of police officers; for example, they provided the suspect with a pen and paper with which to communicate. However, this incident made him wonder whether and at what point he might intervene with police officers, as he explained:

> [I]t [the incident] was interesting because I thought where would it be that I'd intervene? Actually there and then? . . . In those instances would you want to go and say, you're doing it wrong, well you don't want to be saying to a police officer, you're doing it wrong . . . is it something that can be brought up later, for instance if this person isn't at risk or actual harm by the situation . . . in which case would I first take it to a custody sergeant just to report it to them, or is that worse than just trying to intervene there and then? (GMS6)

Later he said that he discussed these matters in his supervisions with his line manager, who said that it was impossible for drug workers to intervene every time they believed that the police had behaved in an unacceptable manner because of the need to maintain their working relationship.

Therefore practitioners felt both powerless to speak up against unacceptable police practices as well as needing to maintain a veneer of cooperation. Like researchers, practitioners in the police custody areas may not want to jeopardize their relationships with the police; they may have spent time cultivating them, against the odds, for the purposes of meeting their own organizational objectives (Skinns, 2005: 254; McConville *et al.*, 1994: 62). That is, those working in the custody areas may not wish to 'rock the boat'. Furthermore, the effectiveness of this form of self-regulation depends on the agencies within the police custody process retaining a sense of their independence, rather than the boundaries between them and the police becoming blurred.

Therefore multi-professional custody areas provide opportunities for practitioners to hold each other to account and to instil in the police self-regulation and self-governance, but power differentials between practitioners, the authority of the police and a desire to 'not rock the boat' meant that such opportunities were probably not realized in practice.

Conclusion

This chapter has demonstrated three main areas of complexity and tension in multi-professional relationships in police custody areas. First, these multi-professional relationships were affected by a lack of trust and familiarity between the police and other practitioners. Particularly for legal advisors, these relationships were also affected by the use of negative stereotypes; they were seen as arrogant, pushy and demanding. These relationships were underscored by adversarialism. A second difficulty in the custody area was that of coordinating the arrival of legal advisors, doctors and AAs, sometimes leading to stand-offs about when each practitioner should arrive at the custody area. The coordination of these practitioners was left to the police and they sometimes resorted to lying to the legal advisors and to the AAs about when they should arrive, which left these other practitioners feeling disgruntled about wasting their time waiting at the police station. The underlying issue, however, was that all of the practitioners in the custody area had scarce resources which meant they were understandably reluctant to attend or wait at the custody area unnecessarily. Third, accountability was obfuscated and there was limited scope for practitioners to hold each other to account, given the power imbalances, particularly between the police and other practitioners, as well as the authority of the police and the desire of practitioners to not 'rock the boat' of their working relationship. This ruled out the possibility of 'deliberative accountability' in Roche's terms (2002: 5).

Contrary to their image as joined-up, cooperative, accountable and mutually beneficial, multi-professional relationships can be difficult to initiate, to manage and to sustain. This adds further weight to the growing body of evidence that partnerships, even in the more bounded context of police custody areas, do not provide a magic solution to criminal justice problems. These tensions and complexities also help to explain some of the findings from earlier in the book. For example, the take-up of legal advice explored in Chapter 5 may be partly determined by the complex interactions between legal advisors, suspects, police staff and the police: the police (sometimes rightly) have been found to challenge the competence of legal advisors, or claim that legal advisors take a long time to arrive, or during busy periods the police have failed to keep track of or even make requests for legal advice, in the first place. Suspects' experiences of police custody are undeniably shaped by some of these challenges within the multi-professional environment.

The findings in this chapter also demonstrate that custody areas are police territory, where the police exercise control not just over suspects, as I described in Chapters 4 and 5 but also over other practitioners. Indeed, this, along with custody officers' legal responsibility for suspects, may have contributed to the view among most research participants that the responsibility for the care and fair treatment of suspects lay with the custody officers. At the same time, police dominance of the custody area was tempered to a degree by legal advisors, drug workers and doctors claiming to be professionally independent from the police. This applied to a lesser extent to doctors; researchers observed circumstances in which the doctors helped the police with their prosecutorial goals and research participants said that the doctors colluded with the police in their assessment of the fitness of suspects.

This paints a picture of the custody areas in which practitioners from time to time try to assert their authority over the police, with some having more success than others. The implication is that the maintenance of order in the custody area was largely down to the police and police staff. In terms of their philosophies of control, police staff erred towards the procedurally just end of the spectrum, while police officers used both procedurally, just as well as coercive, punitive and instrumental means when necessary. The strategies of control used by other practitioners (who were neither police nor police staff) were perhaps lost or less visible in this context.

In the next chapter, I examine the implications of the findings discussed in Chapters 3 to 7 for theories about procedural justice and legitimacy which were critically assessed in Chapter 2. Chapter 9, however, outlines key concepts for future research and examines ways of improving the police custody process.

Notes

1 See, for example, Skinns (2005: 315), Audit Commission (2002), Crawford (2001, 1997: 131–2), Crawford and Jones (1995), Sampson *et al.* (1988) and Blagg *et al.* (1988).

2 Doctors are legally responsible for determining fitness for interview and detention, not the police or drug workers.

Chapter 8

Governance and legitimacy revisited

Having empirically examined the custody environment and the relationships between suspects and those working in custody areas, the aim of this chapter is to examine the implications of these findings for theories of governance and legitimacy, the central tenets of which were outlined in Chapter 2. As shown in Figure 8.1, my argument in Chapter 2 was that the actions of the police were governed partially through 'vertical' constitutional and institutional arrangements such as PACE, although the effectiveness of these mechanisms can be undermined by officer's agency, the occupational culture of the police and their positioning in the criminal justice process. Moreover, the multi-professional nature of police custody and other criminal justice settings means that, on their own, constitutional and institutional forms of governance are insufficient to explain how the police are governed. What is also required is an understanding of what I have called relational forms of governance, which concerns the largely horizontal relationships between the police and other criminal justice practitioners. Both of these forms of governance likely influence how the police and police staff use their authority, thereby affecting their legitimacy and contributing to citizen compliance with the law. The aim of this chapter is to explore what the empirical research on police custody examined in the book thus far has added to these ideas about the links between governance and the legitimacy of police/police staff. A further aim is to situate this discussion within the context of managerialism and neo-liberalism (which have contributed to developments such as workforce modernization, partnership-working and governing at a distance).

First, I explore the governance of the police through constitutional and institutional means and, second, the governance of multiple practitioners through relational governance. Third, I examine how police and police staff used their power to 'govern' suspects, looking in particular at

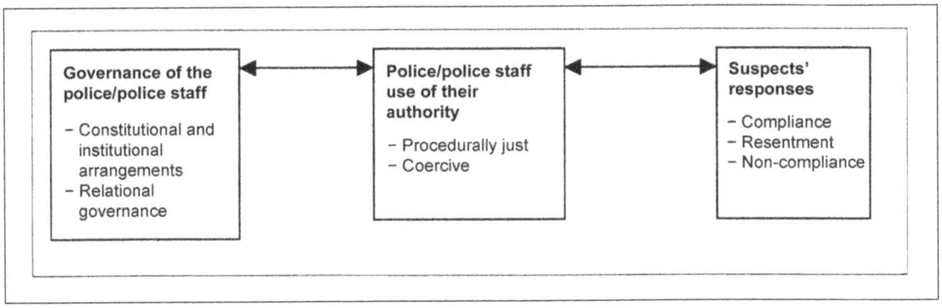

Figure 8.1 Links between governance, the use of authority and suspect responses to police/police staff

whether the police and police staff used strategies of coercion or procedurally fair consensual mechanisms to secure compliance. Fourth, I examine how suspects responded to the power exercised over them by the police, noting the parallels between suspect and prisoner responses to the exercise of authority over them. In particular, I explore how suspects experienced the 'pains of police detention' and whether and how they adapted to these pains. Finally, I critically assess the wider consequences of the police custody process for citizens' relationships with the police and other authorities.

Constitutional and institutional governance of the police

Mostly suspects accessed their rights and entitlements, indicating both that the process was mostly procedurally just and that legal governance, namely PACE, exerted an influence on the police. However, there were occasions when suspects did not access their rights and entitlements. Some suspects were not read their rights, did not have someone informed of their whereabouts when they requested it and were not able to access legal advice when they requested it. Police practices also diverged from the law in their use of informal interviews, which were reportedly used to persuade suspects to talk or to dissuade them from seeking legal advice. The detention review process was also so routinized that it was ineffective as a mechanism for informing suspects about progress with their case.

These divergences from the law were partly enabled by suspects who simply wanted to be out of the custody area as quickly as possible. They were also connected to deliberate and sometimes coercive strategies; for example, some suspects were forcibly taken directly to a cell without being read their rights. These coercive strategies were enabled and justified by a mixture of the demeanour of the suspect (e.g. if they were non-compliant), the culture of the custody area in which these kinds of practices were favoured and the prosecutorial mindset of the police as a result of their structural positioning in the criminal justice process. At the same time, divergence from the law was as much inadvertent as deliberate, as a result of the routinized way the custody process operated, albeit that the impact was largely the same in that suspects were denied access to their rights and entitlements.

However, what was also clear was that whether the police and police staff acted in accordance with PACE was not entirely due to its effectiveness as a form of governance. What also mattered were the complex interactions, shown in Chapter 7, between the police and other criminal justice practitioners. For example, the police were charged with the difficult task of coordinating the arrival of a range of practitioners in order to fulfil requirements under PACE. Whether or not this happened was as much to do with police actions as with the relationships between the police and other criminal justice practitioners and the practitioners themselves. This provides clear evidence for a need to think beyond the constitutional and institutional means of governing the police. In multi-professional contexts such as police custody, relational forms of governance are arguably as important.

Relational governance and multi-professional power relations

As for relational governance, the research showed that practitioners in the custody areas were far from engaged in a partnership of equals. To the contrary, relationships between practitioners were hierarchical in character; the police custody area was regarded by practitioners (and suspects) as police territory into which they were invited so long as they adhered to police rules about acceptable forms of behaviour. For instance, like suspects, legal advisors had to 'toe the line' by not being demanding or pushy, or they could find that they were asked to leave the custody area. Furthermore, when it came to coordinating the arrival of practitioners, this was fitted in the main around police objectives and timescales so that their arrival coincided with when the police were ready to interview the suspect. Consequently, the police were also regarded as being ultimately responsible for the care and fair treatment of suspects, although this also reflected the role ascribed to them in PACE. These tendencies towards the police playing a dominant role have also been documented in other research such as Choongh (1997: 85) and Newburn and Hayman (2002: 136–40).

Together this suggests that police custody areas were largely dominated by police practices and police objectives, but also by police culture, ideologies and normative expectations about suspects and other practitioners. Indeed, the very practice of the police dominating the multi-professional setting is a part of the normative expectations that the police have of themselves; authoritarianism is regarded as a part of police occupational cultures (Skolnick, 2005). To a degree this dominant role is understandable in a police station, that is in a place that the police are likely to regard as their 'own', but this tendency towards taking a dominant role has also been noted in other multi-agency settings, such as Crime and Disorder Reduction Partnerships (Jamel and Mair, 2003; Phillips, 2002; Crawford and Jones, 1995; Liddle and Gelsthorpe, 1994; Sampson *et al.*, 1988). In this context, police domination of the partnerships was further attributed to their construction as 'experts', 'knowledge brokers' or 'specialists' in crime prevention and the main custodians of crime statistics (Crawford, 1997: 131; Tierney, 2001). 'In the face of this "expertise", other partners in inter-agency work are left muted' (Crawford, 1997: 131), albeit that they were also quick to absolve themselves of sole responsibility for tackling racist incidents (Bowling, 1998: 148). Together, this suggests that playing a dominant role is an intrinsic part of the mindset, working practices and culture of the police. If this is so, then it is likely to pose fundamental challenges for cooperative working relationships in multi-agency or multi-professional settings, as well as for parity in relational forms of governance.

That said, there were chinks in the metaphorical armour of the police, meaning that their control of the custody area was far from absolute and suggesting that it was more of a hierarchy of control in which the police were at the helm and below which were other practitioners, some with more power than others. First, to a limited extent police staff threatened the dominant position of the police by taking on additional roles and responsibilities (e.g. designated detention officers in Gormiston had taken on the role of checking on suspects in the cells) and additional powers (e.g. detention supervisors in Sunnyside had begun to read suspects their rights and to use force) for which they did not have a mandate or the authority. Indeed, busyness in the custody areas may have provided an opportunity for police staff to act autonomously from the police. Moreover, the power and mission creep of police staff in police custody may be one of the unintended consequences of workforce modernization, which also applies to other civilianized roles such as police community support officers.

However, these challenges were relatively minimal compared to the power of the police over the police staff. In most other ways the police were the dominant player, with police staff working under their direction and with the police exercising their power *through* the police staff. In addition, the police may also have benefitted from passing on the caring and compassionate part of the job to the police staff and from the 'friendliness' of the police staff in performing this role which was used to secure suspect compliance. Moreover, in ideological terms, the police retained the lion's share of the power since they were almost uniformly regarded by research participants as having ultimate responsibility for suspects. Taken together, these findings suggest that Crawford's (2006: 466) monopolistic model may be the best way of characterizing police–police staff relationships in that police staff were integrated into the police rather than vice versa.

Second, in Sunnyside, Security Ltd also challenged the monopoly of the police, although again this was to a limited extent. This was evident in the disputes about necessary repairs to the building which were not done because it could not be determined who was responsible. This was further illustrated by the fact the police were concerned about 'rocking the boat' in their relationship with Security Ltd, meaning that they did not fine them for failing to meet contractual requirements. This suggests that this relationship between private security companies and the police, if they exist in police custody areas, may be best characterized by Crawford's (2006: 466) market model, which expresses this conflict between different providers.

Third, to a degree, some practitioners more than others were able to stand up to the police while working in the custody area. By virtue of their professional status in the 'harder' sense of the term – that is, they were formally trained and accredited by a professional body – doctors and legal advisors had more power than police staff, drug workers and volunteer appropriate adults in their relationship with the police. At the same time, this still did not offer sufficient protection. Some described the doctor as 'the police doctor', who provided a service to the police, not the suspect. Similarly, legal advisors' professional independence was, in theory, protected by their adversarial role, provided that they acted in this capacity. Yet previous research has shown that some do not always act in an adversarial manner (e.g. Choongh, 1997: 157). As for appropriate adults, they were regarded as 'only volunteers', even by other practitioners like legal advisors. While drug workers' capacity for independence was overtly stated to suspects, it could be compromised by them being permanently based in the custody area and by them lacking professional status in the 'harder' sense of the term.

Taken together this suggests that relationships between the police and doctors may be best characterized by Crawford's (2006: 466) steering model, in which the police steer third parties who act as a 'junior partner' to the police. For drug workers and appropriate adults, it is more likely that they would be co-opted into the police, therefore fitting, like police staff, into the monopolistic model. That leaves legal advisors, whose relative independence from the police, unlike the other practitioners in the custody area, meant that they did not fit readily into any of the types that Crawford describes. One possibility is that legal advisors who failed to act in an adversarial manner could be characterized as a 'junior partner' of the police as part of Crawford's (2006: 466) steering model. Another possibility is that legal advisors who took an adversarial stance could be regarded as equal players in a networked model of governance. Yet this does not sufficiently convey the struggles that arise between the police and legal advisors.

The difficulty with identifying where legal advisors fit in Crawford's (2006) models suggests an underlying deficiency with it. His models explains the various relationships between the state and other policing providers. In fact, the police work alongside a range of practitioners who do not directly engage in policing, in the sense of engaging in mechanisms of social control focusing on inhibiting deviant behaviour. Instead, the legal advisors in the present study viewed themselves as at odds with rather than as part of the policing of suspects. Consequently, perhaps, the models need to be broadened to include the relationship between the state, policing and public sector providers. To do this, the models require an additional category of 'professional independence', which could incorporate actors and organizations without an explicit role in policing, but who have to work alongside the police, providing a different kind of public service, such as welfare, healthcare or legal advice.

Finally, and while there is no need to go into it here at length since it is discussed shortly, suspects also challenged police control of the custody area. This was true for suspects who engaged in a form of 'strategic or manipulative compliance' (Crewe, 2007), in which they played along with what was expected of them while having no normative commitment to the rules of the custody area, simply to pursue their personal objectives. This was also true for suspects who openly expressed defiance of the police, for example by repeatedly pressing the cell buzzer or 'kicking off' during their arrest or in the police station.

The discussion so far shows that there may have been chinks in the absolute control of the custody area by the police, but that the locus of power rested largely in their hands, meaning that the police governed practitioners as well as suspects, rather than practitioners governing each other. The police custody areas in the research provide further empirical evidence which questions whether the police can act as one node in a network of equals involved in governing security. However, whether this is true of other police custody areas remains a question for further empirical research, as police custody areas vary (Phillips and Brown, 1998: 60; Sanders *et al.*, 1989: 183), and because Shearing (2007: 252) notes the answer to the question of whether the police influence events more than others in any given nodal network varies across time and space. Judging by the dominant role played by the police in other multi-agency settings and also by the likely influence of facets of their occupational culture such as authoritarianism, I would hypothesize that the locus of power will rest primarily with the police in other police stations, a matter that is discussed in Chapter 9. Moreover, in the interests of a social democratic approach to the delivery of crime control in which security remains a public good, perhaps this is also where the locus of power should remain (Loader and Walker, 2007: 192–4), as long as the perspectives of other practitioners are not silenced as a result. For the most part, the interviewees in the research also appeared to share this normative position when they almost uniformly pointed to the police as being the bearers of the ultimate responsibility for the care and fair treatment of suspects.

Finally, the research shows that relational forms of governance are arguably as important for understanding multi-professional contexts such as police custody as traditional approaches which have focused on constitutional and institutional arrangements. However, like constitutional and institutional arrangements, relational forms of governance are somewhat imperfect as mechanisms for exerting influence over how the police act, primarily because power differentials tended to silence the voices of other criminal justice practitioners and limit the possibility of them acting as a check and balance on the police in a form of 'deliberative accountability' (Roche, 2003: 5). Even if most decisions about the suspect, in relation to PACE, should be left to the police, this does not mean that other perspectives should not be heard as part of police decision-making.

The use of authority by police and police staff: coercion or consent?

There may have been chinks in the absolute control of the custody area by the police – seeing as they were put in a precarious position by police staff and seeing as their authority was challenged by practitioners such as doctors and legal advisors, as well as to a degree by Security Ltd and by suspects – but the locus of power rested largely in their hands. This meant that the police used their authority over suspects and practitioners in the custody area. However, this did not mean that the way that the police exercised their authority was perceived as legitimate either by suspects (or by other practitioners in the custody area), since there was evidence that police power was wielded in coercive ways, meaning that the suspects needed to engage in an instrumental calculation, if they could, about how best to avoid sanctions and maximize rewards.

Police practices could be coercive in that the police sometimes used force during arrest and/or on arrival at the police station; the researchers observed some suspects being taken directly to the cells and forcibly searched while being pinned down by four or five police officers and/or police staff. It was difficult to say whether this use of force was entirely justified, particularly as the researchers had not been present during the arrest, but Choongh (1997: 83) notes as did some of the interviewees in the present study that they had been man-handled during arrest and even assaulted by the police on previous occasions.

However, coercive police practices were largely more subtle than this and examples of them have been scattered throughout the book. Right from the outset, while they are being booked in, suspects are told where to stand or sit, information is demanded of them, their possessions are removed, and their DNA, fingerprints and photograph taken, with suspects having little choice in the matter. In the cells, much of suspects' treatment depended on whether or not they complied; broadly speaking, suspects that acted up, for example, by repeatedly pressing the buzzer or by being demanding, generally, received less than those who complied with the process. Similarly, since access to showers, to the exercise yard and to cigarette breaks was wholly discretionary, these rewards were only given, if at all, to suspects that had mostly complied with the police and abided by police conceptions of acceptable behaviour. The same was true for suspects and their access to their rights and entitlements; for example, requests for legal advisors could be delayed or forgotten, as could phone calls to notify a suspect's family or friends of their arrest. Informal conversations were also used, for example to dissuade suspects of the need for legal advice or to explore whether they were likely to confess. Moreover, drug-testing on arrest – which, if the suspect refuses, carries a penalty of up to five years' imprisonment – adds another dimension to the coercive nature of police practices.

The custody environment itself was also coercive. The custody areas were frantically busy and austere since they were dirty, noisy, poorly lit and poorly ventilated, particularly in Gormiston. In Sunnyside, the height of the custody desk meant that staff routinely looked down on suspects, sending a clear message to them about who was in control. The cells were no better, with one suspect describing them as 'dead dingy little things', while others felt that they were too cold or too hot and that blankets were dirty or unavailable and that the food was so poor that they refused to eat it. Moreover, the fact that the custody areas were such busy and pressured environments raises questions about why this was so. It suggests that police managers viewed police custody as less of a priority than other aspects of policing when allocating staff and other resources. By the same token, operating police custody areas that are coercive also suits police objectives. These coercive practices and coercive features of the custody environment circumvent the need for legitimacy and for seeking suspects' consent to be policed through, for example, the use of fair procedures.

However, was coercion in the custody area sufficient to make suspects obey the rules? Tyler (1990: 23) argues that what makes people obey the rules is not a fear of the consequences of breaking them or some other estimation of the long-term costs and benefits, in part because the certainty and severity of those punishments are unknown. Instead, Tyler (2003) argues that the key to compliance lies in people's experience of the fairness of criminal justice procedures in terms of the quality of decision-making (including whether it is neutral and unbiased) and interpersonal treatment (including whether they are treated with dignity and respect). However, what is also of importance, according to Beetham (1991: 11), is whether people abide by these decisions because they share the same moral values as the decision-maker and because they believe that it is morally right to do so.

In the present research, while police custody was coercive, this did not preclude it from being procedurally fair. For example, the majority of suspects were read their rights, were not held incommunicado, had access to a legal advisor or an appropriate adult or a doctor, were not interviewed at night-time, were not informally interviewed before their formal interview, etc. Moreover, the police, particularly custody officers and to a lesser extent inspectors, were central in ensuring that the process was fair and that access to these rights and entitlements was not contingent on suspects' compliance. Tyler's (2003) research suggests that it is likely that these kinds of police practices, which enable suspects to assess the quality of the decision-making process, legitimate the exercise of police authority, perhaps making up for any deficits that arise as a result of coercive practices and a coercive environment.

Whether suspects' access to these rights and entitlements amounted to procedural justice or was simply concerned with due process depends in part on the quality of the decision-making process and the interactions between the staff and the suspect in giving these rights. One of the key differences between procedural justice and due process is that within a due process model, it is important to simply abide by rules that are publicly known and fair, while procedural fairness suggests that not only do these rules need to be followed, but people should be treated with dignity and respect in the process. Therefore it is the humanizing aspects of proceedings that are important. In police custody, the system abides by the rules of due process if a suspect is provided with a drink of water in the cells, but it may be procedurally unfair if that suspect has been waiting for a long period of time and has repeatedly pressed the buzzer and requested a drink from staff who have deliberately ignored this request.[1] That is, what is important is not just the giving of rights to suspects, so too is the manner by which they are given.

With regard to the quality of interpersonal treatment by the police, aside from during the booking-in process and the police interview, the police had few dealings with the suspect. It was the police staff in the custody areas who were largely responsible for their welfare while they were in the cells, except in Gormiston where police constables performed this role alongside the police staff. The police staff were relatively uninvolved in actually making any of the fundamental decisions about a suspect's case, such as about whether and when to contact a legal advisor or about whether or not they should receive bail. This suggests that the police were able to make up any deficits in legitimacy and garner their consent to be policed through the quality of the decision-making process, while police staff were able to garner consent through how they treated suspects in the cells.

Indeed, it appeared that police staff adopted a different style of using their authority. To caricature things slightly, the police staff played the 'good cop' and the police played the 'bad cop'. Suspects regarded the police staff as treating them more fairly and with respect than the police. Suspects also reported that they had a better rapport with police staff and could communicate more effectively with police staff, who were more compassionate and polite. Suspects also felt that they were more responsive to their requests and that the police staff were 'more like them', although this may also have been a sign of police staff lacking authority. Police staff were viewed, and indeed positioned themselves, as a neutral buffer in the sometimes fraught relationship between suspects and the police, although this could also be construed as them 'passing the buck'. Therefore it may be that since police staff were not empowered to use force that the police occupied a largely coercive role, which was routinized and efficient in character, while police staff exercised a 'lighter touch' in the way that they used their authority over suspects, relying on words, persuasion, compassion, a sense of equality, responsiveness and neutrality.

On reflection, perhaps this was a deliberate strategy used by police staff to enhance the quality of the interaction between them and the suspect. If this is so, there is a need for a differentiated understanding of how legitimacy is created and maintained in police custody areas which have undergone workforce modernization, as it seemed to vary between police and police staff which was in part connected to their differing roles.

In sum, the two police custody areas involved power being used in coercive and procedurally fair ways. On the one hand, suspects complied with the police because they were coerced through the use or threat of force, through 'punishments' such as cell buzzers being switched off or as a result of the austere police custody environment. On the other hand, suspects complied with the police because police officers (who largely impacted on the quality of decisions) and police staff (who largely impacted on the quality of interpersonal treatment) garnered their consent through the use of fair procedures. This use of fair procedures was not just about access to due process rights, although this was a part of it. Also of importance was the decision-making process and the way suspects were treated in the giving of their due process rights. The implication of all of this is that while procedural fairness legitimized the authority of the police/police staff (in the way that Tyler (2003) suggests), coercive practices simultaneously detracted from these gains in compliance as part of an ongoing and negotiated process involving both police and police staff.[2]

Suspect responses to staff authority

The purpose of this section is to explore how suspects responded to the way that power was exercised over them largely by the police and police staff. The research showed that suspects noticed the more immediate effects of police custody and the pains that this brought. In combination, the uncertainty of their situation, their loss of liberty, their loss of control over what happened to them in the custody area and the paucity of the custody environment as well as the complexity of their needs meant that police custody could be distressing.

Police custody and prisons

It was in suspect responses to the exercise of authority over them that parallels could be discerned with prisoners' responses to prison authorities. Before examining suspect responses to the authority of police and police staff, I briefly consider some of these parallels. Liebling (2004: 462–4) identifies the 'essential similarities' of the five prisons in her research. First, Liebling (2004: 462) suggests that prisons are places of punishment, as well as place-based communities, whose form is shaped by social and political ideas about crime, punishment, social order and human nature. Implicit in the notion of a place-based community, Liebling (2004: 462) argues, are ideas about prisoners observing each other, but also ideas about citizenship and the engendering of civic values. Police custody is not intended as a place of punishment. Indeed, to the contrary, it is supposed to be a place where those suspected of committing a criminal offence, who are also presumed innocent, are detained for short periods of time until a decision is reached about charge. However, this is not how police custody is used in practice; for example, Choongh (1997: 174–5) found the police used custody areas to unlawfully detain suspects who questioned their authority and, in the present study, the police used aspects of the custody process, such as the cell buzzers, to punish suspects who had not complied with their directions. Even so, it is difficult to claim that police custody areas are places of punishment and even more difficult still to claim that they are place-based communities as the police custody population is largely transitory. Even though a small proportion of suspects are likely to be 'regulars', at most suspects are detained for 96 hours, unless they are a terrorist suspect. However, police custody areas are places which contribute to ideas about citizenship and civic values, such as about the relationship between citizens and the police.

Nonetheless, in other respects police custody areas do resemble prisons. Liebling (2004: 462) says that prisoners are generally held against their will and that this contributes to an inherent legitimacy deficit. This is also true for police suspects; those in the present research remarked on the loss of control that they felt in police custody. Indeed, this is connected to the coercive and hierarchical nature of police custody areas, in which both suspects and other practitioners noted that it was police territory and that the police were ultimately responsible for the care and fair treatment of suspects. Similarly, Liebling (2004: 462) argues that prisons are hierarchical, normally having one person in charge, while also meaning that power can be abused, social order can break down and that compliance 'needs to be worked at'.

According to Liebling (2004: 462), prisoners are not only disempowered in their relations with prison staff, they are also constrained by aspects of the prison regime which limit their freedom, but also depersonalize, individualize and responsibilize them. Police custody areas also constrain suspects' freedom whether that is in terms of when and what they eat or when and whether they shower or smoke or take a breath of fresh air. Perhaps they are more constrained than prisoners, albeit for shorter periods of time; indeed, in Chapter 4, one suspect, GMD8, said that police custody was worse than prison because of the greater number of restrictions. Suspects might also experience greater constraint on them because they are kept in solitary confinement, which perhaps most closely resembles a segregation wing in a prison, but without a clock and for some without a clear sense of how long they are likely to be there. Furthermore, police custody areas may be regarded as de-personalizing in a similar way to prisons, as suspects are referred to by police by their custody number or sometimes their surname, although other practitioners checked with suspects about what they preferred to be called.

Like the prisons that Liebling describes (2004: 462), police custody areas are also volatile and fraught places where values are in tension, as well as being places that 'contain and produce pain'. Suspects have been found in previous research to react in an emotional manner to police custody, experiencing it as disturbing, humiliating, intolerable and distressing (Smith and Gray, 1983: 75; Choongh, 1997: 97). Furthermore, suspects in the present study reported in interviews that they found police custody made them anxious, bored, isolated and depressed. Moreover, some events – such as when one of the researchers observed a suspect having to be put on constant watch and eventually taken to hospital after she attempted and then succeeded to repeatedly and deliberately bang her head against the wall – acted as a more poignant reminder of the level of distress that some suspects experienced.

Liebling also notes that prisons are moral and emotional communities where staff–prisoner relationships are central to their 'nature, functioning and quality of life'. Similarly, relationships between the police and suspects, but more importantly between police staff and suspects, contributed substantially to the quality of suspect experiences for the short time that they were there. While these relationships may not be as enduring as for prisoners who are likely to spend longer in contact with the same members of staff, they are nonetheless important in contributing to an overall sense of where that suspect belongs in society and what they can expect from the police and perhaps other kinds of institutional actors in the future.

Based on these characteristics Liebling (2004: 462) argues that prisons differ by degree and that there is remarkable consensus among staff and prisoners about the character of a prison which is not reflected in key performance indicators. She also notes that this character, ethos or culture is difficult for researchers to conceptualize and measure. The present research is the first step in trying to understand how different police custody areas may be characterized, a matter I return to later in this chapter. For the moment, it is important to note that this gradual process of recognizing the importance of prisons for understanding police custody means that this chapter will make more use than heretofore of material from the sociology of prisons.

Suspect responses

The feelings that suspects expressed about being in police custody are reminiscent of the (endogenous) pains of imprisonment identified by Sykes (1958: 63–83) as the deprivation of liberty, the deprivation of goods and services, the deprivation of heterosexual relationships, the deprivation of autonomy and the deprivation of security.[3] This parallel is understandable in the light of the comparability of police custody and prison. Sykes (1958: 63) argues that these modern pains of imprisonment offer supposedly humane alternatives to physical maltreatment and neglect, but that they can be just as painful, particularly because of the threat they pose to an inmate's sense of self-worth. In the context of police custody, perhaps they are painful enough to pressure or coerce suspects into behaving in certain ways. After all, one of their overriding concerns was to leave police custody as quickly as possible, even if this meant declining legal advice or talking to the police, thereby jeopardizing their access to justice. That is, the 'pains of police detention' cannot be underestimated as a form of coercion.

For police suspects, deprivation of liberty, deprivation of goods and services and the deprivation of autonomy were of the greatest relevance, while the deprivation of heterosexual relationships and the deprivation of security were mitigated by the short periods of time that they spent in police custody, as well as by the fact that suspects spent much of their time alone in a cell, where the only threat to their security was from themselves, although this was not an insubstantial threat for some. Sykes (1958: 65) argues that the deprivation of liberty is a double loss as the prisoner is confined to the institution and confined in their freedom of movement within the institution. What is painful about this is being cut off from family and friends and, therefore, the loss of emotional relationships. In police custody, this loss of emotional relationships may only be temporary, but is nevertheless important because it is at a time when a suspect feels vulnerable and in need of more, not less, support. Perhaps this is why it is one of a suspect's three fundamental rights in police custody to have someone notified of their whereabouts, as well as the need to ensure that suspects cannot 'disappear'. Sykes' (1958: 65) analysis suggests that, for the 27 per cent of suspects in the present study whose family or friends were not informed of their arrest after suspects requested that they were, these suspects may have experienced this as one of the pains of their detention. Suspects' discretionary access to a separate right of speaking to someone for a reasonable amount of time on the telephone had similar implications in terms of reducing or adding to this 'pain of police detention'. Indeed, some of the suspects, such as GMD14 in Chapter 4, reported that they felt isolated when they were in the cells.

While the loss of emotional relationships may only be fleeting for police suspects, the moral rejection and social stigma that accompanies the loss of liberty and the sense that the suspect has had to forego their claim to being a fully-fledged and trusted member of society may not. The last may also be further reinforced, according to Sykes (1958: 65–7), by subordination to officials and their physical separation in a subterranean-like custody environment where signs of control are all around them ranging from the height of the custody desk to the taking away of their property to having always to ask for everything that they need. By the time that suspects leave police custody they may have learned a powerful lesson not only about their relationship with the police, but also about their place in society, while this may not necessarily impact on their offending behaviour.

In relation to the deprivation of goods and services, Sykes (1958: 67–70) argues that while prisoners' basic material needs are met (in that they are not hungry, cold, wet, untreated if they are ill nor without exercise), they experience this as painfully depriving, especially in a society that values consumption. However, as the present research has shown, these basic material needs were mostly but not always met in police custody; cells were either too hot or too cold, food and drinks were either inedible or not always forthcoming, depending on how suspects asked for them, suspects were mostly treated if they were ill, but only sufficiently so that they could continue to be detained or interviewed (e.g. dependent drug users had limited access to heroin substitutes) and suspects had limited access to exercise. This suggests that for a minority of suspects this added another dimension to the pains of police detention.

Even for suspects whose material needs were met, according to Sykes' analysis they were still likely to experience this as painful because they were divested of the 'subtle symbolic overtones which we invest in the world of possessions' (1958: 68). The pain of material impoverishment noted by Sykes (1958: 69) through the stripping away of a prisoner's identity seems all the more meaningful both to prisoners and to police suspects, in the light of mass consumerism. Immediate consumption has come to represent an important route to happiness, resulting in multiple opportunities for consumption of goods, services, leisure and pleasure. This can be summarized as a kind of 'I think therefore I shop' mentality. Consumption (not production or working) becomes the central hub around which the world revolves (Lyon, 1999: 21). Indeed, it has become one of the defining aspects of late modernity which extends beyond nation-states to affect global society. Therefore, as Sykes (1958: 70) argues, enforced material impoverishment is an attack on the prisoner's self-image; in a materialistic world, material impoverishment symbolizes personal inadequacy.

Sykes (1958: 73–6) also provides a powerful means of understanding why some police suspects reacted in the way that they did to the in-cell buzzer system and to staff being unresponsive to their requests. Sykes argues that rules which are designed to control behaviour in minute detail are galling to prisoners because of prisoners' 'far-reaching dependence on the decisions of their captors and the restricted ability to make choices' (1958: 73). Perhaps this is what suspects were referring to when they said that they experienced a loss of control. Indeed, one of the suspects, GMD7, who was described in Chapter 4, said that even though it seemed like a silly thing, not having a drink of water when he had a dry throat made him feel annoyed. As Sykes goes on to say:

> The important point . . . is that the frustration of the prisoner's ability to make choices and the frequent refusals to provide an explanation for the regulations and commands descending from the bureaucratic staff involve a profound threat to the prisoner's self-image because they reduce the prisoner to the weak, helpless, dependent status of childhood. (1958: 75)

Moreover, this status also threatens the prisoner's self-image as an adult member of society. Therefore, as with prisoners, this infantilizing of police suspects through their loss of autonomy is crushing and unpleasant, particularly when combined with the other 'pains of police detention' and suspect anxieties about what lies ahead. Moreover, unlike for prisoners, there is little opportunity for suspects to alleviate these pains of police detention through social interactions (Sykes, 1958: 82).

Together these 'pains of police detention' provide an insight into why suspects are in such a hurry to leave custody; it is physically and psychologically painful. Yet it also provides a clue as to why some suspects appeared to resist police coercion, whether that was by repeatedly pressing the in-cell buzzer or smoking crack in the cells, as reportedly happened shortly after the researchers left the custody area when staff failed to find drugs and a crack-pipe during routine searches. As Sykes notes, the pains of imprisonment or of 'police detention', as I have called them, generate a response in prisoners which is necessarily limited by their confinement but leads to either collectivistic or individualistic forms of adaptation and resistance. More recently, Crewe (2007) has provided a more nuanced view of prisoners' adaption to power in prisons, which further shows that the sociology of prisons is helpful for understanding how suspects adapt to their position of powerlessness in the face of police control over them, the custody environment and the police custody regime.

Through ethnographic research Crewe (2007) argues that prisons have become less authoritarian, more civilized and more humane, and although prisoners could see that their behaviour was restricted it was difficult for them to see how power was exercised, operating as it did at a distance through the specialist knowledge of experts such as prison psychologists and through risk assessments. At a glance then, within this reasonably calm atmosphere, it appears that prisoners consent to penal power; in fact, as Crewe (2007) argues, this atmosphere masks various orientations to the prison authorities which express normative consent as well as dissent and resistance. Drawing on Scott's (1990) notion of 'public transcripts', which refer to public acts and performances which can be used to mask whether or not someone conforms to the dominant value system, Crewe argues that '[u]nder conditions of domination, dissent and resistance are likely to be heavily concealed within public discourse or limited to backstage areas' (2007: 257). That is, while resistance was barely visible and prisoners appeared to conform, frustrations bubbled away beneath the surface covered by a veneer of acquiescence.

Crewe (2007) then identifies a typology of adaption, highlighting the distinctions within a single prison community, in terms of prisoners' consent and compliance with prison authorities. First, 'committed compliance' referred to prisoners who blamed themselves for their bad behaviour, leading them to feel that they deserved the punishment that they got and to accept the legitimacy of the prison, seeing it as an opportunity for self-improvement. Their sense of guilt meant that any resentment they expressed was towards themselves and not the prison. Second, 'fatalistic or instrumental compliance' led prisoners to give up resisting the prison authorities and comply with the rules. They complied not because they subscribed to prison rules for normative reasons but because complying enabled a better standard of living through the incentive earned privileges scheme or because it took them one step closer with going home to their families. Resentment about the prison authorities was expressed politely and through the appropriate channels, if they knew about them. But they also expressed resentment about themselves for meekly complying with the rules. Third, there was a small group of prisoners who complied in a detached manner, seeing it as important to rebuild their life in their own way and in their own time, even if this meant knocking back opportunities for parole because they were not ready to be returned to the chaotic life they had lived outside. They were passive and obedient, having sidestepped the need to be governed, thereby offering a form of passive dissent. Fourth, compliance was used strategically and manipulatively to conceal values that were opposed to the dominant values of the prison and to hide resistance, with prisoners, therefore, having little normative commitment to the prison's aims. This group of prisoners recognized that the prison system could not be ignored altogether and so they acted out a 'public script' of obedience (e.g. by attending courses, acting contrite or parroting the requisite language) so as to subvert its aims and advance their personal objectives (e.g. so that they looked good on paper). However, backstage, they were involved in overtly subversive behaviour such as illicit drugs or setting off fire alarms, as well as talking about 'playing the game'. It tended to be higher-status prisoners that manipulated the system in this way.

Crewe (2007) concluded that order in prisons is fragile and that this fourth kind of adaptation involving a 'hollow performance of commitment' undermines the legitimacy of the system as a whole, because, in effect, other prisoners are penalized for their honesty. This conclusion has more relevance, however, for prisons than for police custody areas; as Liebling (2004: 462) notes, prisons are communities where parties observe one another, meaning that prisoners may be more aware than police suspects of the unfair and manipulative behaviour of others. By contrast, in police custody, suspects have few opportunities for interaction with other suspects, with most interaction taking place between them, police staff and police officers. So, whereas in prisons subcultures emerge based on the pains produced as a result of interactions between staff and inmates over time, this is altered in police custody areas because of restricted interactions between staff and suspects and the short timescales.

The present research did not set out to explore, in detail, how suspects responded to being governed or how they adapted to the 'pains of police detention'. However, a few observations are possible in the light of Crewe's (2007) research. Like prisoners and prison authorities, suspects were powerless relative to the police, having a process, a regime and a set of values imposed on them. Like the prisoners in Crewe's (2007) research, it is likely that if suspects were opposed to any aspects of the police custody process, they would have concealed their dissent. Indeed, this was the case. Suspects, such as GMD7 who felt harassed by the police because he was known to them, appeared to engage in a strategic game with staff, which enabled him to assert his agency in the face of more or less total control by the police. He appeared to acquiesce to the power of the police by being seemingly polite and respectful in terms of whether he pressed the buzzer and in how he made his requests and how many requests he made. Yet this was also a strategy to try and get what he wanted because he was aware that the police responded better to those who were overtly compliant and played by the rules. He had learned the hard way: he had been awkward in the past and found that it got him nowhere. He seemed to fall into the category of what Crewe (2007) calls strategic and manipulative compliance. Indeed, since he had been in prison, it is possible that this was a survival strategy that he had developed in prison. This raises the possibility that prison cultures affect police custody and that, presumably, police custody experiences affect prison cultures.

There were also suspects, such as GMD6, who were fatalistic in terms of whether and how they complied with the police, only going through the motions because it was likely to mean that it curtailed their detention. This was apparent in how this suspect responded to the imposition of an appropriate adult on him; he regarded the appropriate adult as there for the sake of it (as he was a schizophrenic), but did not object, even though he saw them as of little use. This fatalism was also expressed in relation to whether or not to request legal advice, with some suspects declining it either because they were innocent, thus making a legal advisor redundant, or because they were guilty and were simply going to admit the offence. These selective illustrations demonstrate that the fatalistic and instrumental compliance that Crewe (2007) noted may be of use in understanding suspect responses to police custody.

By contrast, GMD13 showed 'committed compliance'. He had been accused of assaulting his pregnant girlfriend and eventually accepted a caution for this; but from the outset of the interview with him, it was clear that he blamed himself, as he said that he sat in the cell thinking the worst. He also appeared to accept the legitimacy of the police custody process; for example, he said that while he waited for 30–60 minutes for the police to answer his cell buzzer, he felt this was acceptable as they were simply busy. In addition, he said of the food that while it was poor, it was free and that he expected this as he was not in a 'holiday camp'.

There were no clear examples in the present research of the third typology of detached compliance noted by Crewe (2007). This could be because this was not something that the research systematically set out to explore or perhaps because it is of greater importance for prisoners than police suspects. However, there was possibly a fifth category that could be explored in future research. Some suspects were observed to be repeatedly restrained during arrest or in the police station, such as SND8 or the female suspect in Gormiston who repeatedly banged her head against the wall. There were also others who were openly subversive while they were in the custody area, for example suspects that repeatedly pressed the cell buzzer or demanded things of the police such as SND7, or were caught smoking crack in their cell. It seemed that these suspects had given up or were too distressed and/or intoxicated to care any more about the consequences of what they were doing. This type might be described as (having a commitment to) non-compliance.

This type implies that suspects did not have universal access to their rights and entitlements set down in PACE, or indeed their human rights; in fact, access to human rights was conditional on suspects complying with police conceptions of acceptable behaviour. For some suspects, being able to reason that compliance was what was required of them and that they needed, at the least, to be able to appear that they were playing along with the rules of the 'compliance game' was next to impossible either because they were inexperienced, distressed, intoxicated or mentally ill. It is inappropriate that whether or not someone has access to their right to privacy or their right to not be subject to degrading treatment, or perhaps even to their right to life as it was for Christopher Alder whose case was described in Chapter 1, depends on suspect compliance. As Choongh (1997) argues, suspect rights should be universally available to all suspects and not just those who are perceived by the police as deserving of them. He says '[t]he task is that of raising the fairness of expectations of all suspects, persuading the police that all suspects are entitled to be treated with respect and politeness, and ensuring that investigative powers are not used to punish those who refuse to accede to extra-legal demands' (p. 207). Together this suggests that suspects' social status and police perception of it impacts on access to their due process rights, but also the construction of procedural justice and police legitimacy.

Police custody and its wider consequences

Suspect experiences of police custody may have consequences for their future relationship with the police, in that they contribute to their understanding of what they should expect from the police. These encounters between the police and suspects in police custody areas can be thought about in two different ways, based on whether normative expectations about the police–suspect relationship are *imposed* on them by the police or whether they are mutually constructed and developed through encounters with each other. Normative expectations about the police–suspect relationship undoubtedly exist prior to their encounters with each other in police custody areas, although this is a matter for future research.

First, using the concept of social discipline, Choongh (1997: 227) argues that, particularly for those who are locked into a regular relationship with the police, which itself may be socially constructed based on police perceptions of who is likely to be problematic, the primary purpose of police custody is to *impose* on suspects an understanding of the normative dimensions of their relationship with the police. That is, its purpose is to impose on suspects ideas about what their relationship with the police should be like, for instance imposing on them ideas about the need to obey the authority of the police. The idea that norms are imposed on suspects in order to create social order is also implied by Simon's concept of 'governing through crime' in which institutions, which are not necessarily threatened by crime such as families and schools, are 'using crime to promote governance by legitimizing and/or providing consent for the exercise of power' (2007: 5).

Moreover, it is possible to impose these expectations on suspects, partly because they are coerced into accepting them in the way that Choongh

(1997: 227) argues, but partly because there may be an ideological component to them in the way that Lukes (2005: 25–9, 144) argues with his three-dimensional view of power. Even though they may go against suspects' best interests, normative expectations about the police–suspect relationship are 'sugar-coated', so that suspects accept them all the same, without questioning or even realizing that these expectations are not in their best interests, meaning that conflict is latent not overt. Indeed, procedural justice might be just such an ideology which is used to persuade suspects to accept unfair outcomes (MacCoun, 2005).

The second and less radical version of this argument is that rather than normative expectations about authorities being imposed on suspects by those in positions of power, police custody may be places where these expectations are developed in ways that are mutually beneficial to suspects and the police. For example, Liebling (2004: 461) says that as places of moral performance, prisons are where collective values (e.g. civic or moral values) can be nurtured (as well as threatened). Other research on legitimacy points to similar conclusions, namely that if authority is exercised in ways that are procedurally fair in real terms (not just in ideological terms) and if suspects also believe in the moral rightness of those in authority, this contributes to a belief in the legitimacy of those authorities and therefore to the likelihood that they comply with the law both in the short term (e.g. while they are in police custody) and in the longer term (Sparks and Bottoms, 1995; Tyler, 2003). So, police custody may be a site in which the social contract between suspects and the police is developed.

The present study suggests that relationships between suspects and the police were both mutually beneficial and imposed. There was some imposition of these relationships on suspects through deliberate strategies which were punitive and coercive in character, such as the cell buzzer system and the use of force. To a greater extent, however, this process was inadvertent rather than deliberate, as suspects' ideas about what they should expect from the police arose from the routinized operation of the custody area. Nonetheless, even when this process was inadvertent it meant that the dimensions of the police–suspect relationship were imposed on the suspect. At the same time, the police–suspect relationship was mutually beneficial. Parts of the police custody process were procedurally fair (and were perceived as procedurally fair) in that the majority of suspects accessed their due process rights while being respectfully treated, suggesting that police–citizen expectations were mutually and legitimately constructed. Therefore mutually beneficial and legitimately constructed relationships between suspects and the police should be an ideal to be aimed for, but the use of coercion remains necessary in some circumstances. Punishing suspects (e.g. with the cell buzzer system) is an unacceptable use of coercion, as are the indirectly coercive and unfair aspects of the routinized features of the custody process (e.g. detention reviews), while the use of force to control suspects (e.g. the aggressive and the violent) who have not complied using other means is an acceptable form of coercion.

In addition to police custody contributing to suspects' expectations of the police, police custody may also add to suspects' understandings of what they should expect from other authorities. That is, normative expectations about the police–citizen relationship spill out and spill into their relationships with other authorities, including while in prison, and the police–suspect relationship in police custody is part of a wider nexus of social control.[4] This argument is supported by the comparability between the findings presented here on police custody and the findings on the essential qualities of prisons (Liebling, 2004: 462–4), the pains of imprisonment (Sykes, 1958: 63–83) and prisoners' adaptation to the operation of power (Crewe, 2007). More specifically, police custody can also be regarded as part of the 'carceral archipelago'. In *Discipline and Punish*,[5] Foucault (1991: 293–308) coined this term to illustrate how schools, families, workshops and workhouses began to use similar disciplinary techniques as prisons, thus blurring the boundaries between punishment and other social institutions, a process which was aided by the transfer of people between them. Police custody aids the transfer of suspects between social institutions because it acts as a gateway into the criminal justice process, after which suspects might become defendants and then prisoners. For some suspects it also acts directly as a bridge between the outside world and prison, for example for those who are perceived as unsuitable for bail and are remanded in custody.

Conclusion

In this book it has been argued that suspects experience and perceive aspects of police custody as being procedurally fair in that, for example, most accessed their rights and entitlements. The best available evidence suggests that this is likely to increase whether or not they cooperate with the police and comply with the law. A further implication was that this procedurally just style of policing enabled the police/police staff and suspects to negotiate the boundaries of their relationship in mutually beneficial ways. However, suspects also experienced and perceived aspects of police custody as procedurally unfair, for example when they were denied access to their rights and entitlements, and also as coercive, for example when the cell buzzer system was misused. This was sometimes deliberate and sometimes inadvertent, but either way it *imposed* on suspects expectations about their relationship with the police/police staff. While coercion was sometimes a necessary part of police custody, particularly for the non-compliant, taking a more procedurally just approach provides a better model of how the police should engage with suspects in police custody. Therefore the book has returned to a central theme in policing about the relative balance between policing by consent and policing through coercion.

Importantly, though, it has been argued that social order in police custody was maintained by police and police staff in different ways. The police and police staff employed different philosophies of control. Broadly speaking, police staff acted in ways that were procedurally just and humane, while the police acted in ways that were coercive. This was perhaps because police staff were more restricted in their capacity to use force and the welfarist nature of their role lent itself to being caring and compassionate, but also because this kind of demeanour has not traditionally been a part of the key characteristics of the occupational culture of rank-and-file police officers.

The introduction of a range of criminal justice practitioners into the custody area has done little to shift the likelihood that police custody is police territory. Using Crawford's typology (2006: 466) the police appeared to monopolize police staff, drug workers and appropriate adults while trying to steer doctors as well as having a competitive market-based relationship with Security Ltd. What Crawford's (2006) model cannot encapsulate, however, was the relationship between the police and legal advisors, who were not engaged in policing and deliberately distanced themselves from this. Consequently, a further dimension needs to be added to his model which I call 'professional independence'. Power relations in the custody area did not demonstrate a partnership of equals, leaving little scope for each of the practitioners to govern the other as well as suggesting that police custody areas are not examples of 'networked governance' (Johnston and Shearing, 2003: 25–6), rather of 'anchored pluralism' (Loader and Walker, 2006, 2007: 192–4). There were, however, gaps in the police exercising absolute control over proceedings; for example, police staff had taken on new roles and powers, albeit that these were not officially sanctioned, and the professional status of legal advisors and doctors enabled a modicum of independence. The dominant role of the police, however, meant that the police governed practitioners in the custody area. Nonetheless, in multi-professional contexts such as police custody, relational theories of governance provide an important way of understanding the police, alongside constitutional and institutional arrangements.

The maintenance of order in police custody areas is comparable with prisons. Like prisoners, police suspects appeared to suffer 'pains of police detention' when deprived of their liberty, goods and services and their autonomy, which thus affected their sense of self-worth. They also manifested adaptations to the power exercised over them, which were similar to those identified by Crewe (2007) and some of which may have been learned in prison. The comparability of police custody and prison is revealing, not least because those detained in police custody are only suspects rather than convicted and sentenced offenders. Even though suspects are detained for shorter periods than prisoners it is difficult to justify that the conditions of police custody are similar to, if not worse than, prisons. This further illustrates why police custody can be experienced as punishment.

Finally, police custody is part of a broader nexus of social control which influences what suspects expect from the police and other authorities. These expectations are both negotiated and imposed. More specifically police custody is part of what Foucault (1991) calls the 'carceral archipelago' as it enables the transfer of suspects from the outside world into other criminal justice institutions, acting as a bridge to prison, particularly for those not suitable for bail.

This chapter has identified a number of avenues for future research on the police custody process which are discussed in more detail in Chapter 9, as are the implications of the research for improving the police custody process.

Notes

1 This incident happened in Gormiston and was described in Chapter 4.
2 Sparks and Bottoms (2008) also argue that legitimacy is only one element contributing to order in prisons, albeit a crucial one, but so too is coercion.
3 Sykes (1958) explores the pains of imprisonment by focusing on the internal workings of the prison, but says little about factors external to the prison such as ethnicity or gender.
4 This idea that the police–suspect relationship is part of a wider nexus of social control is raised by Choongh's (1997: 100) concept of social discipline, which has Foucauldian connotations, although he does not explore this.
5 Foucault (1977, cited in Garland, 1990: 143–50) used the term discipline to refer to individualized and moralistic training of the body and the soul, hierarchical observation and 'normalization' of the deviant, and is epitomized in Bentham's Panopticon, whose 'hub and spoke' model permits almost total surveillance, resulting in a self-disciplining dynamic.

Chapter 9

The future of police custody

The purposes of this final chapter are threefold. First, the aim is to examine the implications of the present research for making immediate improvements to police custody for practitioners and for suspects. Second, the aim is to examine the possibilities for further research. I argue that future research could be harnessed to a framework which reflects not only understandings of how the police custody process works, but also how it *should* work. Third, I explore how a clear understanding of police custody could be used in ongoing assessments of its quality and in ongoing reforms.

It is important that the present research might contribute, in the future, to normative insights about how the police custody process should work. In a conference in December 2009, James Sheptycki used a powerful, albeit esoteric, analogy between a painting of the *Raft of Medusa* by Géricault and the criminal justice process to argue that without what he called 'good policing', academics and the police are complicit in the inhumanity portrayed on the *Medusa*, and in decreasing the number of people included in the term 'us' and increasing the excluded and those considered as 'them'. What he showed with the analogy was that the creation and maintenance of social order requires constant attention, is always undertaken with a mixture of despair and hope, and has, in any circumstances, a human cost. Sheptycki (2009) argued that an awareness of the normative dimensions of policing may help reduce any surplus human cost as well as the complicity of the police and academics in an oppressive system. For fear of being complicit in loading suspects onto the 'raft of the *Medusa*', it is important to think about the normative dimensions of police custody.

Before examining the future of police custody, it is worth recognizing the contributions and limitations of the present study. Police custody is an area that has received scant empirical attention since the flurry of research in the 1980s and early 1990s, meaning that it is ripe for further enquiries, especially in view of some of the changes to the custody process that were reviewed in Chapter 1, including workforce modernization and the rationalization of spending on legal advisors. The present study (together with Kemp and Balmer (2008) and Kemp (2010)), therefore, offers a contribution to a relatively neglected but changing field. While the mixed-methods research, which explores the custody process from the viewpoint of suspects and criminal justice practitioners, has strengthened its validity, the research offers only a snapshot of the police custody process in two sites in England and Wales at two points in time, and thus the results probably cannot be generalized except to areas that have similar features to Gormiston and Sunnyside. In addition, the research is based on a number of data sources and tried to examine a number of perspectives, but it did not deal with two particular aspects of police custody, namely the police interview and the role of the Crown Prosecution Service. Nonetheless, the research has much to offer as a theoretically situated in-depth socio-legal account of police custody in England and Wales.

Improving police custody in the immediate term

In this section, I provide some tentative ideas about what might be done to improve the police custody process. While it is unconventional to return to empirical material in the final chapter, it is important to give a central place to the meanings that research participants ascribed to changes to police custody. This is partly because these meanings have not yet been discussed, but also because changes to the physical environment may not be enough if this fails to alter what these changes *mean* to suspects in terms of fairness and legitimacy. Their views are also important given the connections that were drawn in Chapter 8 between suspects' experiences of police custody and the wider consequences for their relationships with the police and others in positions of authority. Moreover, unnecessary suffering is unpalatable and inhumane, as Shep-tycki's (2009) analogy poignantly highlights.

One of the questions asked of all interviewees was what would improve police custody. This was a way of asking them to reflect on the negative aspects of the custody process, but in a constructive way. Their responses were related either to the custody environment or how they were treated by staff. Drawing on these data and also the key findings from the research, I explore changes that could be made to the custody environment and their likely meanings for suspects.

In terms of the custody environment suspects wished for improvements to be made. GMD8 said that since he was young he had been involved in 'quite a few crimes', meaning that he spent a lot of time in police custody, and that 'those police cells are worse than living in a cardboard box'.

Others such as GMD2, GMD5, GMD9 and GMD12 wished that cells were cleaner, warmer and more comfortable, for example having a radio or a television in them to occupy them while they waited, as well as for cleaner and larger blankets and more edible and readily available food. Staff, however, wanted a custody area that was better ventilated; for example, GMS5 said that the fans in the custody area were 'like putting fans on in the Millennium Dome'. GMD10 wanted padded cells for people intent on 'head-butting the wall', while a doctor wanted a window in the door of his consultation room with a curtain on it, so that it could be left open on occasions if he felt in need of extra safety. To make cells cleaner, warmer and more comfortable could be solved relatively quickly, if resources were allocated for the 'power-cleaning' of the custody area on a regular basis and to extra clean blankets. The same can be said of the food. After all, police suspects are not there for punishment and altering these aspects of the custody environment would make this principle clearer, as well as making it feel fairer and more humane.

Another change that could be made to the custody area would be to introduce telephone booths. Indeed, GMD5 said 'with the telephone thing, it's on the wall. I think they should have like a private room for that, a quiet private room'. Current arrangements are unlawful in that suspects cannot consult with their legal advisor in private if this consultation takes place over the telephone (Pattenden and Skinns, 2010). If the Legal Services Commission rolls out the use of mandatory legal advice over the telephone for those suspected of offences other than the limited range of less serious ones for which it is currently used, having telephone booths will become all the more important. Telephone booths will not only increase the opportunities for private consultations, but also reduce the likelihood that the police are challenged in court for unlawful practices, as well as being and feeling fairer for suspects. Another option would be to explore whether CCTV links between courts and police custody areas, which are known as 'virtual courts', could also be used for private legal consultations (Pattenden and Skinns, 2010).

However, there were other areas of improvement that cannot be as easily addressed as they are connected to the attitudes of staff and to the wider culture of the custody area. Suspects SND7, SND8, GMD2, GMD4, GMD7, GMD9, GMD11 and GMD12 wished that the police were more polite, even-handed, compassionate and cognizant of them being a suspect (presumed to be innocent), and less authoritarian in how they treated them, especially in relation to the cell buzzers, as well as wishing that the police were faster in responding to cell buzzers and to their requests and also in dealing with their case. This suspect encapsulated some of these views:

> People with a more caring attitude, the police are there to do their job which is basically catch people doing no good and get them locked

> up, and in the meantime they have to stay in a police cell . . . and the people who are looking after people need to be people with a bit more of a caring attitude, not necessarily nurses and doctors, but that kind of person rather than someone who's intent on locking up criminals, someone who looks at someone as an innocent person rather than, you're a criminal because you're in a cell. (GMD2)

There are also harm-reductive benefits of responding promptly to cell buzzers, given that Leigh *et al.* (1998) found a quick response to calls for help may be one way of preventing deaths in custody. Apart from the harm-reductive benefits, these aspects of interpersonal treatment between staff and suspects might also make custody feel more procedurally just and contribute to a greater sense of police legitimacy.

The same can be said of suspects' wishes to be provided with more information about their rights and entitlements, for example by making it mandatory for all suspects to be given the PACE Codes of Practice to read in the cells. SND4 said that if suspects did not know what was available to them then the police simply provided the bare minimum. He said: 'I've read that code and rights book, and there's so much in it that you can ask for, and the food, and the drinks, and when you do ask for it and they know you haven't read it, they just . . . put the phone down . . . they just leave you rotting really.' For this to be an effective strategy, the PACE Codes of Practice would also have to be rewritten in more accessible language.

As has been already argued, the pressure on staff in custody areas is partly as a result of how managers prioritize resources, yet this also affects the stress levels of both operational staff and suspects. Suspects' suggestions about improving the police custody process also highlight a deeper issue connected to staff attitudes. As Choongh (1997: 205, 235) argues, the solution to some of these difficulties lies in persuading the police that *all* suspects are entitled to be treated with respect and politeness and are deserving of access to their rights and entitlements. There are no quick or easy solutions for this.

From the perspective of plural policing, an important issue to address is whether workforce modernization should continue unabated and if so what form it should take. As argued in Chapter 6, there were clearly some advantages to having police staff in police custody areas, not least because they were liked by suspects who reported that they felt more fairly treated by the police staff than by the police. However, it was troubling that these police staff had begun to take on new roles and powers for which they were not trained. In addition, in Sunnyside, there were uncertainties about line management and contractual accountability mechanisms were largely ineffective. Taken together this suggests that if police staff are to be used in police custody areas, then the police should employ them rather than contracting-out the work to private security companies. The police might also consider rotating the police staff that they employ between different roles, such as between being a civilian investigator, custody assistant and police community support officer so as to prevent burn-out and to ensure that staff have a more rounded set of skills. Ultimately, this could mean that they continue to treat suspects in a way that is fair and for which they were liked. That said, it is important to note that if police staff are simply used to improve suspect experiences of fairness and, by implication, the likelihood that they accept decisions which are unfavourable to them, then this should not overshadow the importance of substantive justice.

Improvements might also be made in relation to access to legal advice, given the likely contribution it makes to the legitimacy of authorities and to substantive justice. In part and, as one of the suspects suggested, this could involve the provision of more detailed information in police custody areas about how long suspects are likely to wait for a legal advisor, why they are waiting and what time their legal advisor is due to arrive. In the light of changes to the way legal advice is provided, it is essential that the independent role of (duty) solicitors in defending the rights of their clients, regardless of guilt, is clarified so as to increase the likelihood that suspects will trust duty solicitors and to address suspects' concerns about the police inferring guilt from their request for legal advice. Moreover, given that the use of telephone legal advice is inevitable for some suspects it is also of importance to eliminate opportunities for illegal practices, such as eavesdropping on private conversations between legal advisors and their clients, rather than increasing them through the use of cell intercoms.

Relationships between the police, police staff and legal advisors also require attention if access to custodial legal advice is to be improved. This research has shown that familiarity between legal advisors and police/police staff and an appreciation of each other's roles and responsibilities was facilitated by legal advisors having an office in the custody area. This approach could perhaps be trialled in other custody areas, space permitting. Moreover, negative stereotypes of legal advisors might be challenged by informing the police about their roles and responsibilities and about the pressures legal advisors face as a result of reforms to legal aid provision. Lessons could be learned perhaps from drug workers in custody areas, who have tried to improve their relationships with the police by informing the police about their role and the impact of their work (Hunter *et al.*, 2005).

There are also glaring inadequacies in the service provided by appropriate adults. Appropriate adults, are mandatory for juveniles and required for vulnerable adults and yet appropriate adult services have limited statutory funding and are expected to rely on volunteers. This shows the lack of priority they are afforded by government which is reflected in their devalued status in the custody area. Overall, the principle of having an appropriate adult is correct, but their role requires some major changes to increase uptake. Changes are required to clarify the role of appropriate adults. They also require more resources so that appropriate adults are more readily available. Furthermore, police officers need to be better able to recognize mental disorder and to trust their own judgement when requesting an appropriate adult, rather than relying on doctors to make the decision, some of whom may also lack sufficient training in mental illness and intellectual impairment.

There are also grounds for improving multi-professional relationships in police custody areas. When asked about how to improve working relationships, staff firstly talked about communication and information sharing. For instance, drug workers wanted to be able to speak to doctors when they made decisions about a suspect's fitness. A number of practitioners wanted improvements to information-sharing processes so that when a suspect arrived in the custody area, medical information would be more readily available about them so that they would not have to start from scratch. Legal advisors wanted improvements to communication with police, so that they could more easily contact staff in the custody area and the investigating officers.

The second main theme in the data on improvements to multi-professional relationships related to the need to capitalize on the opportunity to address suspects' multiple needs which might underlie their offending behaviour. It would mean, therefore, taking a more preventative and long-term approach to suspects' needs in which police custody was seen as a one-stop shop where suspects could engage with a 'welfare officer' who could refer them to helping agencies once they left police custody.

Finally, the review of PACE implies that there are grounds for improving the legal framework within which police custody is situated. While there is not space for a detailed assessment here, the present research suggests that PACE could be reworded so that it specified the roles and responsibilities of the police and police staff, which might reduce the likelihood of 'power creep' and 'mission creep' or, at the least, describe what each of these players should be doing. Moreover, provided it is not used as 'window dressing' so that old practices continue under a different guise, PACE could be reworded using language which expresses a concern with ideas from the present research, such as fairness and legitimacy, as well as to reflect concepts such as human rights, which have begun to percolate through to the custody process as a result of rulings in the European Court of Human Rights and joint inspections by HMIC and HMIP. Of course, these changes may not be implemented as intended, judging by the deviations from the law that have been documented throughout this book and given the limits of legal regulations (e.g. Choongh, 1997: 229, 235), but it would offer more clarity about what should be important in the police custody process in England and Wales.

Towards an agenda for future research

Future research on the police custody process needs to be guided by a model of what the police custody process is like. By specifying what police custody is like, it may also be possible to begin to explore what the police custody process should be like. For example, Liebling's (2004: 473) concept of the 'moral performance' of prisons has directed attention to the possibility of using it not only to describe what prisons are like, in terms of how things work and fail, but also to examine the normative dimensions of prisons, and the gap between how prisons are and what prisons should be like (Sparks and Bottoms, 2008).

The present exploratory study suggests that social order is the key to understanding police custody areas and that social order is produced through the use of persuasion and fair procedures, with coercion being reserved for the recalcitrant minority of suspects. The present research has also provided a number of ideas about concepts central to order maintenance in the police custody process which are discussed shortly. Further research needs to be directed at validating these concepts and to testing the relationships between them, including the idea that persuasion and coercion are central to the production of social order.

To do this, the first step would be to survey all police services in England and Wales to find out about current police custody provisions, focusing particularly on designated facilities (i.e. those that are normally fully operational all of the time). This would enable researchers to develop a typology of the different kinds of arrangements, for example whether and how many custody areas are entirely run by the police or part-run by the police and by civilians paid by the police or part-run by the police and a private security company or entirely run by a private security company and so on. Once a typology of this kind had been identified, one of each type of police custody area could be selected for more in-depth empirical research – this would be the second stage in the research. In each, in-depth, exploratory and possibly ethnographic work could be used to further identify and define concepts central to the creation and maintenance of order in police custody areas which I discuss shortly. The third and final stage of the research would be to test these concepts through a survey of police, police staff and possibly other practitioners, as well as of suspects in a number of police custody areas, to see whether these concepts are generalizable. Data analysis could then be used to examine the links between these concepts and to develop them into a model which could be used as a tool for assessing the quality of the police custody process.[1]

The concepts that could be explored at the second stage of the research process include: perceptions of the police and the custody environment; the loci of power and whether it rested with the police or elsewhere; the different ways that power is used whether that is coercively or fairly; how suspects respond to the power exercised over them – whether they act out of 'dull compulsion' or comply with, adapt to or resist it; and the moral, emotional and relational aspects of the police custody process. I discuss each of these in turn below.

Perceptions of the custody environment

The research showed that what was important about the custody environment to suspects and staff were things like its busyness, cleanliness, ventilation, temperature and light. These matters were also connected to who and how many people worked there, as well as the number and kind of people that were detained there and for how long. These matters could be directly observed, and staff and suspects' perceptions of them could also be sought and verified by examining police records. This concept would be deliberately descriptive.

Occupational cultures

The occupational cultures of police and police staff are another important dimension of police custody affecting the treatment of suspects. We do not know yet whether police and police staff have comparable cultures to each other, although Chapter 6 hinted that there may be some similarities but also subtle differences between them, suggesting that the police staff have not straightforwardly been absorbed into the occupational culture of rank-and-file police officers who worked in the custody area. The structural conditions of police and police staff – which refer to the organizational, historical, legal and political conditions of their work and which are anchored in certain forms of power – are different in that police staff have different conditions of service, unions and distinct powers (Chan, 1997: 71). The cultural knowledge or 'habitus' of police staff also showed similarities to and differences from the police. On the one hand, their 'axiomatic knowledge' or mandate is different. Rather than it being based around a 'crime-fighting' sense of mission which involves the efficient, apolitical and professional enforcement of the law, as is arguably the case for the police (Chan, 1997: 76–80), the mandate of police staff revolved around suspect welfare, requiring a different set of skills such as being caring and compassionate. On the other hand, police and police staff shared similar methods for describing how things are done and similar values for assessing how to deal with different situations. For example, like the police, police staff showed a similar dislike of legal advisors, stereotyping them as obstructive, as well as demonstrating a territoriality about the custody area. Perhaps police staff learned these categories, methods and values from the police.

To explore the contours of the occupational cultures of the police relative to police staff would make an interesting study in and of itself.

However, in a study of social order in police custody areas, the point would be to examine how these occupational cultures contribute to suspect cooperation and compliance.

The loci of power

In spite of the involvement of police and police staff as well as legal advisors, doctors, drug workers and appropriate adults in custody areas, the research showed that power mostly rested with the police and that the police relationship with other practitioners depended on who they were. This suggests four hypotheses:

- *Hypothesis 1*. Crawford's (2006: 466) monopolistic model in which police staff are integrated into the police rather than vice versa will best characterize relationships between police and police staff in police custody areas, as well as between the police and drug workers and appropriate adults.
- *Hypothesis 2*. Crawford's (2006: 466) steering model in which the police govern at a distance the policing activities of others will best characterize relationships between police and doctors.
- *Hypothesis 3*. Crawford's (2006: 466) market model, in which the police compete, as well as cooperate with other policing providers will best characterize the relationship between the police and private security companies involved in the police custody process.
- *Hypothesis 4*. Crawford's (2006: 466) models cannot adequately theorize the relationship between the police and legal advisors, who distanced themselves from being seen to engage in policing. A further dimension is required to theorize this relationship which I have called professional independence.

Coercion

Coercion was an intrinsic part of the custody process, alongside procedural fairness, making this a vital component to explore in future research. Throughout the book, various examples of coercion were identified, including not only police practices (e.g. the use of force or the use of informal conversations to encourage suspects to admit to an offence or to dissuade suspects from seeking legal advice) and the practices of police staff (e.g. if they, as well as police officers, deliberately ignored cell buzzers and suspects' requests), but also aspects of the custody environment (e.g. the layout and austerity of the conditions). These different forms of coercion could be assessed more thoroughly in future research to explore whether in fact they were coercive and how and, therefore, whether they should be included in this concept. It is also vital to examine the impact of coercion relative to procedural fairness on police legitimacy and how this, in turn, impacts on suspect compliance.

Fairness

The research showed that there were a number of situations in which the different dimensions of procedural fairness and unfairness, as defined in Paternoster *et al.* (1997), were played out. In fact, procedural fairness in police custody might be measured with reference to these situations as follows:

- *representation* – the operation of the buzzer system and detention reviews;
- *consistency* – access to showers and smoking;
- *impartiality and neutrality* – staff responses, particularly to drug users, women and suspected illegal immigrants who were stereotyped by the police;
- *correctability* – the operation of the buzzer system, detention reviews, but perhaps also the police complaints system, in which CCTV evidence may play a part;
- *ethicality* – staff responses to suspect requests and whether they were timely and appropriate, but also suspect access to key rights and entitlements such as legal advice.

However, accuracy or the quality of decision-making and whether it is based on valid information would be more difficult to measure in the police custody process. One possibility would be to examine the quality of decisions made about charge or bail, but this would involve looking at a broad range of information including the evidence against the suspect, their prior history, whether or not the person had a legal advisor and the quality of the advice they received. As with occupational cultures, the complexity of this decision-making process would require a separate study in and of itself.

Compulsion

The research showed that some suspects expressed a form of 'fatalistic or instrumental compliance', but other than this the idea that suspects complied with the police out of a sense of dull compulsion was little explored. However, in relation to prisons it has been identified as important. Sparks and Bottoms (1995: 53) found that vulnerable prisoners who were separated from other prisoners felt relatively powerless, as they were reliant on the prison authorities to act in their best interests. Yet they expressed little resistance and posed minimal challenges to prison staff, even when they experienced changes to the prison regime as unfair. This was because, Sparks and Bottoms (1995: 53) argue, that they simply accepted these changes as inevitable. Therefore dull compulsion could also be an important concept in future research on order and the police custody process, particularly for suspects that have learned this strategy having been in prison and given the similarities the research found between prison and police custody. The hypothesis is that some suspects are compelled to comply with the police in the custody area because they feel that police control over them is inevitable and immutable.

Compliance

This is a central concept in a study of order and the police custody process. Compliance with the police, which was the main reaction of suspects found in this research, cannot be viewed as necessarily immediate – such that it occurs as the suspect walks through the door. Instead, it is processual, whether created through consent or coercion (as argued in Chapter 9). What is less clear is the relation between that process and suspects' perceptions of how the police do and should use their authority, before, during and after they leave police custody. Nor do we entirely know how these perceptions accord with police and police staff perceptions, and so whether the different people present in the custody area vary from each other in their normative understandings of what the police should do. It is a key question – previous research has concentrated upon police–suspect mutual perceptions and interactions. However, the custody area is now populated by many more people, all of whom have some role to play in creating or destroying compliance. The process of negotiating compliance is work done by all these actors on an ongoing basis rather than being a one-off outcome, a theme which is missing from Tyler's (2003) work on police–citizen relationships.

Compliance could be measured by asking suspects to self-report on their offending behaviour a short time before and a short time after leaving police custody and, in the absence of self-report data, it may be possible to use police and court records to ascertain whether and on how many occasions they were arrested and convicted again. While in custody, rather than asking suspects to self-report about their offending, it would be more appropriate to ask them about whether they followed police directions and why, for example was it because they believed that it was the right thing to do or because they felt they had little choice or because it meant some kind of reward (e.g. leaving custody) or punishment (e.g. because they were trying to make a point of resisting the police). The hypothesis is that coercion, fairness and compulsion all contribute in varying degrees to whether suspects comply with the police while in custody and once they leave police custody.

Adaptation and resistance

The research showed that suspects adapted in various ways to the power exercised over them by the police and police staff. Of Crewe's (2007) typology, three categories – namely, committed, strategic and fatalistic compliance – bore resemblance to some of the suspects in the research. What is less clear, however, is whether this typology adequately characterizes the experiences of a broader range of suspects, as it was not systematically examined in the research. Moreover, there may be other dimensions that might be added to the typology given the police-dominated world of police custody, such as more overt forms of resistance (as described in Chapter 8). The hypothesis is that suspects, particularly those who have been in prison, adapt to the police custody process using 'committed compliance', 'fatalistic or instrumental compliance' and 'strategic or manipulative compliance', as well as forms of overt resistance. Furthermore, some of the deviations between the law and practice documented throughout the research suggest that these categories may be of relevance not just to suspects but also to police officers and police staff.

Beyond power: emotions and relationships

The research demonstrated that suspects reacted to police custody in an emotional way, experiencing it, for example, as frightening, isolating and boring. More importantly, suspect experiences expressed different kinds of 'pains of police detention'. Of Sykes' (1958) 'pains of imprisonment', the deprivation of liberty, goods and services, and autonomy showed the greatest similarity with suspect experiences in the present study. As with the adaptation strategies that Crewe (2007) assesses, it may be that there is a degree of transference of these responses between prison and police custody or vice versa for suspects who have experienced both. The hypothesis is that suspects, particularly those who have been in prison, experience 'pains of police detention'.

Drawing on Liebling's (2004) work, future police custody research could also explore some of the other emotional and relational factors that she has identified in prisons using the concept of 'moral performance'. This concept highlights a need to go beyond power relations and their connection with legitimacy; she notes the importance of also considering the moral, emotional and relational dimensions of prisons, which are implicated in whether or not someone feels committed to prison authorities (Liebling, 2004: 473–5). More specifically, Liebling (2004: 458) found that what matters in prisons are things like 'respect', 'humanity', 'fairness', 'order', 'personal development' and 'well-being'. Therefore, moral performance is used to mean 'those aspects of a prisoner's mainly interpersonal and material treatment that render a term of imprisonment more or less dehumanizing and/or painful' (2004: 473). It is likely, in view of the discussion in Chapter 8 about the similarities and differences between prisons and police custody (e.g. in terms of the distress that suspects experienced) that these moral and emotional dimensions of prisons are of importance for understanding police custody. That is, whether suspects feel committed to the authority of the police will be partly determined by the operation of power (either coercion or persuasion), but also by these moral and emotional responses to the police custody process. Consequently, future research might examine, for example, how police custody affects suspects' psychological well-being, as well as the other procedurally just and coercive means that add to and take away from legitimacy.

Ongoing assessment and reform

As for further and ongoing assessment and reform, this chapter has examined some of the immediate improvements that could be made to the custody process based on the findings from the book. I have also outlined key components of social order in the police custody process which, in future research, could be validated and developed into a model that explores the relationships between them. Future research would also take us nearer to a better understanding of what the police custody process should be like.

Examining the gaps between what police custody is like and what it should be like opens up the possibility of an agenda for ongoing assessment and reform. For example, research led by Alison Liebling shows that empirical and normative concerns *can* contribute to change. The evaluation that she led of the pilot of the Safer Custody Programme in six local prisons contributed to the development of Measuring the Quality of Prison Life (MQPL) questionnaire (Prison Service News, 2004). A version of it was subsequently adopted for the ongoing auditing of prisons, and the MQPL is now widely used not only as a tool for measuring the quality of prison life, but also as a platform for ongoing reform (Home Affairs Select Committee, 2004).

If the concepts outlined above can be validated and if they can be developed into a model that looks at the relationships between them, this suggests a clear role for researchers in contributing to ongoing auditing and reform of the police custody process. In this sense, research and researchers may become embedded in police accountability mechanisms. However, it may be that the police do not allow such a close and critical connection with researchers or alternatively that researchers are reluctant too, for fear that they may lose control over the research process (e.g. the research instrument may become distorted to suit police objectives in terms of what they wish to be measured) or struggle to retain an objective and critical view of police practices. Moreover, relationships between researchers and 'the police' are more complicated than with other criminal justice agencies. After all, there are 43 police services in England and Wales, and the police are not represented by a single national body. This raises questions about how well-intentioned researchers can make themselves heard. There are two possibilities, namely the Association of Chief Police Officers (ACPO) and the National Policing Improvements Agency (NPIA). With their backing and with further research, the police custody process could be made less painful, safer, fairer and more just, and the police – and perhaps other kinds of authorities – could be made more legitimate in the process.

Note

1 An alternative approach, once the key concepts have been firmly established, would be to try to manipulate aspects of the custody process through the use of an experimental design. While a design of this kind could establish, for example, whether or not certain experimental conditions enhanced suspect experiences of fairness and compliant behaviour, it could also be unethical, as well as focusing on police custody as an event, not a process. As this study has shown, police custody is composed of different layers and perspectives and this depth would be lost, making it difficult to say anything about how or why the experimental conditions were effective. In an experimental design, the manipulation of the custody environment would also fail to capture the lived realities of the custody process for staff and for suspects.

Appendix

The research base

The objectives of the research on which the book is based were:

1. To describe the organizational objectives, roles and responsibilities of key practitioners in police custody areas.
2. To describe the experiences of suspects in police custody, in particular their experiences of the practitioners they encountered therein.
3. To describe and appraise the meaning of due process in the context of police custody areas.
4. To describe and appraise multi-professional relationships and cooperation in custody areas.
5. To describe and appraise the governance of police custody areas in view of the changing context of civilianization and privatization.

The study used what Creswell and Plano Clark (2007: 65–6) call multi-level triangulation in which different methods are used to address different levels within the study, although these levels are merged together into one interpretation.

Data were collected in two sites, which were deliberately chosen because, while they both had a similar throughput of around 12,000 suspects per year, one was publicly run and one predominantly privately run. In order to maintain anonymity, the publicly run custody area was given the pseudonym Gormiston and the privatized custody area and the private security company were given the pseudonyms Sunnyside and Security Ltd, respectively. Sunnyside is in a city in the South-East of England while Gormiston is in a London borough. Sunnyside was purpose-built containing 36 cells through a public finance initiative in 2001, whereas the custody area in Gormiston had only 26 cells and was refurbished in the 1980s. The majority of staff on any one shift in the custody area in Sunnyside were civilians employed by Security Ltd who worked alongside three custody officers and one inspector. By contrast, the majority of staff on any one shift in Gormiston were police sergeants who worked alongside two inspectors and one civilian employed by the police. Both sites were busy, but Gormiston was slightly busier as it had fewer staff and fewer cells per suspect, thus creating more pressure to process suspects quickly.[1]

In each site, data were collected in sequence: a week-long period of participant observation undertaken by three researchers was followed by qualitative interviews with staff and suspects undertaken by one researcher, and this was followed by the collection of quantitative data from police custody records, for example about how long suspects were detained, whether they consulted with a doctor or a legal advisor and so on. It is difficult to measure the reliability of the custody record data. However, PACE requires a custody record to be opened for all arrestees and for it to log the main events relating to their time in police detention, including suspects' requests, the provision of food and drinks, and visits to the cell by staff or when they leave their cell to consult with a legal advisor, take a shower or visit the exercise yard.

The interviews were semi-structured and based on an interview guide, which was used to ensure that similar questions were asked in a similar order. To ensure reliability between the data collected by the three observers, an observation guide, which provided a framework of the main areas of interest, was used to structure data collection. Observers were also asked to separate, as far as possible, their interpretations from the factual recounting of what they saw. When possible, the observers took notes unobtrusively and these were supplemented by a comprehensive write-up at the end of each shift that they observed. Observer effects are inevitable, but it was hoped that they would diminish the more time that was spent in the custody area by the researchers. Moreover, the custody record data suggested that, for example, in terms of access to legal advice, there were few differences between when the researchers were then and when they were not.

Table A.1 Data collected in the research

Type of data	*Sunnyside*	*Gormiston*	*Total*
Week-long participant observation	February 2007 (week one)	July 2007 (week two)	Two-weeks participant observation
Interviews with practitioners	15	15	30
Interviews with suspects	9	14	23
Custody records for February 2007	234	200	434
Custody records for July 2007	232	217	449
Total no. of custody records	466	417	883

In total, 336 hours of observation and 53 interviews were conducted and quantitative data were extracted from 883 custody records (see Table A.1). Each type of data was given equal weighting in the research. The rationale for this approach was that each type of data addressed most, if not all, of the research questions for the study but from different perspectives, and that together they would be able to provide as complete a picture as possible of the week-long police custody process observed in each site. The qualitative data were analysed thematically, while descriptive and inferential statistics were produced from the custody record data. The aim was to integrate these different types of data and perspectives into one overall interpretation, while also comparing and contrasting between them. The research was situated within the framework of Adaptive Theory (Layder, 1998: 143), which merges constructivist and positivist paradigms. Adaptive theory acknowledges the coexistence of the objective and subjective dimensions of social reality, in which the researcher is encouraged to fuse inductive with deductive forms of reasoning and to use multiple strategies of research.

While it may not be possible to generalize the findings from this research to all other custody areas in England and Wales, particularly given the variations that occur between police custody areas even in the same police service (e.g. Phillips and Brown, 1998: 60; Sanders *et al.*, 1989: 183), by describing each of the custody areas (in terms of staff, suspects and the environment), it is hoped that lessons may be drawn for other similar custody areas.

Note

1 The ratio of suspects to cells each day was 1.2:1 in Gormiston and 0.93:1 in Sunnyside; that is, each day Gormiston had more suspects than there were cells. In addition, the staff to suspect ratio was higher in Gormiston (1:1.6) than in Sunnyside (1:1.2).

References

ACPO (2006) Retention guidelines from nominal records on the Police National Computer. ACPO (online). Available at: www.acpo.police.uk/policies.asp (accessed 15 February 2010).

An Garda Síochána (2008) *Guidance Notes on the Implementation of the Criminal Justice Act 1984 (Treatment of Persons in Custody in Garda Síochána Stations Regulations, 1987 and 2006)*. Dublin: Garda Síochána.

Antoniou, N. (2008) 'Factors Influencing Whether Suspects Seek Legal Advice in the Police Station'. Unpublished MPhil dissertation, University of Cambridge.

Ashworth, A. and Von Hirsch, A. (2005) *Proportionate Sentencing: Exploring the Principles*. Oxford: Oxford University Press.

Audit Commission (2002) *Community Safety Partnerships*. London: Audit Commission.

Baldwin, J. (1992) *The Conduct of Police Investigations: Records of Interview, the Defence Lawyer's Role and Standards of Supervision*, Royal Commission on Criminal Justice, Research Study Nos. 2, 3 and 4. London: HMSO.

Baldwin, J. and McConville, M. (1979) 'Police interrogation and the right to see a solicitor', *Criminal Law Review*, March, pp. 145–52.

Bayley, D. and Shearing, C. (2001) *The New Structure of Policing: Conceptualization and Research Agenda*. Washington, DC: National Institute of Justice.

Beetham, D. (1991) *The Legitimation of Power: Issues in Political Theory*. Basingstoke: Palgrave Macmillan.

Bittner, E. (1970) *The Functions of the Police in Modern Society*. Washington, DC: National Institute of Mental Health.

Blagg, H., Pearson, G., Sampson, A., Smith, D. and Stubbs, P. (1988) 'Inter-agency co-operation: rhetoric and reality', in T. Hope and M. Shaw (eds), *Communities and Crime Reduction*. London: HMSO.

Bottomley, K., Coleman, C., Dixon, D., Gill, M. and Wall, D. (1991) 'The detention of suspects in police custody: the impact of the Police and Criminal Evidence Act 1984', *British Journal of Criminology*, 31(4): 347–64.

Bottoms, A. E. (1983) 'Neglected features of contemporary penal systems', in D. Garland and P. Young (eds), *The Power to Punish: Contemporary Penality and Social Analysis*. London: Heinemann.

Bottoms, A. E. and Tankebe, J. (2010) *Understanding Legitimacy: A Dialogic Relationship within Institutional Normative Order*. Public Seminar at the Institute of Criminology, University of Cambridge. 20 October 2010.

Bottoms, A. E. and McClean, J. D. (1976) *Defendants in the Criminal Process*. Abingdon: Routledge.

Bowling, B. (1998) *Violent Racism*. Oxford: Clarendon.

Bowling, B., Parmar, A. and Phillips, C. (2008) 'Policing minority ethnic communities', in T. Newburn (ed.), *Handbook of Policing*, 2nd edn. Cullompton: Willan.

Bridges, L. and Cape, E. (2008) *CDS Direct: Flying in the Face of the Evidence*. London: Centre for Crime and Justice Studies, King's College London.

Bridges, L. and Sanders, A. (1990) 'Access to legal advice and police malpractice', *Criminal Law Review*, July, pp. 494–509.

Britton, N. J. (2000) 'Race and policing: a study of police custody', *British Journal of Criminology*, 40(4): 639–58.

Brodeur, J.-P. (2007) 'An encounter with Egon Bittner', *Crime Law and Social Change*, 48: 105–32.

Brown, D. (1989) *Detention at the Police Station under the Police and Criminal Evidence Act 1984*, Home Office Research Study No. 104. London: HMSO.

Brown, D., Ellis, T. and Larcombe, K. (1992) *Changing the Code: Police Detention under the Revised PACE Codes of Practice*, Home Office Research Study No. 129. London: HMSO.

Bucke, T. and Brown, D. (1997) *In Police Custody: Police Powers and Suspects' Rights under the Revised PACE Codes of Practice*, Home Office Research Study No. 174. London: Home Office.

Bullock, S. (2008) *Police Service Strength*, Home Office Statistical Bulletin. London: Home Office.

Button, M. (2002) *Private Policing*. Cullompton: Willan.

Button, M. (2003) 'Private security and the police of quasi-public space', *International Journal of the Sociology of Law*, 31: 227–37.

Button, M. (2007) *Security Officers and Policing: Powers, Culture and Control in the Governance of Private Space*. Aldershot: Ashgate.

Button, M. and John, T. (2002) '"Plural policing" in action: a review of the policing of environmental protests in England and Wales', *Policing and Society*, 12: 111–21.

Button, M., Frimpong, K., Smith, G. and Johnston, L. (2007) 'Professionalizing counter-fraud specialists in the UK: assessing progress and recommendations for reform', *Crime Prevention and Community Safety*, 9: 92–101.

Button, M., Williamson, T. and Johnston, L. (2007) '"Too many chiefs and not enough chief executives": barriers to the development of PFI in the police service in England and Wales', *Criminology and Criminal Justice*, 7(3): 287–305.

Cape, E. (2002) 'Incompetent police station advice and the exclusion of evidence', *Criminal Law Review*, June, pp. 471–84.

Cape, E. (2004) 'The rise (and fall?) of a criminal defence profession', *Criminal Law Review*, June, pp. 401–16.

Cape, E. (2006) *Defending Suspects at Police Stations: The Practitioner's Guide to Advice and Representation*. London: LAG Education and Service Trust Ltd.

Carlen, P. and Powell, M. (1979) 'Professionals in the magistrates' courts', in A. Parker (ed.), *Social Work and the Courts*. London: Edward Arnold.

Carrabine, E. (2004) *Power, Discourse and Resistance: A Genealogy of the Strangeways Prison Riot*. Aldershot: Ashgate.

Chan, J. (1996) 'Changing police culture', *British Journal of Criminology*, 36(1): 109–34.

Chan, J. (1997) *Changing Police Culture*. Cambridge: Cambridge University Press.

Choongh, S. (1997) *Policing as Social Discipline*. Oxford: Clarendon.

Clare, I. and Gudjonsson, G. (1992) *Devising and Piloting an Experimental Version of the 'Notice to Detained Person'*, Royal Commission on Criminal Justice, Research Study No. 7. London: HMSO.

Clayman, S. and Skinns, L. (2011) 'To snitch or not to snitch? An exploratory study of the factors affecting active youth co-operation with the police', submitted to *Policing and Society*.

Cohen, S. (1985) *Visions of Social Control: Crime, Punishment and Classification*. Cambridge: Polity Press.

Commission for Racial Equality (2004) *The Police Service England and Wales: An Interim Report of a Formal Investigation by the Commission for Racial Equality*. London: CRE.

Crank, J. P. (1989) 'Civilianization in small and medium police departments in Illinois, 1973–1986', *Journal of Criminal Justice*, 17(3): 167–77.

Crawford, A. (1997) *The Local Governance of Crime: Appeals to Community and Partnerships*. Oxford: Oxford University Press.

Crawford, A. (2001) 'Joined-up but fragmented: contradiction, ambiguity and ambivalence at the heart of New Labour's "Third Way"', in R. Matthews and J. Pitts (eds), *Crime, Disorder and Community Safety*. Abingdon: Routledge.

Crawford, A. (2006) 'Networked governance and the post-regulatory state? Steering, rowing and anchoring the provision of policing and security', *Theoretical Criminology*, 10: 449–79.

Crawford, A. (2007) 'Reassurance policing: feeling is believing', in D. Smith and A. Henry (eds), *Transformations in Policing*. Aldershot: Ashgate.

Crawford, A. (2008) 'Plural policing in the UK: policing beyond the police', in T. Newburn (ed.), *Handbook of Policing*. Cullompton: Willan.

Crawford, A. and Jones, M. (1995) 'Inter-agency co-operation and community-based crime prevention: some reflections on the work of Pearson and colleagues', *British Journal of Criminology*, 35(1): 17–33.

Crawford, A., Lister, S., Blackburn, S. and Burnett, J. (2005) *Plural Policing: The Mixed Economy of Visible Patrols in England and Wales*. Bristol: Policy Press.

Creswell, J. W. and. Plano Clark, V. L. (2007) *Mixed Methods Research*. London: Sage.

Crewe, B. (2007) 'Power adaptation and resistance in a late-modern men's prison', *British Journal of Criminology*, 47: 256–75.

DCA (2006) *Lord Carter's Review of Legal Aid Procurement: Legal Aid – A Market-Based Approach to Reform*. London: DCA.

Dixon, D. (1991) 'Common sense, legal advice and the right of silence', *Public Law*, pp. 233–54.

Dixon, D. (1997) *Law in Policing: Legal Regulations and Police Practices*. Oxford: Oxford University Press.

Dixon, D. (2008) 'Authorise and regulate: a comparative perspective on the rise and fall of a regulatory strategy', in E. Cape and R. Young (eds), *Regulating Policing*. Oxford: Hart.

Dixon, D., Bottomley, K., Coleman, C., Gill, M. and Wall, D. (1990) 'Safeguarding the rights of suspects in police custody', *Policing and Society*, 1: 115.
Duff, P. (1998) 'Crime control, due process and the case for the prosecution', *British Journal of Criminology*, 38(4): 611–15.

Elmsley, C. (1991) *The English Police: A Political and Social History*. Hemel Hempstead: Harvester Wheatsheaf.
Evans, R. (1993) *The Conduct of Police Interviews with Juveniles*, Royal Commission on Criminal Justice, Research Study No. 8. London: HMSO.

Field, A. (2005) *Discovering Statistics Using SPSS*. London: Sage.
Flanagan, R. (2008) *The Review of Policing: Final Report*. London: Home Office.
Forst, B. and Manning, P. K. (1999) *Privatization of Policing: Two Views*. Washington, DC: Georgetown University Press.
Foster, J. (2003) 'Police cultures', in T. Newburn (ed.), *Handbook of Policing*. Cullompton: Willan.
Foucault, M. (1991) *Discipline and Punish*. London: Penguin.

Garland, D. (1990) *Punishment and Modern Society*. Oxford: Oxford University Press.
Garland, D. (1996) 'The limits of the sovereign state: strategies of crime control in contemporary society', *British Journal of Criminology*, 36(4): 445–71.
Garland, D. (2001) *The Culture of Control*. Oxford: Oxford University Press.
Gearty, C. (2007) *Civil Liberties*. Oxford: Oxford University Press.
Gelsthorpe, L. and Padfield, N. (2003) 'Introduction', in L. Gelsthorpe and N. Padfield (eds), *Exercising Discretion: Decision-Making in the Criminal Justice System and Beyond*. Cullompton: Willan.
Genders, E. (2002) 'Legitimacy, accountability and private prisons', *Punishment and Society*, 4: 285–303.
Genders, E. and Player, E. (2007) 'The commercial context of criminal justice: prison privatization and the perversion of purpose', *Criminal Law Review*, July, pp. 513–29.
Gleeson, E. and Grace, K. (2009) *Police Complaints: Statistics for England and Wales 2008/9*. London: IPCC.
Greasley, A. and Barlow, S. (1998) 'Using simulation modelling for BPR: resource allocation in a police custody process', *International Journal of Operations and Production Management*, 18: 978–88.
Guardian (2008) 'European court rules DNA database breaches human rights', *Guardian* (online). Available at: www.guardian.co.uk/uk/2008/dec/04/law-genetics (accessed 4 December 2008).
Guardian (2009) 'Family claim cover-up over death in police custody', *Guardian* (online). Available at: www.guardian.co.uk/uk/2009/aug/21/sean-riggs-police-death-cctv (accessed 20 October 2009).
Gudjonsson, G., Clare, I., Rutter, S. and Pearce, J. (1993) *Persons at Risk During Interviews in Police Custody: The Identification of Vulnerabilities*, Royal Commission on Criminal Justice, Research Study No. 12. London: HMSO.

Hall, N. (2005) *Hate Crime*. Cullompton: Willan.
Harding, R. (2001) 'Private prisons', in M. Tonry and J. Petersilia (eds), *Crime and Justice: A Review of Research*. Chicago, IL: University of Chicago Press, pp. 265–346.

Hauber, A., Hofstra, B., Toornvliet, L. and Zandenbergen, A. (1996) 'Some new forms of functional social control in the Netherlands and their effects', *British Journal of Criminology*, 36(2): 199–219.

Hirst, J. (1993) *Royal Commission Research Papers: A Policing Perspective*, Police Research Series No. 6. London: Home Office Police Department.

HMIC (2004) *Modernising the Police Service: Role, Management and Deployment of Police Staff in the Police Service of England and Wales*. London: HMIC.

Hodgson, J. (2004) 'The detention and interrogation of suspects in police custody in France', *European Journal of Criminology*, 1: 163–99.

Hodgson, J. and Bridges, L. (1995) 'Improving custodial legal advice', *Criminal Law Review*, February, pp. 101–13.

Hofstra, B. and Shapland, J. (1997) 'Who is in control?', *Policing and Society*, 6(4): 265–81.

Holdaway, S. (1980) 'The police station', *Urban Life*, 9(1): 79–100.

Home Affairs Committee (2008) *Policing in the Twenty-First Century*, Seventh Report of Session 2007–8. London: Stationery Office.

Home Affairs Select Committee (2004) *Fifth Supplementary Memorandum Submitted by Her Majesty's Prison Service*. Home Affairs Select Committee (online). Available at: www.publications.parliament.uk/pa/cm200405/cmselect/cmhaff/193/193we61.htm (accessed 3 February 2010).

Home Office (1981) *Report of the Royal Commission on Criminal Procedure*. London: HMSO.

Home Office (1991) *Safer Communities: The Local Delivery of Crime Prevention through the Partnerships Approach*, Standing Conference on Crime Prevention chaired by James Morgan. London: Home Office.

Home Office (2007) *Review of the Police and Criminal Evidence Act 1984: Summary of Responses to the Public Consultation Exercise (16 March–31 May 2007)*. London: HMSO.

Home Office (2008a) *PACE Codes of Practice, 2008*. London: TSO.

Home Office (2008b) *PACE Review: Government Proposals in Response to the Review of PACE 1984*. London: Home Office, Policing Powers and Protection Unit.

Home Office (2009) *Police Powers and Procedures England and Wales 2007/8*, Home Office Statistical Bulletin. London: HMSO.

Home Office (2010) *Public Confidence in the Police: Findings from the British Crime Survey Year Ending September 2008*. Home Office (online). Available at: www.crimereduction.homeoffice.gov.uk/ (accessed 13 January 2010).

Hood, C. (1991) 'A public management for all seasons?', *Public Administration*, 69 (Spring): 3–19.

Hough, M. (2007) 'Policing, new public management and legitimacy in Britain', in T. Tyler (ed.), *Legitimacy and Criminal Justice*. New York: Russell Sage Foundation.

Hughes, G. (2006) *The Politics of Crime and Community*. Basingstoke: Palgrave Macmillan.

Hunter, G., McSweeney, T. and Turnbull, P. (2005) 'The introduction of drug arrest referral schemes in London: a partnership between drug services and the police', *International Journal of Drug Policy*, 16(5): 343–52.

IPCC (2006) *Report Dated 26th February 2006 of the Review into the Events Leading Up to the Death of Christopher Alder on 1st April 1999*. London: IPCC.

IPCC (2008) *Near Misses in Police Custody: A Collaborative Study with Forensic Medical Examiners in London*. London: IPCC.

Irving, B. L. (2007) Personal communication, 8 October.
Irving, B. L. and McKenzie, I. (1989) *Police Interrogation: The Effects of the Police and Criminal Evidence Act 1984*. London: Police Foundation.

Jacobson, J. (2008) *Police Responses to Suspects with Learning Disabilities and Learning Difficulties: A Review of Policy and Practice*. London: Prison Reform Trust.
Jamel, J. and Mair, G. (2003) 'Crime and Disorder Partnerships in a Large Northern City. Unpublished report.
Johnston, L. (1992) *The Rebirth of Private Policing*. Abingdon: Routledge.
Johnston, L. (2007) 'Keeping the family together: police community support officers and the "police extended family" in London', *Policing and Society*, 17(2): 119–40.
Johnston, L. and Shearing, C. (2003) *Governing Security*. Abingdon: Routledge.
Johnston, L., Button, M. and Williamson, T. (2008) 'Police, governance and the Private Finance Initiative', *Policing and Society*, 18(3): 225–44.
Jones, T. (2003) 'The governance and accountability of policing', in T. Newburn (ed.), *Handbook of Policing*. Cullompton: Willan.
Jones, T. (2008) 'The accountability of policing', in T. Newburn (ed.), *Handbook of Policing*, 2nd edn. Cullompton: Willan.
Jones, T. and Newburn, T. (2002) 'The transformation of policing: understanding current trends in policing systems', *British Journal of Criminology*, 42: 129–46.
Jones, T. and Newburn, T. (2006a) 'Understanding plural policing', in T. Jones and T. Newburn (eds), *Plural Policing: A Comparative Perspective*. Abingdon: Routledge.
Jones, T. and Newburn, T. (2006b) 'The United Kingdom', in T. Jones and T. Newburn (eds), *Plural Policing: A Comparative Perspective*. Abingdon: Routledge.
Jones, T. and. Newburn, T. (1998) *Private Security and Public Policing*. Oxford: Oxford University Press.

Kemp, V. (2010) *Transforming Legal Aid: Access to Criminal Defence Services*. London: Legal Services Research Centre.
Kemp, V. and Balmer, N. (2008) *Criminal Defence Services: Users' Perspectives*, Research Paper No. 21. London: Legal Services Research Centre.

Layder, D. (1998) *Sociological practice: linking theory and social research*. London: Sage.
Legal Services Commission (2007) *Duty Solicitor Call Centre and CDS Direct Expansion*. London: Legal Services Commission.
Legal Services Commission (2008) *DSCC Statistics 27 April 2008*. Available at: www.legalservices.gov.uk/criminal/defence_solicitor_call_centre.asp.
Leigh, A., Johnson, G. and Ingram, A. (1998) *Deaths in Custody: Learning the Lessons*. London: HMSO.
Leng, R. (1993) *The Right to Silence in Police Interrogations: A Study of Some of the Issues Underlying the Debate*, Royal Commission on Criminal Justice, Research Study No. 10. London: HMSO.
Leo, R. (2008) *Police Interrogation and American Justice*. Cambridge, MA: Harvard University Press.
Liberty (2008) *The Rights of Suspects in the Police Station*. Liberty (online). Available at: www.yourrights.org.uk/yourrights/the-rights-of-suspects/the-rights-of-suspects-in-the-police-station/in dex.html (accessed 15 February 2010).

Liddle, M. A. and Gelsthorpe, L. (1994) *Crime Prevention and Inter-Agency Co-operation*, CPU Paper 53. London: HMSO.

Liebling, A. (2006) *Prison, Outcomes and Concepts of Moral Performance*. Talk given at the Institute of Criminology, University of Cambridge, 23 November.

Liebling, A. (2010) *Distinctions and Distinctiveness in the Work of Prison Officers: Legitimacy and Authority Revisited*, Nigel Walker Lecture, 26 May, Institute of Criminology, University of Cambridge.

Liebling, A. assisted by Arnold, H. (2004) *Prisons and Their Moral Performance: A Study of Values, Quality and Prison Life*. Oxford: Oxford University Press.

Loader, I. and Walker, N. (2006) 'Necessary virtues: the legitimate place of the state in the production of security', in J. Wood and B. Dupont (ed.), *Democracy, Society and the Governance of Security*. Cambridge: Cambridge University Press.

Loader, I. and Walker, N. (2007) *Civilizing Security*. Cambridge: Cambridge University Press.

Loftus, B. (2008) 'Dominant culture interrupted: recognition, resentment and the politics of change in an English Police Force', *British Journal of Criminology*, 48(6): 756–77.

Loftus, B. (2009) *Police Culture in a Changing World*. Oxford: Oxford University Press.

Loftus, B. (2010) 'Police occupational culture: classic themes altered times', *Policing and Society*, 20(1): 1–20.

Lukes, S. (2005) *Power: A Radical View*, 2nd edn. Basingstoke: Palgrave Macmillan.

Lustgarten, L. (1986) *The Governance of the Police*. London: Sweet & Maxwell.

Lyon, D. (1999) *Postmodernity*. Buckingham: Open University Press.

McClean, C. and Liebling, A. (2007) 'Prison staff in the public and private sector', in B. Crewe, J. Bennett and A. Wahidin (eds), *Understanding Prison Staff*. Cullompton: Willan.

McConville, M. and Hodgson, J. (1993) *Custodial Legal Advice and the Right to Silence*, Royal Commission on Criminal Justice, Research Study No. 10. London: HMSO.

McConville, M., Sanders, A. and Leng, R. (1991) *The Case for the Prosecution*. Abingdon: Routledge.

McConville, M., Sanders, A. and Leng, R. (1997) 'Descriptive or critical sociology', *British Journal of Criminology*, 37(3): 347–58.

McConville, M. and Hodgson, J. with the assistance of Jackson, M. and Macrae, E. (1993) *Custodial Legal Advice and the Right to Silence*, Royal Commission on Criminal Justice, Research Study No. 16. London: HMSO.

McConville, M., Hodgson, J., Bridges, L. and Pavlovic, A. (1994) *Standing Accused: The Organisation and Practices of Criminal Defence Lawyers*. Oxford: Oxford University Press.

MacCormick, N. (2008) *Institutions of Law*. Oxford: Oxford University Press.

MacCoun, R. J. (2005) 'Voice, control and belonging: the double-edged sword of procedural fairness', *Annual Review of Law and Social Science*, 1: 171–201.

McLauglin, E. and Murji, K. (2001) 'Lost connections and new directions: neo-liberalism, new public managerialism and the "modernization" of the British police', in K. Stenson and R. R. Sullivan (eds), *Crime, Risk and Justice: The Politics of Crime Control in Liberal Democracies*. Cullompton: Willan.

McLauglin, E., Muncie, J. and Hughes, G. (2001) 'The permanent revolution: New Labour, new public management and the modernization of criminal justice', *Criminal Justice*, 1(3): 301–18.

Maguire, M. (1988) 'Effects of the PACE provisions on detention and questioning: some preliminary findings', *British Journal of Criminology*, 28: 19–43.

Maguire, M. (2002) 'Regulating the police station: the case of PACE 1984', in M. Maguire and G. Wilson (eds), *The Criminal Justice Process*. Oxford: Oxford University Press.

Marshall, J. and Scott, G. (2009) 'Professionals', *A Dictionary of Sociology*. Oxford Reference, Oxford University Press (online). Available at: www.oxfordreference.com/ (accessed 21 January 2010).

May, T., Gyanteng, T. and Hough, M. (2010) *Differential Treatment in the Youth Justice System*. London: ICPR, King's College London.

Medford, S., Gudjonsson, G. H. and Pearse, J. (2003) 'The efficacy of the appropriate adult safeguard during police interviewing', *Legal and Criminological Psychology*, 8: 253–66.

Merritt, J. (2009) 'Legislating for police powers, a cautionary note from England and Wales', *Policing: An International Journal of Police Strategies and Management*, 32(2): 377–94.

Moston, S. and Stephenson, G. M. (1993) *The Questioning and Interviewing of Suspects Outside the Police Station*, Royal Commission on Criminal Justice, Research Study No. 22. London: HMSO.

Newburn, T. and Hayman, S. (2002) *Policing, Surveillance and Social Control: CCTV and Police Monitoring of Suspects*. Cullompton: Willan.

Newburn, T. and Reiner, R. (2004) 'From PC Dixon to Dixon Plc: policing and police powers since 1954', *Criminal Law Review*, August, pp. 601–18.

Noaks, L. (2000) 'Private cops on the block', *Policing and Society*, 10: 143–61.

Noaks, L. (2004) 'The diversification of British police: the citizen's experience', *Policing: An International Journal of Police Strategies and Management*, 27(2): 264–74.

Noaks, L. (2008) 'Private and public policing in the UK: a citizen perspective on partnership', *Policing and Society*, 18(2): 156–68.

Norris, C. and Armstrong, G. (1999) *Maximum Surveillance Society: The Rise of CCTV as Social Control*. Oxford: Berg.

O'Malley, P. (1992) 'Risk, power and crime prevention', *Economy and Society*, 21(3): 252–75.

O'Neill, S. (2010) 'More power to the people in "new deal" for the police', *Times Online*. Available at: www.timesonline.co.uk/tol/news/uk/crime/article 7130750.ece (accessed 20 May 2010).

Ocqueteau, F. (1990) 'The state facing the security industry', *L'Année Sociologique*, 40(1): 97–124.

Office of the United Nations High Commissioner of Human Rights (2009) *Optional Protocol to the Prevention Against Torture*. OHCHR (online). Available at: www2.ohchr.org/english/bodies/cat/opcat/index.htm (accessed 30 September 2009).

Osborne, D. and Gaebler, T. (1992) *Reinventing Government: How the Entrepreneurial Spirit is Transforming the Public Sector*. Reading, MA: Addison-Wesley.

Packer, H. (1968) *The Limits of the Criminal Sanction*. Oxford: Oxford University Press.

Padfield, N. (2006) 'A critical perspective on private prisons in England and Wales', in N. Capus *et al.* (eds), *Public-Privé: vers un nouveau partage du contrôle de la criminalité?* Chur/Zürich: Rügger Verlag.

Paternoster, R., Bachman, R., Brame, R. and Sherman, L. W. (1997) 'Do fair procedures matter? The effect of procedural justice on spouse assault', *Law and Society*, 31(1): 163–203.
Pattenden, R. and Skinns, L. (2010) 'Choice, privacy and publicly-funded legal advice at the police station', *Modern Law Review*, 73(3): 349–70.
Phillips, C. (2002) 'From voluntary to statutory status: reflecting on the experience of three partnerships established under the Crime and Disorder Act 1998', in G. Hughes, E. McLaughlin and J. Muncie (eds), *Crime Prevention and Community Safety: New Directions*. London: Sage.
Phillips, C. and Brown, D. (1998) *Entry into the Criminal Justice System: A Survey of Police Arrests and Their Outcomes*. London: HMSO.
Pierpoint, H. (2006) 'Reconstructing the role of the appropriate adult in England and Wales', *Criminology and Criminal Justice*, 6: 219–37.
Pierpoint, H. (2008) 'Quickening the PACE? The use of volunteers as appropriate adults in England and Wales', *Policing and Society*, 18(4): 397–410.
Pleasence, P., Kemp, V. and Balmer, N.J. (2011) 'The justice lottery? Police station advice 25 years on from PACE', *Criminal Law Review*, Issue 1, 2011.
Prison Service News (2004) 'MQPL plays a part in revised suicide prevention plan', *Prison Service News* (online). Available at: www.hmprisonservice.gov.uk/prisoninformation/prisonservicemagazine/ (accessed on 3 February 2010).

Reiner, R. (1992) 'Policing a postmodern society', *Modern Law Review*, 55(6): 761–81.
Reiner, R. (2010) *The Politics of the Police*. Oxford: Oxford University Press.
Rigakos, G. S. (2002) *The New Parapolice: Risk Markets and Commodified Social Control*. Toronto: University of Toronto Press.
Robertson, G. (1992) *The Role of Police Surgeons*, Royal Commission on Criminal Justice, Research Study No. 6. London: HMSO.
Roche, D. (2003) *Accountability in Restorative Justice*. Oxford: Oxford University Press.
Rose, N. (2000) 'Government and control', *British Journal of Criminology*, 40(2): 321–39.
Rowe, M. (2007) 'Rendering visible the invisible: police discretion, professionalism and decision-making', *Policing and Society*, 17(3): 279–94.
Royal Commission on Criminal Justice (1993) *Royal Commission on Criminal Justice Report*, chaired by Viscount Runciman of Doxford. London: HMSO.
Royal Commission on Criminal Procedure (1981) *The Investigation and Prosecution of Criminal Offences in England and Wales: The Law and Procedure*. London: HMSO.

Sampson, A., Stubbs, P., Smith, D., Pearson, G. and Blagg, H. (1988) 'Crime localities and the multi-agency approach', *British Journal of Criminology*, 28(4): 478–93.
Sanders, A. (2008) 'Can coercive powers be effectively controlled or regulated? The case for anchored pluralism', in E. Cape and A. Sanders (eds), *Regulating Policing: The Police and Criminal Evidence Act 1984 Past, Present and Future*. Oxford: Hart.
Sanders, A. and Young, R. (2003) 'From suspect to trial', in M. Maguire, R. Morgan and R. Reiner (eds), *The Oxford Handbook of Criminology*, 3rd edn. Oxford: Oxford University Press.
Sanders, A. and Young, R. (2006) *Criminal Justice*. London: Butterworths.
Sanders, A., Bridges, L., Mulvane, A. and Crosier, G. (1989) *Advice and Assistance at Police Stations and the 24-hour Duty Solicitor Scheme*. London: Lord Chancellor's Department.

Scott, J. and Marshall, G. (2009) 'Professions', *A Dictionary of Sociology*. Oxford: Oxford University Press, *Oxford Reference Online* (accessed 13 February 2010).

Shaw, G.B. (1911) *The Doctor's Dilemma*. London: Constable & Co.

Shearing, C. (2007) 'Policing our future', in D. Smith and A. Henry (eds), *Transformations of Policing*. Aldershot: Ashgate.

Shearing, C. and Stenning, P. (1983) 'Say "cheese!" The Disney order that is not so Mickey Mouse', in C. D. Shearing and P. C. Stenning (eds), *Private Policing*. Newbury Park, CA: Sage.

Shefer, G. and Liebling, A. (2008) 'Prison privatization: in search of a businesslike atmosphere?', *Criminology and Criminal Justice*, 8(3): 261–78.

Sheptycki, J. (2009) *Constabulary Ethics and Transnational Policing in Europe*. Paper presented at Conference on Police Governance, Accountability, Developments, Challenges and Outlook, University of Limerick, 4 December.

Shicor, D. and Gilbert, M. J. (2001) *Privatization in Criminal Justice: Past, Present and Future*. Cincinnati, OH: Anderson.

Sigurdsson, J. and Mulchandani, R. (2010) *Police Service Strength in England and Wales, 30 September 2009*. London: HMSO.

Skinns, L. (2005) 'Cops, Councils and Crime and Disorder: A Critical Review of Three Community Safety Partnerships'. Unpublished PhD dissertation, Cambridge University.

Skinns, L. (2008) 'A prominent participant? The role of the state in police partnerships', *Policing and Society*, 18(3): 311–21.

Skinns, L. (2009a) '"Let's get it over with": early findings on the factors affecting detainees' access to custodial legal advice', *Policing and Society*, 19(1): 58–78.

Skinns, L. (2009b) '"I'm a detainee get me out of here": predictors of access to custodial legal advice in public and privatized police custody areas', *British Journal of Criminology*, 49(3): 399–417.

Skinns, L. (2010) '"Stop the clock": predictors of detention without charge in police custody areas', accepted by *Criminology and Criminal Justice*.

Skinns, L. (2011) 'The right to legal advice in the police station: past, present and future', *Criminal Law Review*, Issue 1, 2011.

Sklansky, D. A. (1999) 'Private police', *UCLA Law Review*, 46(4): 1165–87.

Skolnick, J. (2005) 'A sketch of the policeman's "working personality"', in T. Newburn (ed.), *Policing: Key Readings*. Cullompton: Willan.

Smith, D. J. (1997) 'Case construction and the goals of criminal process', *British Journal of Criminology*, 37(3): 319–46.

Smith, D. J. (1998) 'Reform or moral outrage – the choice is yours', *British Journal of Criminology*, 38(4): 616–22.

Smith, D. J. (2007a) 'The foundations of legitimacy', in T. Tyler (ed.), *Legitimacy and Criminal Justice*. New York: Russell Sage Foundation.

Smith, D. J. (2007b) 'New challenges to police legitimacy', in D. Smith and A. Henry (eds), *Transformations of Policing*. Aldershot: Ashgate.

Smith, D. J. and Gray, J. (1983) *Police and People in London: The Police in Action*. Aldershot: Gower.

Sparks, R. (1994) 'Can prisons be legitimate? Penal politics, privatization, and the timeliness of an old idea', in R. D. King and M. Maguire (eds), *Prisons in Context*. Oxford: Clarendon.

Sparks, R. and Bottoms, A. E. (1995) 'Legitimacy and order in prisons', *British Journal of Sociology*, 46(1): 45–62.

Sparks, R. and Bottoms, A. E. (2008) 'Legitimacy and imprisonment revisited', in J. M. Byrne, D. Hummer and F. Taxman (eds), *The Culture of Prison Violence*. Boston, MA: Pearson.
Spencer, J. R. (2005) 'Introduction', in M. Delmas-Marty and J. R. Spencer (eds), *European Criminal Procedure*, 2nd edn. Cambridge: Cambridge University Press.
Sullivan, R. R. (2001) 'The schizophrenic state: neo-liberal criminal justice', in K. Stenson and R. R. Sullivan (eds), *Crime, Risk and Justice: The Politics of Crime Control in Liberal Democracies*. Cullompton: Willan.
Sunshine, J. and Tyler, T. (2003) 'The role of procedural justice and legitimacy in shaping public support for policing', *Law and Society Review*, 37(3): 513–48.
Sykes, G. M. (1958) *The Society of Captives*. Princeton, NJ: Princeton University Press.

Tankebe, J. (2007) 'Policing and Legitimacy in a Post-Colonial Democracy: A Theoretical and Empirical Study of Ghana'. Unpublished PhD thesis, University of Cambridge.
Tankebe, J. (2008) 'Police effectiveness and police trustworthiness in Ghana: an empirical appraisal', *Criminology and Criminal Justice*, 8(2): 185–202.
Tankebe, J. and Gelsthorpe, L. (2007) 'Legitimacy', *Dictionary of Probation and Offender Management*. Cullompton: Willan.
Thacher, D. (2001) 'Conflicting values in community policing', *Law and Society Review*, 35(4): 765–98.
Tierney, J. (2001) 'Audits of crime and disorder: some lessons from research', *Crime Prevention and Community Safety: An International Journal*, 3(2): 7–17.
Turnbull, P. and Skinns, L. (2010) 'Drug Intervention Programme', in A. Hucklesby and E. Wincup (eds), *Drug Interventions in Criminal Justice*. Buckingham: Open University Press.
Tyler, T. R. (2003) 'Procedural justice, legitimacy and the effective rule of law', in M. Tonry (ed.), *Criminal Justice*. Chicago, IL: University of Chicago Press.
Tyler, T. R. and Huo, Y. J. (2002) *Trust in the Law: Encouraging Public Cooperation with the Police and the Courts*. New York: Russell Sage Foundation.

Waddington, P. A. J. (1999) *Policing Citizens*. London: UCL Press.
Wakefield, A. (2003) *Selling Security: The Private Policing of Public Space*. Cullompton: Willan.
Wakefield, A. (2008) 'Private policing: a view from the mall', *Public Administration*, 86(3): 659–78.
Warr, J. (2008) 'Understanding prison staff', in J. Bennett, B. Crewe, B. and A. Wahidini (eds), *Prison Staff*. Cullompton: Willan.
Williams, C. (2008) 'Constables for hire: the history of private "public" policing in the UK', *Policing and Society*, 18(2): 190–205.

Zander, M. (2005) 'Unwise move', *Police Review*, 14 January.
Zander, M. (2007) *Cases and Materials on the English Legal System*. Cambridge: Cambridge University Press.
Zander, M. (2010) *PACE: Past, Present and Future*, Second Cambridge Law Lecture by the Cambridgeshire and District Law Society, Law Faculty, University of Cambridge, 13 May.
Zedner, L. (2006) 'Policing before and after the police', *British Journal of Criminology*, 46(1): 78–96.

Index

Added to the page reference 'f' denotes a figure, 'n' denotes a footnote and 't' denotes a table.